Improving Passions

Dedicated to all the adjuncts and limited-term faculty who keep our universities running

Improving Passions
Sentimental Aesthetics and American Film

Charles Burnetts

EDINBURGH
University Press

Edinburgh University Press is one of the leading university presses in the UK.
We publish academic books and journals in our selected subject areas across the
humanities and social sciences, combining cutting-edge scholarship with high editorial
and production values to produce academic works of lasting importance. For more
information visit our website: edinburghuniversitypress.com

© Charles Burnetts, 2017, 2019

Edinburgh University Press Ltd
The Tun – Holyrood Road
12 (2f) Jackson's Entry
Edinburgh EH8 8PJ

First published in hardback by Edinburgh University Press 2017

Typeset in Monotype Ehrhardt by
Servis Filmsetting Ltd, Stockport, Cheshire,
and printed and bound by CPI Group (UK) Ltd
Croydon, CR0 4YY

A CIP record for this book is available from the British Library

ISBN 978 0 7486 9819 6 (hardback)
ISBN 978 1 4744 3169 9 (paperback)
ISBN 978 0 7486 9820 2 (webready PDF)
ISBN 978 1 4744 1396 1 (epub)

The right of Charles Burnetts to be identified as author of this work has been asserted
in accordance with the Copyright, Designs and Patents Act 1988 and the Copyright and
Related Rights Regulations 2003 (SI No. 2498).

Contents

Acknowledgements

This project has benefited greatly from the help and support of a number of different people and organisations. I would first like to thank my thesis advisor Barry Langford for his invaluable advice and attentive support. I would also like to thank Daniella Berghahn for her assistance throughout my doctoral studies. I would also like to thank countless other members of the Royal Holloway Department of Media Arts, University of London for their help and advice at away-days and at the odd tea-break down the road from the BFI Library. The latter of course has been an invaluable resource for me while in London. I would also like to thank Mandy Merck, who has offered much of her time in advising me on the foundational chapters of this study.

I would also like to extend my gratitude to the members of the Department of Communication and Culture at Indiana University, USA, particularly those who attended a scholarly writing group that met every fortnight or so, for accepting me as one of their own and providing me with some great advice on the project. I would like to thank Joan Hawkins in particular for her patient and generous contributions to various chapters. Thanks also to Kyle Tabbernor for his very helpful feedback.

Finally, I would like to thank my family for their kind patience and support throughout this process. My wife Chaya, in particular, has always been there for me, helping me through the tough times and assisting me in this project in so many ways.

Introduction

Schindler's List, the 1993 film by Steven Spielberg, tells the story of a businessman and member of the Nazi party who finds moral purpose through the discovery of his altruism towards Jews in wartime Poland both before and during the Holocaust. It was a film that famously divided the critics, particularly its tearful ending and its alleged descent into bathos and sentimentality.[1] At this point in the film, the Schindler Jews have been saved from extermination at Auschwitz, the Allies have finally won the war, and so Schindler (Liam Neeson) decides to take his leave. Before doing so, however, Schindler tearfully berates himself for not having saved more Jews with the remainder of his wealth. This takes place in front of the Jews he has saved, including his closest aid Itzhak Stern (Ben Kingsley), who are there to present him with a collective symbol of their gratitude (a gold ring forged from a Jewish man's gold tooth) and to bid farewell to their benefactor. This scene confirms Schindler as a good man who realises the moral stakes of what he has successfully or, in his estimation, unsuccessfully achieved. The film as a whole has taken Schindler through a narrative of redemption, from the charming, egocentric, and self-serving entrepreneur at the film's outset to a heroic, self-sacrificing man of compassion at the end. For the critic David Thomson, however, this scene is excessive. He argues,

> In the end, this Schindler sacrifices his all to be good, even to the point of a breakdown scene that is beyond Neeson and which is the most pointed failure in the picture.
> How much truer it might have been if this Schindler had stayed matter-of-fact and jovial to the end, laughing off the chance of friendship with Stern (for, really, Stern isn't his type) and recollecting – as a rough joke – that the getaway car might have meant another handful of lives. But Spielberg won't permit that brusqueness with his big finish in sight. So Schindler becomes, simply, a ruined but saved man, a character such as Capra might have liked. (Thomson 1994: 44–6)

Thomson's mention of Capra immediately invokes a tradition of sentimental narrative and characterisation in Hollywood cinema that, for Thomson, hangs over Spielberg's film. Capra's *It's a Wonderful Life* (1946), it should be noted, has become a paradigm of Hollywood sentimentality to which all other films within such a 'mode' are often compared. Both *Schindler's List* and *It's a Wonderful Life* tell stories of men who come to realise the 'important things in life', such as family, community, or charity, over the more materialistic concerns of finance, business, or pleasure. Thomson asks how fitting it is, however, for Spielberg to overlay a generic, sentimental, narrative arc of moral redemption for its central character over the historical events and traumas of the Holocaust. Considering the redemptive climax inappropriate, Thomson focuses on what would have been, as he says, 'truer'. He wants more of a continuity between the cynical, business-like Schindler of earlier on in the film and his character in the farewell scene, and no doubt beyond. He does not believe in the central character's sudden overwhelming sadness at the gift upon his departure. He hints that Spielberg is pulling the strings, manipulating the narrative in order to produce his 'big finish'.

This 'big finish' is furthermore situated here as the climax of a film whose theatricality and sense of melodrama is deemed particularly salient, most strikingly evidenced for many critics by Spielberg's choice of emphasising the survival of a select group of Jews compared to the mass murder of millions. Despite the wide sweep of the prior narrative through key historical events of the Holocaust (the deportation from the Warsaw Ghetto, graphic murders, children separated from their parents, Jews entering the Auschwitz gas chambers) *Schindler's List* controversially looks to those who survive. The tracking shot in the sequence outlined above, showing the faces of the Schindler Jews reflected in his car's windows as it moves along, gives the impression of abundance and plenitude. Their number exceeds what can be taken on in the frame, delivering a catharsis of virtue rewarded. Through its emphasis on rescue and survival, *Schindler's List* indeed contrasts markedly with many other films about the Holocaust. Thomas Elsaesser, for instance, contrasts Spielberg's 'theodicy' with the European modernism of Claude Lanzmann's *Shoah* (1985, France) as follows:

> By affirming that whoever saves one life, saves mankind, Spielberg accepts the principle that the one can represent the many, that the part can stand for the whole. *Shoah* is based, explicitly and emphatically, on the exact opposite premise: that no one can stand in for anyone else, no one can speak for anyone else. (Elsaesser 1996: 178)

Focalisation on a moral hero is foregrounded by Elsaesser here then as part of a broader aesthetic, with explicitly Talmudic underpinnings, that runs counter to the austere anti-mimeticism of modernist film aesthetics. *Shoah* largely favours a modernist aesthetic of emptiness, faded memories, and distorted testimonies, all of which signify the stark absence of those who have perished. Spielberg's finale does the inverse. Where six million have died, Spielberg focuses on more than 1,200 who survived. While many and most Germans are understood to have been unambiguously obedient to the Nazi party, Spielberg presents just one who acted against such ghastly conformism.

The conflict of responses to this hugely successful film about the Holocaust is one example then of the complex ethical and aesthetic debates surrounding sentimentalism at the cinema, a mode described by Joanne Dobson as an 'imaginative orientation . . . premised on an emotional and philosophical ethos that celebrates human connection, both personal and communal, and acknowledges the shared devastation of affectional loss' (Williamson 2014: 266). Outrage at *Schindler's List* would be fuelled indeed by the sense of its invoking very different feelings to those usually attached to the Holocaust in critical discourse, an event that has become in many ways paradigmatic of modernity's rupture of 'human connection' and of the impossibility of celebrating any kind of essential human 'ethos'. As Miriam Hansen notes, the film was deemed excessively melodramatic in its deployment of a classical (German) protagonist, a last-minute rescue, and an upbeat ending. At the same time, it was also deemed 'too "realistic"' (1996: 300) in its daring to offer a 'direct representation' (301) of events that defy representability in the extent of their horror. While the film aimed ostensibly to educate and inform its audience about the Holocaust, its 'feelgood' tropes and classical realism were deemed by many to falsify the legitimate affectivity of the events that the film depicts. The male liberal subject emerged specifically in this discourse as a problematic influence in two interrelated ways: first, in terms of the problematic universality of its chief protagonist (Schindler) and, second, in terms of its director, Steven Spielberg, and his alleged transgression of a representational ethics.

Realism and Film Reviewing

At the core of these objections is indeed an adherence to realism that often yields hostility towards the sentimental narrative patterns surrounding what M. W. Disher once referred to as 'Virtue Triumphant' (cited in Elsaesser 1985: 188). At the same time, sentimentality is difficult to define precisely and is often, as Jennifer Williamson argues, about more than just 'plot' or 'bad writing' (Williamson et al. 2014: 4). Its common association with adjectives like 'trite' and 'mawkish' reveal, for instance, that sentimentalism has a lot to do with feelings, particularly those attached to conveying an (often excessively) optimistic, idealistic, or Utopian reflection upon the world, a mode that is often enough deemed manipulative or ideological in its allegedly wilful departures from social and political reality. Alongside such objections, however is the related, although more formal, problematic of cinema's representationalism and its links with a humanist philosophy critiqued by modernist practices and theories. If we return momentarily to the sequence discussed in *Schindler's List*, it is as much to do with its 'direct representation' of a traumatic event that the film courts criticism rather than merely its choices concerning narrative, character, or style.

This book examines a complex contemporary disenchantment about sentimentality then to the extent that it is understood as both a mode of narration and a representationalist philosophy, a problem negotiated with particular power and sophistication I suggest by film and those who have thought seriously about its distinct affective appeals. V. F. Perkins, for instance, in his seminal *Film as Film: Understanding and Judging Movies*, offers an influential definition of 'sentimentality' in film as a 'disproportion between pathos asserted (in music, say, or image or gesture) and pathos achieved, in the action' (1993: 132). Here is a framing of sentimentalism that distinguishes between a film sequence's legitimate elicitation of pathos or emotion (derived from the 'action' of the film) and an illegitimate variant that brackets the pathos elicited by an excessive, or cheap, deployment of music or imagery. The sense of proportionality informing Perkins' model is a criterion that is far more common in film criticism than the specific charge of sentimentality itself, despite the latter's common ground with a logic of balance and justified pathos. In Warren Buckland's utilisation of Perkins' approach, for instance, sentimentality is one of various problems that may arise from a film's failure to achieve 'organic unity' (2006: 31), a criterion that both he and Perkins define in relation to a formalist ideal of balance between cinema's 'realist' and 'expressive' capacities. Thus:

> The skilled filmmaker reconciles film's conflicting tendencies by maintaining a credible world and, at the same time, using film's expressive capacities to achieve heightened coherence – or organic unity. An unbalanced, incoherent film is one that either pulls too much toward realism and credibility and does not exploit film's expressive capacity, or one that overuses its expressive capacity at the expense of realism and credibility. (Buckland 2006: 37)

The overuse of music or imagery in Perkins' definition of sentimentality clearly relates here then to Buckland's analogous problematisation of a film-maker's over-deployments of film's 'expressive capacity', to the extent that such excesses risk an undermining of 'realism and credibility'. An example that Buckland provides of imbalance (although not necessarily sentimentality specifically) is Steven Spielberg's use of 'extravagant overabundant spectacle' (128) in the final sequence of *Close Encounters of the Third Kind* (1977), where the aliens and their enormous mothership finally appear on-screen in their first direct encounter with humankind at the summit of Devils Tower, Wyoming. For Buckland, this scene undermines the film's otherwise admirable deployments of off-screen space (in its depiction of Unidentified Flying Objects) in favour of an excessive visibility that takes away from the 'dramatic possibilities' (ibid.) of the film's subject. While Spielberg is praised by Buckland for his inspired use of on-screen/off-screen space to fuel the spectator's imagination in most of *Close Encounters*, the climax is criticised as an excessive spectacle of the visible that, extending Buckland's argument, may shift spectatorship towards the response of sentimentality.

The approach to film sentimentality discussed above is marked then by critical assessments of formal excess at the level of the text under analysis, such as of 'pathos in music and imagery' that makes a film jarring in its apparent imbalance of realism and expressivity. It is this definition that corresponds most closely to popular understandings and deployments of the term, particularly in relation to the way sentimental films (or sequences within films) are frequently deemed to manipulate the spectator, most paradigmatically to tears. Such films are jarring, mawkish, maudlin, sickly, or saccharine because spectators detect an ingenuous intentionality and motive on the part of a film-maker in a film's imbalance of either narrative or spectacle. In *Schindler's List*, the sequence discussed above is deemed excessive in its focus on the character of Schindler at the expense of the Jewish victims of the Holocaust, compounded, moreover, by its fore-grounding of his departure and its moving musical score. The sequence becomes jarring in its potential distortion of the narrative information presented thus far in the film, such as in its earlier characterisation of Schindler as a pragmatic entrepreneur or of the Schindler Jews as a group of people who have been utterly traumatised and spiritually destroyed by their experiences. Instead, the sequence is deemed to stand on ceremony, we may say, foregoing its well-publicised claims to representation and realism with a kind of emotional correctness.

Such text-based determinations of sentimentality can nevertheless become highly ambiguous and unreliable when we consider that spectators do not respond emotionally to films in the same ways. Carl Plantinga, for instance, offers two parallel routes to feeling sentimental about the final scene of Charles Chaplin's *City Lights* (1931) that culminate in somewhat of a paradox, discussing the scene where the tramp finally reveals himself to the once-blind flower girl (whose sight he had helped to restore) in relation to both narrative distortion and spectator emotion. Plantinga notes in the first instance that the sequence avoids one sort of sentimentalism by leaving the relationship between these two characters ambiguous and unresolved at the film's close, avoiding the bathos (and possible imbalances) invoked by a happy romantic union that strains credulity. Plantinga notes, however, that sentimentality may equally be invoked by the tramp character's mere invocation of goodwill, virtue, and hope as he awaits his beloved flower girl's reaction at the scene's fade to black, regardless of whether we see an outcome or not. Thus, 'through our allegiance with the tramp and our experience of congruent emotions', writes Plantinga, 'we celebrate a gratifying image of ourselves as compassionate, righteous, and just – because we recognise his selfless love in a cruel world and respond to it emotionally' (1997: 386).

Sentimentality can be deemed operative here then both at the level of the text and/or at the level of reception, and, thus, for Plantinga causes difficulties about being accurate about the tonal imbalances such a sequence may be accused of making. This problem of definition between a narrow, text-determined form of sentimentalism and a broader, and in some ways more structural/subjective process, raises problems about gauging the kinds of sentimentalism described in Perkins' model. If sentimentality can be invoked despite an absence of excess at the level of the text, and can be related equally to the sensitivities and cultural background of the spectator, we are in murky territory about what we're objectively referring to as critics or theorists when we deploy the term in either a descriptive or evaluative sense. Indeed, all too often, calling a film or film sequence sentimental tells us more about the critic than the film itself, especially in cases where the term is used at the expense of substantive textual analysis. Ed Tan and Nico Frijda, for instance, characterise a certain spectator's feelings about sentimentality in film in relation to an embarrassment and 'helplessness' before filmic events, leading to condemnation of the film's apparent undermining of the spectator's preferred self-image as an 'autonomous self' (1999: 55). Such an attitude, they continue, is traditionally gendered male in its resistance to what they refer to as the 'submission response' (53) of sentimentality, a resistance to being moved (sometimes to tears), that prejudices the spectator from cues (both in terms of the current text and future texts with similar narrative patterns) that may invoke a similar set of cognitive tensions.

Such observations may certainly raise less than surprising concerns when we come to consider the undeniable dominance, as with many other professions, of white, male, heteronormative subjectivity in film criticism and its affective preferences and biases. Film reviewers, in particular, who are most often in the business of evaluation and taste-making, espouse values and judgements that will be either shared or rejected by us when we become the spectators of the same films they have seen and reviewed. If a critic we respect charges a film sequence with an (excessive) sentimentalism, we will often accept this charge as representative of feelings and thoughts that will likely mirror our own in relation to the same data, especially if we feel they have been proven to have done so (and justifiably) in the past with previous films. The charge also serves in many cases to preclude the need for further analysis, wherein the reviewer's judgement of sentimentalism stands in for proof as such, as may be expected by a more stringent textual analysis of the sequence or film in question. The charge of sentimentality serves in such respects as a rhetorical shortcut, combining a cognitive and emotional response to arrive at a particular critical judgement, much in the same way that the film review serves in itself as a shortcut we use as prospective film-goers to decide which films are worth watching over those that aren't.

But what if we don't agree with the above critic, or perhaps even most critics, about a certain film, sequence, or performance? What if a critic we are usually entertained by and/or whose opinions we respect seems to completely undervalue a film we loved, or persistently heaps scorn on a genre or film-maker we like? More acutely, what if a critic finds something in a film sentimental that we found genuinely moving, or perhaps even integral to the film's meaning? This is when we begin to need a more objective or critical approach to film emotion that can give us a better perspective on what seems at issue for the available critics. The academic study of film serves in such respects as an obvious port of call for us, thanks to its methodological scrutiny of cinematic texts, audiences, and the various cultural histories they negotiate. This book's focus on sentimentality serves in such a vein to unpack the critical and popular discourses attached to feeling manipulated by film's emotional appeals to virtue, morality, and communality, of its pretensions to improve or educate the spectator, and the stakes of feeling, thinking, and acting in resistance to such models. Responding to the often vexed question of what the sentimental means to various critical and popular constituencies, it argues that a value remains in the sentimental, less as an evaluative term (with its ongoing connotations of a stoical critical elitism), but as a critical concept and cinematic 'mode' (Williams 1998; Williamson 2014) that has long spoken to the analytical and popular dimensions of affect and cognition in film and its spectatorship. The sentimental, in other words, both animates our anxieties about film (in its relationship to the maudlin or contrived, for instance) and fuels our deepest affective engagement with it.

Melodrama and the Bourgeois Body

A fruitful approach to film sentimentalism becomes available then when we pursue a line of enquiry that takes us away from diagnosing sentimentality for the purpose of evaluation per se, and where instead we come to understand it as a category of address with a particular history and an identifiable set of rhetorical patterns. Tom Gunning, for instance, discusses sentimentality through Charlie Chaplin and the great film-maker's negotiation of the melodramatic rhetorical tradition. As part of a wider discussion of Chaplin's 'body of modernity' (2010), Gunning foregrounds the tramp as a figure of complexity and subversion in his physical deviations from genteel decorum and propriety, discussing a scene in *The Pawnshop* (1916) that shows the tramp weeping at a poor beggar's tale of woe while eating crackers, only for the half-chewed crackers to comically fly out of his mouth when he can no longer control his hysterical sobs. Opposed to the 'body of bourgeois individualism, cosmetically enclosed and complete unto itself', the tramp's vulgarity and physicality is foregrounded by Gunning here in terms of a carnivalesque theatrics – a body that 'remains open to the world and merges with other bodies, both biologically and socially' (239). Thus:

> This body, which Chaplin shares with the long tradition of carnival clowns, contrasts sharply with what, Julia Kristeva, one of Bahktin's critical heirs, calls 'the clean and proper body' – the body of bourgeois individualism, cosmetically enclosed and complete unto itself, never openly emitting noises, smells or embarrassment. Chaplin's bodily humor was the 'nasty' Chaplin, rather than the sentimental Chaplin, that cliché that so many critics use to avoid dealing with Chaplin's actual complexity. (Gunning 2010: 239)

Gunning refers specifically to the sentimental here then in relation to the affective tensions engendered by Chaplin's film and the cultural history his tramp character speaks to. In analogous terms to Buckland's insistence on 'organic unity' between realist and expressivist tendencies in film, Gunning foregrounds the sequence as a dialectical negotiation of melodrama and slapstick as distinct rhetorical modes. The discussion extends moreover to the ways that such negotiations speak to a far longer history of struggle between the body and its legibility, where sentimentality is aligned here with the stagnant conventions of melodrama and its insistence on a tearful, decorous sympathy for the other, subverted as always by the tramp's inability to remain within its genteel parameters. The tramp's 'body of modernity' serves here as counterpoint to an otherwise maudlin scene, foregrounding a sophisticated self-reflexivity in the film that stands in for, and negotiates, the critic's distaste about sentimentalism's excessive codification of human behaviour and its obviousness.

The use of humour in Chaplin is framed here then as a means by which sentimentalism is bracketed or contextualised by this and other Chaplin films as a hackneyed mode of address that often 'strains' for feeling. Such self-reflexivity is related in turn to the kinds of 'excess' noted in the films of Douglas Sirk, Vincente Minnelli, George Cukor, and Nicholas Ray by such critics as Thomas Elsaesser (Elsaesser 1985) and Geoffrey Nowell-Smith (1977) in their seminal writings on film melodrama. Film's expressive properties in mise en scène, colour, or music could be conceived analogously as ironic commentary or materialist 'excess' (Elsaesser 1985: 170) in relation to the classical realist narrative and its reproduction of dominant bourgeois ideology. Where an affirmative 'classical realist' mode of narration (ostensibly adhered to by these same Hollywood films) allowed character desire and pleasure to be indulged and 'sublimated' by the illusionistic thrust of classical narrative,[2] melodrama for Elsaesser and other theorists strove to give expression to the social and ideological contradictions lying below the surface.[3] Sentimentalism indeed may be posed as a good term for denoting that body of ideology (equated from Marxist perspectives with bourgeois or classical realism) that this radicalised melodrama seemed to be subjecting to critique, according to such accounts. Elsaesser argued, for instance, that the stylistic excesses of 'sophisticated melodrama' displayed a 'modernist sensibility working in popular culture' that ironically problematises the 'incurably naive moral and emotional idealism in the American psyche' (Elsaesser 1985: 182). In such respects, cinematic melodrama could be claimed to be providing a set of devices for making salient and problematising the sentimental culture invoked by Hollywood's narrative mode, wherein the latter's affirmative idealism would be deconstructed by the genre's displacements and ironies.

Problematically, however, the extent to which sentimentalism has historically been considered 'excessive', or even indeed itself melodramatic, muddies any easy mapping of a sentimental/melodrama dichotomy to a norm versus critique model, notwithstanding their disparate genealogies. Debates were focused indeed on a relatively narrow range of Hollywood films to support a model that tended to equate 'melodrama' with a critique of the bourgeois family and oppressed womanhood. thereby putting the term under particular strain. In response to this 'Phantom Genre' (Merritt 1983), more recent scholarship has indeed re-emphasised melodrama's roots as a theatrical and cinematic genre that had as much to do with sensationalism, elaborate stage mechanics, and robust heroics as with the intimacies and ironies of its more domestic, 'maternal' variants.[4] More damaging to such political-modernist approaches to melodrama have been challenges from cognitive film theorists on what they deem an 'orthodoxy' of film theory to draw on continental philosophy and its 'Grand Narratives' to symptomatise Hollywood films and their ideology. Such interpretative analysis is deemed in turn to be biased (like the film critic described above) by an apparent distaste, or 'ideological stoicism' (Plantinga 1997: 373) towards cinema's affectivity, one argued to renew Plato's original scepticism about poetry and the arts. Derived from 'neo-Freudian' models of pleasure and desire and the theatrical aesthetics of Bertolt Brecht, an 'orthodoxy' of 'ideological film criticism' is targeted specifically here as a body of scholarship that 'fails to account for the complexity and diversity of spectator emotion' (377). Whether the spectator adopts a critical attitude autonomously or is entreated to do so through Brechtian distanciation, Plantinga argues (along with other broadly cognitivist scholars) that such theory rests on a flawed 'apparatus' discourse of cinema as 'epistemic delusion' (ibid.).[5]

Questions are raised here specifically then about the rubric of 'excess', part indeed of a larger debate concerning the alleged reliance of film theory, and political-modernist approaches, on rubrics of epistemic negation and anti-signification. Put differently, such approaches pose the valid question as to why a sequence's sentimentalism is deemed legitimate on the necessary condition of its narratological or stylistic bracketing, as if its own mode of address is in some way inadequate, incomplete, or ideologically compromised. Tom Gunning's example of the tramp's comic subversion of sympathy for a beggar comes under scrutiny here, too, for instance, for it arguably also relies on a rubric of bracketing or irony as the condition for critical detachment from an otherwise hackneyed scene. If a sentimental scene can only be discussed within the context of its auto-subversion or irony, doubt is raised here about the norm/excess dichotomy that seems implied by such analysis, and the presumption of 'illusion' or even brainwashing with which that norm becomes aligned.

Another way of thinking about such challenges, as Linda Williams has argued, is that they question the helpfulness of differentiating between a '"bad" melodrama of manipulated, naively felt, feminine emotions and a "good" melodrama of ironical hysterical excess thought to be immune to the more pathetic emotions' (1998: 44). Such objections, as well as shifts in the field towards 'affect' and a cultural historicism, have indeed precipitated several correctives to both theories of melodrama and the wider 'excess' or 'attraction' model in film theory. For Linda Williams, melodrama is better understood as an accommodation of different levels of realism, thus collapsing distinctions between spectacle and narrative. Thus:

> The notion that the classical Hollywood narrative subordinates spectacle, emotion, and attraction to the logic of personal causality and cause and effect assumes that the 'action' privileged by the form is not spectacular. However, we have only to look at what's playing at the local multiplex to realise that the familiar Hollywood feature of prolonged cinematic action is, and I would argue has always been, a melodramatic spectacle (and Gunning's notion of attraction) no matter how goal-driven or embedded within narrative it may be. (Williams 1998: 70)

By foregrounding melodrama as an overarching logic of Hollywood cinema, rather than one constituted by the exhibitionistic tendencies of 'attraction' and excess, Williams calls into question the adequacy of a narrative versus 'attractions' binary, and its correlative model of norm versus critique. Returning to earlier theories of melodrama by Steve Neale (1986) and Franco Moretti (1983), and her own work on 'body-genres' (1991), Williams foregrounds both narrative and spectacle, or 'action' and 'pathos', as co-dependent factors in the mode's affectivity. Thus, in relation to the common weeping that characterises the mode, Williams argues:

> It is this feeling that something important has been lost that is crucial to crying's relation to melodrama. A melodrama does not have to contain multiple scenes of pathetic death to function melodramatically. What counts is the feeling of loss suffused throughout the form. (Williams 1998: 70)

The importance of melodrama relates here then not merely to its stylistic departures from classical narrative (as excessive spectacle), but rather the form's overall invocations of 'loss', echoing more now the affects associated explicitly with sentimentalism and the 'shared devastation of affectional loss' described by Dobson cited above. 'Scenes of pathetic death', echoing Samuel Richardson's infamous deathbed scene in his novel *Clarissa, or, the History of a Young Lady* (published in 1748), can certainly invoke such feelings through the potential mirroring of facial expression and emotion between character and spectator, but Williams underlines here the more pervasive sense of bereavement for a character or idea to which spectators develop moral allegiance through the melodrama's narrative procedures.[6] Alluding to the arguments of Peter Brooks, melodrama's historical purpose of making morality 'legible' (1976: 42) is foregrounded by such revisions to the melodramatic model. Whether an ending is happy or sad becomes secondary to the salience of a clearly desired outcome (a new imaginary 'schemata' to use a cognitivist term) and its persistence as a sentimental, but no less valid, 'fantasy' or desire (Neale 1986) on the part of the spectator. Christine Gledhill argues in a similar vein that the mode depicts 'less how things ought to be than how they should have been' (1987: 21), the form resting on tensions between a moral idealism and the representation of social realities that too often fall short of such ideals. Steve Neale, in *Screen*'s special issue on 'Melodrama' in 1986, similarly accounts for melodrama as a discourse of the 'if only' (1986: 12) in relation to a variety of narrative contexts, where justice is challenged and sometimes goes unfulfilled despite narrative 'closure'.[7] 'Justice in Jeopardy', or 'Virtue in Distress' have likewise been discussed specifically in relation to film sentimentalism by cognitivist scholars Ed Tan and Nico Frijda (1999), who perhaps are most explicit in their alignments of melodrama with its specifically 'sentimental' appeals.[8]

'Thinking With and Through Our Bodies'

Debates about film sentimentalism are marked then by tensions between a modernist 'attractions'-oriented discourse of excess and irony and more historicist, cognitivist, or phenomenological explorations of melodrama's wide-ranging aesthetics, a mode that for Barry Langford is 'at once before, beyond and embracing the system of genre in US cinema as a whole' (2005: 31). Recent studies of 'melodrama' meanwhile shift focus beyond film entirely in their attention to the cultural genealogy and persistence of America's melodramatic imaginary as a historical phenomenon. Most significant here are works by Williams herself, as well as Lauren Berlant, and the political scientist Elizabeth Anker, all of whom centralise the melodramatic imaginary as a dominant of American cultural politics, whether in terms of the historical treatment of race (Williams 2002), the essentialisation of female identity and nationality (Berlant 2008), or even the legitimation of Western foreign policy in relation to the terrorism of the last thirty years (Anker 2014). Anker notes, for instance, in explaining the rationale for the US-led wars in Iraq and Afghanistan, that the US's melodramatic culture promotes 'a specific type of citizenship, in which the felt experience of being an American comprises not only persecuted innocence and empathetic connection with other Americans' suffering but also the express demand to legitimate state power' (4). 'Virtue Triumphant', in other words, is recognised as a discourse that all too often serves power to the detriment of more nuanced or reflective modes of engagement with the Other, reducing such negotiations to an 'us versus them' schema. Sentimentalising nation through the self-adoption of victimhood and

persecuted innocence is posed merely as the recto here to the verso of a
defensive unilateralism in foreign policy.

But what is sentimentality in particular and can it be profitably differentiated from melodrama, 'classical narrative', or 'excess'? These are
questions that animate the discussion below, whether with reference to
the 'Cult of Sensibility' in eighteenth-century European salon cultures,
or the kinds of 'sensual thinking' formulated by Sergei Eisenstein in his
reconsiderations of montage. Without preempting these arguments in too
much detail here, the book offers a cautious answer to the affirmative while
foregrounding too the problems of making concepts mean (somewhat)
new things when they have already been around for a long time. In the
case of sentimentalism, it's contemporary meanings in many ways do little
justice to both its history as a concept and a cultural mode of address, and,
in some ways, speak to persistent biases with regards to the rationalism and
stoicism of critical discourse. Linda Williams, for instance, defends the
specifically sentimental emotions of the 'maternal melodrama' against the
de rigueur feminist response of critical distance, for instance, by posing
the problematics of reason and emotion as central to its spectatorship. Did
'emotion swallow us up, or did we have room within it to think?' (1998:
47) Williams asks about the much-debated ending of *Stella Dallas* (Vidor,
1935), where a mother sacrifices her relationship with her daughter so
the latter may marry into US East-coast high society. She articulates a
dilemma here that both acknowledges the possibilities of a manipulative
'submission response' (which she aligns precisely with the risks of an
ideological 'false consciousness' (70)), while articulating one of the defining features of the melodramatic imagination and its apparently 'pathetic'
emotions.[9] In a similar vein, Mandy Merck (1998) interrogates the death
of Diana, Princess of Wales, and its infamous outpouring of public grief in
the UK, as an event that foregrounded the affective power and problematics of her being positioned as 'virtue in distress'. Focusing in particular on
the 'authoritarian populism' (12) the event seemed to precipitate, Merck's
'Irreverent Elegies' foreground the contradictions (and possible interdependence) between the 'kindlier, less stuffy society' (12) that her death
seemed to inaugurate and the renewed conservatism of British politics in
the New Labour government of late 1990s Britain.

Such studies importantly foreground the intersections between the
concerns of film studies (with its rich interrogation of spectatorship) and
those of cultural studies in its attention to subjectivity and public rhetoric.
This book occupies a similar space in its focus on the historical meanings
of staged grief and loss, using cinema as one of various cultural spaces
around which public emotion is orchestrated and debated. As the studies

cited above indicate, sentimentalism has a particularly contemporary significance as a key affective mode within the West's increasingly liberalised public rhetorical culture. From Oprah to the rise of Donald Trump, unbridled emotion is 'popular' and often signifies honesty or individuality in a culture that is deemed increasingly autonomic and mechanised, where a true display of authentic 'humanity' is deemed all too rare. The sense to which a globalised system of free market capitalism overrides all human intervention and desire marks the mood of our post-millennial cultures, where the politics of the body and the 'gut', as opposed to the abstracted 'expert' discourses of law, economics, and politics, have come centre stage. Slavoj Žižek's highly controversial comments about immigration and the inadequacy of political correctness, for instance, make sense only alongside the backdrop of a radical disenchantment with rubrics of 'tolerance' and a philosophy of multicultural universalism, which are increasingly put under strain by the austerity-driven inequalities of the new neoliberal world order.[10] As with Merck's observations above, theorists are focusing here on the adequacies of a multiculturalist identity politics once it crosses over to 'official' policy and becomes mere lip-service under the aegis of 'respect' or tolerance, finding a dangerous embrace of political inertia and status quo below its 'liberal' surface.

Theorists of film and other melodramatic cultures are responding therefore to pervasive movements in contemporary culture and the humanities, where issues of 'affect' and the body have emerged as important considerations. In the academy, this reorientation has been referred to in terms of a variety of 'turns' – the affective, ethical, philosophical, or phenomenological turns being the most recognised banners, each of which signify a recasting of the psychoanalytic/Marxian/structuralist approach without abandoning its core hermeneutic concerns. Key to these areas, however, is a shift away from what Robert Sinnerbrink describes as film theory's established 'suspicion of emotion as the pernicious "other" of a critical reason that would emancipate oppressed subjects through theoretical illumination and ideological demystification' (2015: 81). The possibility, as Linda Williams puts it in her summation of the *Stella Dallas* debate, to 'think both with and through our bodies' (1998: 47), summarises succinctly indeed the stakes of this important shift, mirroring more recent writing about a 'cultural politics of emotion' (see Ahmed 2004) that interrogates the role of affect in cultural discourse. In many such formulations, the notion of a private, individuated subject who is either manipulated or enlightened by discourse gives way to considerations of the important contextual and cultural factors that 'construct' meaning. Such shifts are presaged by the philosophical work of Stanley Cavell and Gilles Deleuze

in their common foregrounding of 'Immanence' over 'Being', the unconscious, 'deterritorialized' strands of social thought over the reflections of
an individuated rational agent. In all such formulations, the body emerges
as a vital mediator to thought, the privileged boundary or 'screen' between
self and world that mirrors the work of cinema itself.

I suggest indeed that, in the light of the 'New Humanities', the philosophy of sentimentalism emerges as an important theoretical antecedent
to such renewed emphases on the body and emotion. James Chandler,
for instance, aligns Deleuze's influential film theory with the 'sentimental vehicularity' of Laurence Sterne's *A Sentimental Journey* (2013, 195),
focusing in particular on a model of sympathy that functions through the
'translative movement' of vehicles and moving-image technology (201).
Such emphasis on sentimentalism as a complex 'conceptual repertoire'
of movement and becoming echo new, 'postmodern' configurations of
emotion that decentre the humanist-cognitive subject in favour of a more
radical affectivity. Thus, Steven Shaviro comments:

> There are good reasons why we can no longer take emotions seriously. We are far too
> jaded, cynical, and ironic ever to trust the heart rather than the head. And a good
> thing too. But this condition of terminal irony is also what allows us to reinvent the
> much-maligned state of aesthetic disinterest. And in that cool, impersonal, and
> disaffected state we encounter the life (after death) of postmodern emotions. I am
> calling, therefore – and I think that Warhol would have approved – for a new sort
> of emotionalism or even *sentimentalism*, that is to say, for feelings that are playful,
> perverse, whimsical, wasteful, futile, dysfunctional, extravagant, and ridiculous.
> (Shaviro 2004: 131; my emphasis)

Shaviro recovers 'sentimentalism' here then as a kind of modern, sensual
eclecticism that induces what he further goes on to describe as 'Kantian
disinterest' (137), an affect that is disengaged enough from commodity
culture to allow for more creative, desubjectivised responses. The emotions
of the 'heart' remain critically inadequate if they must remain embedded
within more traditional formulations of the sentimental – complicit, as
they would be for Shaviro with ultimately more utilitarian and instrumen-
talist regimes of value and consumption (see also Sconce 2002).

The 'terminal irony' to which Shaviro refers, by contrast enables the
subject to productively disengage from the various investments and mis-
recognitions of a commodified consumer culture, precipitating a more post-
human, de-cognitivised emotional landscape. This 'disinterest' may sound
like a return to the Stoical formulations critiqued above in their recourse
to disengagement and irony, but there are important elements to consider
in this potential reorientation of sentimentalism, an approach indeed that
informs the analysis below of various post-classical positions and films in

Chapters 4, 5, and 6. The first consideration relates to the way that post-Deleuzian metaphysics of this kind is removed from the reason–passion binary, allowing for 'affect', rather than either reason or cognitivist emotion, as a mediating term in its denotations of embodied thought. Affect here refers not merely to the individual subject's 'cognitive' processes of apprehension and inference-making, but rather to a more immediate and unconstrained reactivity to aesthetic phenomena. The second consideration concerns the ways that Deleuzian models allow theorists like Shaviro to recentralise aesthetics in place of politics, particularly in the way that film and other cultural experiences become validated precisely in their autonomy from conditions of legibility and rational discourse. Thus, Shaviro writes elsewhere:

> To have an aesthetic experience is many things; but at the limit, it is to feel – and perhaps thereby to cry, to laugh, or to scream. As Deleuze says, 'it makes us grasp, it is supposed to make us grasp, something intolerable and unbearable' (18). But the intolerable and unbearable is also the unactable and the untenable: that which we cannot affect or act upon. (Shaviro 2007: 12)

Removed precisely from a 'functionalist' conception of spectatorship that privileges both the politically emancipatory message (of an ethics-based film theory) and the conscious, legible emotions of cognitivism, the 'aesthetic experience' is reaffirmed here as an emotionally autonomous and disinterested phenomenon. In answer to William's question as to whether the emotions of melodrama merely 'swallow us up', aesthetics returns here to reaffirm the disinterest and possibilities of non-conscious emotion, displacing politics while upholding the importance of bodily engagement and an unconstrained field of affect. This form of disinterest relates importantly also to issues of 'camp' and its political ambivalence, a mode of affect that informs many of the films examined in later chapters in their deviation from a more classical or realist mode of address. Camp's importance will be underlined most specifically in terms of its ambiguous embrace of irreverence through its complex breaking of taboos and politically correct codes.

What is shared by theorists like Williams, Shaviro, and Deleuze therefore is a recasting of film and cultural theory that I suggest is animated at core by compromises and correspondences with sentimentalism. They emphasise processes of 'becoming' and re-engagement over the more static legitimacies of rationalised discourse and institutionality, while acknowledging the inadequacies of merely repudiating the 'pathetic' and its strong affective charge. The philosophical return represented by such thinkers, and the 'affective-turn' more broadly understood, signals an ongoing negotiation between questions of cognition and more culture-focused approaches in film theory, around which the sentimental is well placed.

In its casting of 'orthodox' film theory as a neo-Platonist philosophy that insists on the upholding of a reason–emotion dichotomy, cognitivist approaches often overlook and trivialise important contributions to contemporary film and cultural studies that have sought to re-contextualise the potentially rationalist biases of film theory through considerations of embodiment (Sobchack 1992; Marks 1999) or cinema's negotiation of other audiovisual forms (Bolter and Grusin 2000; Shaviro 2010). In doing so, it has all too often swerved towards the 'Post-Theory' discourse of what David Bordwell describes as 'finding causal, functional, or teleological explanations' (1989: 17) about film and its spectatorship, to the detriment of film theory's valuable attention to more general questions concerning subjectivity, emotion, and becoming, or, as Shaviro notes, of 'dysfunction' and 'hermeneutic unfoldings' (2008: 50).

Put differently, there is something to be gained by being stuck between the rock of medium-specific approaches and the hard place of a more generalised cultural enquiry, notwithstanding the ominous spectre of interdisciplinarity. In what follows in the chapters below are analyses that therefore work within the spirit of the 'radical pluralism' (Martin-Jones 2016: 10) that now characterises the study of affect in film and cultural studies. This book examines sentimentalism 'against the grain' of its contemporary meanings, charting a field that draws on the body, gender, ethics, and narrative as constitutive discourses.

Outline of the Book

Chapter 1 charts a genealogy of the sentimental mode, from the sentimental literary cultures of eighteenth-century Europe through to the widespread success of popular melodrama in Europe and America. It draws connections between the sentimental novel, 'Moral Sense' philosophy of the eighteenth-century 'Scottish Enlightenment', and nineteenth-century melodrama, as discourses and traditions each bound up with questions relating to affect, the subject, and society. While textual analysis of specific texts seeks to draw out the continuities and problematics of sentimentalism as a literary and theatrical genre, a focus remains on establishing the critical contours of the term's cultural history. The section's particular aim is to trace the term's fall from grace while nevertheless establishing its full theoretical significance to film theory. It will also review influential literary scholarship on the cultural gendering of sentimentalism of the period, whether discerned in the ideological consolidation of bourgeois society, the continuance of sentimental narrative in theatrical melodrama and the novel (Stowe, Dickens), or in the various periodicals, guidebooks, and assorted paraphernalia that make up a feminising culture for theorists like Ann Douglas, Jane Tompkins, and Lauren Berlant.

Chapter 2 explores the extent to which film theorists of the early-to-mid twentieth century were able to conceive of cinema as a sentimental medium alongside the socio-cultural and intellectual backdrop of modernity and modernism, respectively. I select theory drawn from both formalist and realist traditions, both familiar and less well-known texts, using a critical lens attuned to the representation of individual virtue, the face, the sympathetic 'auteur', and cinematic pedagogy. Key work by such theorists as Sergei Eisenstein, the writers of *Close-Up* magazine, André Bazin and Béla Balázs, are examined in terms of a revisionist understanding of modernist emotion and intimacy. Such theory can be aligned in turn I suggest with sentimental principles introduced in the first chapter; for instance, in relation to the face in close-up (Balázs on Dreyer's *The Passion of Joan of Arc* (1928)), 'sentimental humanism' (Eisenstein on Dickens), the importance of a virtuous hero or heroine (Balázs' critique of avant-garde film), and notions of 'sympathetic' film-making (Bazin on Chaplin and De Sica).

Chapter 3 focuses on the critical functions of comedy in relation to sentimental narrative structures in the early and classical Hollywood eras, focusing on how humour is both celebrated and critiqued in terms of its counter-balancing, compensation for, or even negation of the sentimental in film. The chapter starts by analysing Chaplin's adoption of a melodramatic style in his feature films, as understood in terms of Linda Williams' arguments for melodrama as a dominant 'mode' of popular Hollywood cinema. Chaplin's early work will be analysed with particular reference to the critical opposition to his features on the part of intellectuals wedded to a more 'naturalistic' cinema or to Chaplin's more 'anarchic' deployment of slapstick, such as the American writer Gilbert Seldes and the early work of Siegfried Kracauer. The discussion then turns to the classical genres of Hollywood's 1930s and 1940s period, using sequences from John Ford's *Stagecoach* (1939) as an exemplary negotiation of sentiment and slapstick. Focus is maintained on the way that such categories are influenced by sentimental codes, particularly in terms of the persistence of genteel sensibilities and/or moralistic narrative structures. The chapter draws in such respects on key theorists of film comedy of that era, such as Stanley Cavell, Henry Jenkins, and Lea Jacobs.

Chapter 4 provides a wider theoretical basis for the 'sophistication' and self-consciousness that characterises post-classical or postmodern forms of sentimentality in US film culture, with particular attention paid to notions of 'excess' and distanciation. It accounts in particular for the influence of key modernists like Adorno, Benjamin, and Brecht on taste

INTRODUCTION

19

categories that persist in contemporary film studies, with particular reference to the 'ideological stoicism' that is alleged to predominate in critical film culture. The discussion will provide a context for a discussion of the 'affective' turn in film theory, around which the contributions of Gilles Deleuze and Stanley Cavell loom large in their centralisation of a film-as-thought paradigm.

This provides the theoretical basis for case studies in Chapters 5 and 6, both of which circulate around the predominance of 'camp' in contemporary US genre films. Chapter 5's discussion turns to two 'post-classical' examples of Hollywood's war/combat genre, examining their problematic negotiation of sentimentality as fundamentally melodramatic films. The 'camp' appropriation of violence and identity of Quentin Tarantino's *Inglourious Basterds* (2009) is conceived in such respects as an apparent rhetorical antidote to the 'New Sincerity' of Steven Spielberg's *Saving Private Ryan* (1998), a negotiation that I suggest is problematised by its own reliance on gendered discourses of action and resistance as adequate responses to trauma and memory. Chapter 6 examines the 'camp' sensibility of two contemporary art films, Lars von Trier's *Dancer in the Dark* (2000) and Todd Solondz' *Palindromes* (2004), focusing in particular on their respective treatments of melodrama as a genre attuned to the experience and suffering of women in US society. Meditating on the problem of gender and childhood in pastoral America, the analysis seeks to explore the negotiation of sentimentalist conventions borrowed from traditional film genres like the musical and the 'maternal melodrama', focusing in particular on issues of 'play' and camp performance. The discussion thus raises problems introduced in earlier chapters with regards to the self-reflexive bracketing of sentimentality as a discourse of sincerity and ethical subjectivity, emphasising its ambiguous presence in the art film as a mode of fantasy and self-reflexive mythologising.

I argue in the chapters below indeed that, notwithstanding wide-ranging dismissal of sentimentalism by popular and critical voices, the concept represents a fertile mode of discourse for considering the affective dimensions of film. Indeed, I would suggest that a discursive grey area exists between critical dismissal and euphoric celebrations/recuperations of melodramatic pathos, requiring a more fine-tuned, media-specific, and historically sensitive analysis of its tropes and paradigms. In relation to film specifically, sentimentalism aspires to what the medium was almost destined to embody in terms of its eclectic sensual palette, while at the same time a property of predecessor arts that many may have wished film to one day overcome entirely. In such respects, I have situated my discussion specifically around debates that animate theorists of cinematic and political modernism, examining how sentimentality has been both quarantined or dismissed by realist and modernist sensibilities, at the same time that it shares certain historical precursors and aesthetic concerns. As a body of theory that both validates 'feeling' in its pedagogical and idealist aims while remaining problematic ideologically, the sentimental demands a renewed critical scrutiny.

Notes

1. For criticisms of Spielberg's treatment of the Holocaust in *Schindler's List*, see Bill Nichols, 'The 10 Stations of Spielberg's Passion: "Saving Private Ryan." "Amistad." "Schindler's List."', *Jump Cut* 43 (July 2000), pp. 9–11; Leon Wieseltier, 'Close Encounters of the Nazi Kind', *The New Republic* 210, no. 4 (1994), p. 42.

2. Examples of which Elsaesser provides in relation to the 'strong actions' of the traditional Western, Gangster, or Noir genres, where 'central conflicts' are 'successively externalised and projected into direct action'. See Thomas Elsaesser, 'Tales of Sound and Fury', in Bill Nichols (ed.), *Movies and Methods. Vol. 2*, Berkeley and Los Angeles: University of California Press, 1985, p. 177.

3. Applying Peter Brooks' discussion of literary melodrama, Elsaesser in particular proposed melodrama as a 'mode of experience' derived from the sentimental novel and popular nineteenth-century theatre, a 'sophisticated' dimension of which was manifest in the 'family melodrama' of the 1940s and 1950s. Such films, among others, were claimed to foreground middle-class American family life as a site of individual struggle, frustration, and psychological turmoil, despite the nuclear family's valorisation elsewhere within the American culture of the 1950s (especially on television). See also Laura Mulvey, 'Notes on Sirk and Melodrama', *Movie* 25 (winter 1977/8), pp. 53–6; Geoffrey Nowell-Smith, 'Minnelli and Melodrama', *Screen* 18, no. 2 (1977), pp. 113–18; Chuck Kleinhans, 'Notes on Melodrama and the Family under Capitalism', *Film Reader*, 3 (1978), pp. 40–7; D. N. Rodowick, 'Madness, Authority and Ideology: The Domestic Melodrama of the 1950s', in Marcia Landy (ed.), *Imitations of Life: A Reader on Film and Television Melodrama*, Detroit: Wayne State University Press, 1991, pp. 237–47.

4. Steve Neale's analysis of reception materials surrounding the release and circulation of early film melodrama shows in a similar vein how an understanding of the genre can no longer be confined to the categories of the 'maternal' or 'family' melodrama. He shows, for instance, how the term 'melodrama' was used in cinema's early years as much in relation to early Westerns, crime dramas, and adventure films as to domestic or maternal dramas. See Steve Neale, 'Melo Talk: On the Meaning and Use of the Term "Melodrama" in the American Trade Press', *Velvet Light Trap* 32 (1993), pp. 66–89.

5. This particular application of critical theory, moreover, has come under severe criticism in the last twenty years of film scholarship, in terms of its alleged failures in addressing issues surrounding filmmaking and developments in film technology with sufficient historical scrutiny, as critiqued most forcefully by such figures as David Bordwell and Noël Carroll. See David Bordwell and Noël Carroll, *Post-Theory: Reconstructing Film Studies*, Madison, WI: University of Wisconsin Press, 1996.

6. Williams, for instance, recognises melodrama's logic in such traditionally male-oriented tales as Mark Twain's *Adventures of Huckleberry Finn* or films such as *Rambo* (1982). See Linda Williams, 'Melodrama Revised', in Nick Browne (ed.), *Refiguring American Film Genres: History and Theory*, Berkeley: University of California Press, 1998, pp. 42–88; pp. 1–39.

7. Neale draws in particular on Franco Moretti's narrational analysis of melodrama's 'tears', defining its high emotions in terms of where the 'point of view of one of the characters comes to coincide with the point of view of the reader as established by the narrative' (7).

8. Such emphasis on the melodrama's affinities with loss and the 'if only' has gone some way in shifting debate away from feminist film theory's initial focus on the 'Women's Film', a genre conceived of in relation to the critical analysis of women's experience under patriarchy (both in terms of female protagonists and in reference to real women audiences of the 1930s and 1940s). With a focus on women's experience as a site of suffering and pathos, such films were initially polemicised by feminist film theorists as articulations of a specifically feminist response to capitalism, patriarchy, class, and family. Foregrounding the female experience in American society, melodrama, and the 'Woman's film' (the latter referring to films such as *Stella Dallas* (Vidor, 1937), *Now Voyager* (Rapper, 1942), and *Mildred Pierce* (Curtiz, 1945), provided a gendered expression of the problematics of female identity with a specifically modernist attention to image and ideology. See Linda Williams, 'Something Else Besides a Mother: "Stella Dallas" and the Maternal Melodrama', *Cinema Journal* 24, no. 1 (autumn 1984), pp. 2–27; Mary-Ann Doane, *The Desire to Desire: The Woman's Film of the 1940s*, Bloomington: Indiana University Press, 1987; Gaylyn Studlar, *In the Realm of Pleasure: Von Sternberg, Dietrich and the Masochistic Aesthetic*, New York: Columbia University Press, 1988.

9. By fostering identification with victims and resolving conflict within their micro-situations (that is the family unit) the melodrama seemed to avoid a more complex articulation of women's oppression under patriarchy, a pathos that was as much the problem as the solution. See Williams' discussion of her disagreements with E. Ann Kaplan (44–6).

10. Žižek argues, for instance, that 'critical energy has found a substitute outlet in fighting for cultural differences which leave the basic homogeneity of the capitalist world-system intact' (2000: 218).

CHAPTER 1

Towards a Genealogy of Sentimentalism in the Eighteenth and Nineteenth Centuries

> Standing all alone in the midst of the business and bustle of the street, the house looked a picture of cold desolation; and Kit, who remembered the cheerful fire that used to burn there on a winter's night and the no less cheerful laugh that made the small room ring, turned quite mournfully away.
>
> It must be especially observed in justice to poor Kit that he was by no means of a sentimental turn, and perhaps had never heard that adjective in all his life. He was only a soft-hearted grateful fellow, and had nothing genteel or polite about him; consequently, instead of going home again, in his grief, to kick the children and abuse his mother (for, when your finely strung people are out of sorts, they must have everybody else unhappy likewise), he turned his thoughts to the vulgar expedient of making them more comfortable if he could.
>
> (Dickens, *The Old Curiosity Shop*, 2001: 105–6)

This passage reveals the sentimental here as a mere mask of gentility in Dickens' world, the underside of which is characterised precisely as the cruelty of abusing one's own family members. To be 'soft-hearted' and 'grateful' is contrasted here with the artifices of a 'sentimental turn' – the latter is a socially appropriate reaction to Little Nell's absence from her house, while Kit's feelings are genuine and true. Dickens is clearly in sympathy here with those who may never have heard of the word 'sentimental' or learnt its codes of appropriate emotionality, and contrasts them with a 'finely strung' class who have learnt its mannerisms but are in essence morally bankrupt. This framing of sentimentality echoes that described by philosopher Mary Midgley, who equally aligns its codes with an attitude of 'brutality' (1979), as echoed furthermore in Oscar Wilde's dismissal of sentimentality as the mere 'bank holiday of cynicism' (2005: 353).

Nevertheless, to be 'sentimental', or to have 'sensibilité', would be associated in the mid-eighteenth century with the cultivating of precisely that sympathy written of in relation to Kit: a goodwill towards the other and a moral purity of spirit towards reform and the alleviation of misfortune. It would become the mark of bourgeois civility, through the approval and tearful enjoyment of the capacity for sympathy with others' tales of woe and suffering. This ambiguity surrounding the ethical components of sentimentalism is reflected indeed in one of the first written deployments of the term, by a close correspondent of the novelist Samuel Richardson, Lady Bradshaigh, where she enquires of him:

> What, in your opinion, is the meaning of the word *sentimental*, so much in vogue among the polite . . . Every thing clever and agreeable is comprehended in that word . . . I am frequently astonished to hear such a one is a *sentimental* man; we were a *sentimental* party; I have been taking a *sentimental* walk. (*OED* 2017; emphasis in the original)

No sooner has the 'sentimental' entered language, therefore, than a question is raised as to its meanings. Would it denote a property of the subject's character or would it have more to do with the nature of a collective group, activity, or event? Does it denote the intellectual refinement signified by what is 'clever', or does it have the more taste-based valency of the 'agreeable'? What seems notably absent from Bradshaigh's question is indeed any direct indication of sentiment's ethical or moral dimensions. In its place is the revealing deployment of 'polite' in reference to those for whom the word is in 'vogue', indicating the term's possible exclusivity to the fashionable and cultivated upper classes.

Indeed, although the sentimental presents difficulties of definition in one of its first coinages, something that seems assured in Bradshaigh's questions is its association with the various activities and tastes of an urbane and refined portion of British society. The current *Oxford English Dictionary*'s (*OED*'s) definition of 'sentimental' retains such associations, at least in its 'originally . . . favourable' sense, to people characterised by 'exhibiting refined and elevated feeling', or to those whom the Romantic poet Robert Southey, in 1823, would refer to rather more disdainfully as the 'sentimental classes' (*OED* 2017). It is precisely in this invocation of the patrician upper classes of eighteenth-century Britain that an ethics of sentiment, and its fallacies, seem often to go hand in hand. As an ethics indexed problematically to the tastes and discrimination of a particular social group, sentimentalism often signifies the discrimination and tastes of a historical social group with its own biases, tastes, and preferences as much as a more generalisable standard.

Uncovering the history of sentimentality as a category of taste is indeed an important first step in understanding the role that cinema would come to play in both representing and eliciting emotions, allowing us to draw connections between older aesthetic debates and ongoing questions raised by affect-oriented approaches to film. This chapter therefore traces sentimentalism as it reached its apex in the moral philosophy and literature of the eighteenth century, considering specifically the ways that sentimentalism became respectable as well as how it came to attain its more contemporary alignments with bad taste and excessively mannered approaches to writing and other artistic output. Focus is then broadened to account for the ways that nineteenth-century melodrama, and later cinema, served as important negotiations and inheritors of the sentimental tradition, underlining its particular significance to the emergence of American narrative film.

Virtue Imperilled

Sentimentalism, or the 'Law of the Heart', to use Terry Eagleton's term (1990: 33–71), would be in vogue for much of the mid-eighteenth century in Britain, France, and Germany. It represented a particular stance in relation to the ethical possibilities of emotion, strongly identified with the rise of the novel (although sentimental tropes were certainly present in all art forms including poetry, theatre, and painting). It was also integral to much of the eighteenth-century's moral philosophy, especially in its concerns with the possibility of a virtuous subject in an increasingly urbanised and pragmatised society. The complex historical, political, and philosophical antecedents leading up to the coming to prominence of this 'law' falls outside the scope of this chapter, but two things are worth emphasising here. The first regards the intervention that such a school of thought represents in relation to the 'egoistic' philosophy of Hobbes; the second regards the relation to the absolutist rule of the Stuarts and the aristocracy of sixteenth- and seventeenth-century England and France, as represented in the courtly wit and libertinism of the period's 'Restoration drama' in Britain. Sentimental literature is indeed closely indexed to the rise of bourgeois economics and Enlightenment morality, symbolised by the overthrow and demonisation of the feudalist aristocracy of previous centuries. In the sentimental novel, young women are vulnerable to the desires and pursuits of the 'libertine' aristocrat of the previous century's excesses: a misogynistic male aristocrat who considers himself intellectually and legally free of moral constraints, and runs amuck to the detriment of the lower orders. Seducing lower-class women without any further commitments, such as marriage or family, the libertine is a recurring figure in Samuel Richardson's novels, typified by Mr B (in *Pamela*) and Lovelace (in *Clarissa*). The 'sentiments' that such eponymous heroines live by in turn embody principles that, when challenged by the rake's sexual advances, are defended by weeping, wordless sighs, and confidences made by the heroine to her diary, comprising a language of virtue imperilled, and eventually either rewarded (by marriage) or redeemed (by saintly death). Counterposed to the linguistic and intellectual dexterity of the rake, virtue becomes aligned here with the visuality, and thus legibility, of a (feminised) emotion, an alignment that the melodrama of later eras (and the cinema, of course) comes to exploit in their own contributions to the sentimental tradition.

In France, in 1762, the *philosophe* Denis Diderot (1713–84) would write of a benevolence felt vicariously through his emotional responses to Richardson's novels. He claims that 'the passions he portrays are those I feel within me; the same things arouse them, and I recognise their force in myself' (Diderot 1994: 83). Moreover, such praise is characterised by a strong conviction of the moral worthiness of reading the novels. As an elegy to Richardson, who had died in 1761, he writes:

> How good I was! How just I was! Wasn't I pleased with myself! When I had been reading you, I was like a man who had spent the day doing good. (Diderot 1994: 83)

The proud celebration of reading as an explicitly moral activity may seem slightly absurd and reductive of literature's wider aesthetic aims by today's standards, yet typifies the values of those who recommended the practice, as attributed to Samuel Johnson, of reading 'for the sentiment'.[1] To read of virtuous characters is conceived here as a vicarious practice of those same good deeds without the attendant difficulties of doing the same in reality. Reading becomes a moral act through the assumed transmission of virtue between text and reader. Diderot thus elsewhere offers a definition of 'sensibilité' that is thoroughly infused with moralistic discourse. Thus:

> Sensibilité is that tender and delicate disposition of the soul which renders it easy to be moved and touched . . . It gives one a kind of wisdom concerning matters of virtue and is far more penetrating than the intellect alone. People of sensibility because of their liveliness can fall into errors which men of the world would not commit; but these are greatly outweighed by the amount of good that they do. Men of sensibility live more fully than others . . . Reflection can produce a man of probity; but sensibility is the mother of humanity, of generosity; it is at the service of merit, lends its support to the intellect, and is the moving spirit which animates belief. (Diderot cited in Brissenden 1974: 115)

With this definition of sensibilité, the *philosophe* asserts the superiority of a subject who lives by feeling to one who lives by 'reflection', or the intellect, alone. This privileging of feeling or 'passion' over reasoned 'reflection' is indebted in turn to various positions in the British 'Moral Sense' school of philosophy, also known as the 'Scottish Enlightenment', as represented by such figures as Anthony Cooper (third Earl of Shaftesbury), Francis

Hutcheson, Lord Kames, David Hume, and Adam Smith. Indeed, Diderot had translated Shaftesbury's *Inquiry Concerning Virtue* into French, and in his own writings extols the virtues of a subject who acts with affective humanity and benevolence. With influences as diverse as the liberal 'empiricist' doctrines of John Locke and seventeenth-century Deism and Platonism, 'Moral Sense' philosophy is concerned above all with the importance of emotion to the moral efficacy of reason, as popularised by Shaftesbury's *Characteristics of Men, Manners, Opinions*, published in 1711. Like the 'Deists' before him, Shaftesbury's philosophy is shaped by the theological doctrines of reward, punishment, and self-preservation that underpin Christian orthodoxy and Locke's empiricism.

Shaftesbury's main argument turns indeed on the possibility of a life of virtue that can be eventually followed through instinct rather than having to be enforced by a system of incentives, penalties, and obedience to authority. In this, Shaftesbury sets a template for the 'Moral Sense' school in its foregrounding of emotion and compassion as integral components of ethical conduct. David Hume in turn relates Shaftesbury's model of innate ethical instinct to aesthetics and the function of art in cultivating taste, thus claiming that

> nothing is so improving to the temper as the study of the beauties, either of poetry, eloquence, music, or painting. They give a certain elegance of sentiment to which the rest of mankind are strangers. The emotions which they excite are soft and tender. (Hume 1987)

Aligned thus with a cultivating function, art serves for Hume as a negotiation between raw 'passions' and the formal structures of reason, through the intermediaries of 'elegance' and 'eloquence'. Hume's theory shares here with Diderot an emphasis on 'sensibility' and the affective, a shared conviction in the 'improving' powers of 'beauty' as vital components to truth and moral value. Like Diderot, too, Hume deploys a sentimentalist language in his extended analyses of human psychology and emotion. In his essay 'On Goodness and Benevolence', for instance, when he describes our innate approval for the expression and display of 'love', he argues:

> The tears naturally start in our eyes at the conception of it [Love]; nor can we forbear giving a loose to the same tenderness towards the person who exerts it. All this seems to me a proof, that our approbation has, in those cases, an origin different from the prospect of utility and advantage, either to ourselves or others. (Hume 1896)

For Hume, then, tears become evidence of a subject's genuine and disinterested approval of a benevolent concept like love. Aligned with 'sympathy', love is explained (true to the style of 'moral sense') as something that lies beyond perceived self-interest, inspiring 'tender' as opposed to rational or self-directed cognitions. The key anchor of Hume's argument rests on what he terms a 'spark of friendship' between subjects, or 'contagious' (Hume 1896) passions, that in his terms:

> pass with the greatest facility from one person to another, and produce correspondent movements in all human breasts. Where friendship appears in very signal instances, my heart catches the same passion, and is warmed by those warm sentiments, that display themselves before me. (Hume 1896)

'Warm sentiments' and 'correspondent movements' signal thus a mode of interpersonal engagement that differs radically from the registration of more intellectual concepts or doctrines. This great optimism in 'friendship' is grounded in an assumed inevitability with which emotions can be transmitted between subjects. Importantly, such 'correspondent movements' are pre-cognitive, that is, they are shared bodily experiences rather than necessarily shared beliefs or ideas.

Emotion thus takes on a particularly important function in Hume here, with the body and its tender registration of reality privileged over mind and concept. As Hume famously claims, 'reason ought only be the slave of the passions, and can never pretend to any other office than to serve and obey them' (Hume 1896). This is often cited as evidence of Hume's unambiguous privileging of feeling over reason, but on various levels this simplifies Hume's sentimentalism. As Michael L. Frazer argues of Hume, moral sentiments 'are not merely passions, but products of the mind as a whole, reason and imagination included. It is from passion alone that these sentiments get their motivational impetus, but moral sentiments are much more than mere impetus' (2010: 6).

Hume elsewhere advances a thesis that asserts the 'delicacy of taste' as ultimately superior to 'delicacy of the passions'. 'Taste' refers principally here to the sensitivity of those who respond to life aesthetically, and echoing film theorists like Béla Balázs, is described specifically in terms of the subject's apprehension of life's minutiae. Thus, he argues:

> It is remarkable, that nothing touches a man of humanity more than any instance of extraordinary delicacy in love or friendship, where a person is attentive to the smallest concerns of his friend, and is willing to sacrifice to them the most considerable interest of his own. Such delicacies have little influence on society; because they make us regard the greatest trifles: But they are the more engaging, the more minute the concern is, and are a proof of the highest merit in any one, who is capable of them. (Hume 1896)

Such attention to detail, or as Hume claims, the 'greatest trifles', as a criterion of 'delicacy' aligns Hume quite closely therefore to theories of cinema that similarly emphasise the cinema's foregrounding of life's 'smallest concerns', such as in Balázs, where a sentimentalist language is invoked in relation to the close-up's revelation of human action and feeling. What unites these thinkers is a shift in emphasis towards questions of emotion and ethics over matters of reason and impartiality, particularly in relation to interpersonal communication. The chief function of art emerges here as the fostering or cultivation of sensibility or delicacy, an enhancement of our better faculties as sensitive spectators.

France and the 'Cult of Sensibility'

If the theory emerges from Scottish Enlightenment thinkers, it is France that most clearly embraces sentimentality as a cultural practice in mid-eighteenth century Europe. Anne Vincent-Buffault shows, for instance, that, in France, the event of eliciting tears in public audiences attains the status of communal ritual by 1730, fulfilling the sentimental ideal of shared, 'contagious effects' (1991: 243). Friedrich Melchior, Baron von Grimm would claim thus:

> Men are all friends when leaving a play. They have hated vice, loved virtue, cried together, developed the good and just elements of the human heart side by side. They have found themselves to be far better than they thought, they would willingly embrace each other... (Grimm cited in Vincent-Buffault 1991: 67)

In order to satisfy the requirements of this collective ritual, Vincent-Buffault argues thus that the elicitation of tears becomes an essential criterion for new plays. In about 1730, a new tragic-comic genre arises, with a plot that in Gustave Lanson's words, 'incites us to virtue in feeling for their misfortunes and in applauding their triumphs' (cited in Vincent-Buffault 1991: 60). The bourgeois family home becomes the key setting for this 'Comédie Larmoyante', and tearful scenes become highly conventionalised. The misfortune of innocent victims and the defeat of social prejudice (such as the victory of romantic love over class prejudice and financial considerations) become common narrative tropes for the elicitation of tears. Like the 'sentimental comedy' of British theatre at the time, the form constitutes also an obvious precursor to the following century's melodramas.

In 1769, in his *Paradoxe sur le Comédien* (Paradox of Acting), Diderot also praises a style of acting that has the maximisation of audience emotion as its key aim, using techniques such as 'cries, inarticulate words', or 'broken voices' (Diderot 1936: 576–7). Aristotle, in his *Poetics*, famously advised caution about the excessive gesticulations of some actors,[2] yet Diderot gives the actor here the task of accentuating the spectacle of suffering through 'a splendid aping', a dramatic style that is larger than life. Thus:

> A gladiator of ancient times is like a great actor, and a great actor is like an ancient gladiator; they do not die as people die in bed. They must portray before us a different death so as to please us, and the viewer feels that the bare, unadorned truth of movement would be shallow and contrary to the poetry of the whole. (Diderot 1936: 581)

By contrast, Jean-Jacques Rousseau, in 1758, frames theatrical sentiment alongside other problematically conventionalised artifices of civil society. Concerned about the theatre spectator who has 'wept over imaginary ills' without feeling any inclination for applying the same emotions to his own social reality, Rousseau claims:

> We believe that we are drawn together at a performance, when it is there that each of us becomes isolated, it is there that we will forget our friends, our neighbours, our dear ones, and direct our interest towards fables, weep over the misfortunes of the dead or laugh at the expense of the living. But I feel that this language is no longer in season in our century. (Rousseau cited in Vincent-Buffault 1991: 119)

In the above passage, the sentimental theatre (and its attendant 'language') is framed by Rousseau as an apparatus of alienated subjectivity in its elicitation of individuated pleasures, a corruption of a more authentic sensibility that would reside for Rousseau in the connections between friends and neighbours within a simpler, rustic society. In his second preface to *La Nouvelle Heloise*, urban and rural existence are thus polarised, with the unthinking virtue of the naïve rustic held up as the ideal of sensibility in contrast to the mannerisms of the city-dweller. Those who live outside an abstracted world of corruption, beyond artificial models of sociality, are applauded for a natural common sense. Rousseau's preferred mode of representation is thus diametrically opposed to Diderot's prescriptions for acting the pathetic scene:

> Do you believe that really impassioned people have those intense, strong, colorful ways of speaking that you admire in your Dramas and Novels? No: passion wrapped up in itself expresses itself with more profusion than power. (Rousseau 2010: 10)

The language and performance of sensibility therefore occupy for Rousseau one extreme of a marked opposition between a decadent, emotionalist world and a virtuous form of spiritual existence, the latter removed from the former both physically and semiotically. His sentimentalism is thus both continuous with an Enlightened opposition of 'reason to privilege, equality to hierarchy' (Howard 2010: 249) yet also singularly sceptical about the systematicity of civil society, wherein the 'goodness of nature (and natural man)' is privileged over the 'artificial conventions of civilisation' (ibid.). In terms of a theatrical aesthetics, the display of tears by the spectator becomes suspect here for Rousseau, a superficial substitute for a more effective (because more deeply felt) response to social or ethical problems.

A 'Sickly Sort of Refinement'

Invoked above in Rousseau are distinctions retained by much contemporary criticism between the authenticity of naturalism as opposed to more melodramatic or mannerist styles of acting, with importance attached above all to standards of verisimilitude and realism. Rousseau's comments also provide a template for sentimentalism's dismissal in later centuries as a reliable philosophical system, wherein issues of pleasure surrounding spectatorship come to sit in tension with the ethical imperatives of a 'Law of the Heart'. In Britain in the 1750s, Rousseau's comments are mirrored by the writings of numerous moralists who attempt to distinguish authentic from false feeling. In an anonymous letter to the journal *Man* would be one of the first instances of the use of the term 'sentimental', in praise of 'Moral weeping':

> We may properly distinguish weeping into two general kinds, genuine and counterfeit; or into physical crying and moral weeping. Physical crying, while there are no real corresponding ideas in the mind, nor any genuine sentimental feeling of the heart to produce it, depends upon the mechanism of the body: but moral weeping proceeds from, and is always attended with, such real sentiments of the mind, and feeling of the heart, as do honour to human nature; which false crying always debases. (Anonymous cited in Lutz 1999: 31)

The Scottish moralist David Fordyce would later on in the decade write the following concerning the 'Enjoyments' of a moral subject's 'Sympathy' and, specifically, the emotional discharge that characterises such moments of compassion. Thus:

> It is such a Sorrow as he loves to indulge; a sort of pleasing Anguish, that sweetly melts the Mind, and terminates in a Self-approving Joy. Though the good Man may want Means to execute, or be disappointed in the Success of his benevolent

Purposes, yet . . . he is still conscious of good Affections. (Fordyce cited in Crane 1934: 205)

As in Hume, compassionate sorrow is allowed to be 'agreeable' and 'pleasing' because it is never not aligned with the 'good' and is always praiseworthy. Crane nevertheless points to Fordyce's 'complacent emphasis' on 'Self-Approving Joy'. The danger of sentiment, as detected by Rousseau above and others discussed below, is that it may constitute a narcissistic indulgence in self-regarding moralism as opposed to a critical engagement with the socio-political contexts of a sorrowful scene. If such a critical exercise required an intellectual analysis of the scene as well as an emotional connection to its sadness, how would such analysis be possible if the subject is overwhelmed by an 'Anguish' that 'melts the Mind'?

Following the notoriety of Richardson and his epistolary novels (*Pamela: Or, Virtue Rewarded* (1740), *Clarissa: Or the History of a Young Lady* (1748), and *The History of Sir Charles Grandison* (1753),) and the public appetite for sentiment, many imitations of his novels come to proliferate. They would come to suffer for many from a 'moral bankruptcy' (Brissenden 1974: 125), exploiting the pleasures of tearful readership without the 'psychological realism and moral seriousness' of the earlier novels of sentiment. Plot and character conventions come to be recognised and deployed for their capacity to elicit emotions as ends unto themselves, such as the abduction of women, cynical attacks on provincial families by rakish aristocratic men (see Henry Mackenzie's *The Man of the World*), or the lament of the impossibility of real friendship in the city in Henry Brooke's *The Fool of Quality* (1770). The heroes of these novels display a characteristically maudlin innocence about society and its evils. A language of tears, sighs, and gestures becomes generic, a recurrent convention of representing feelings too deep for verbal expression. Fainting, swooning, or crying are resorted to frequently, in order to be replicated in the reactions of its own readers who have learned a bodily code of refined feeling. A critic in the *Monthly Review* of 1771 approves of Henry Mackenzie's *Man of Feeling*, and its hero, Harley, for instance, owing to its specific appeal to the emotions, arguing that 'the Reader, who weeps not over some of the scenes it describes, has no sensibility of mind' (cited in Brissenden 1974: 254).

The elicitation of tears, at the time, was indeed still widely regarded as a worthy aim of fiction that traded in pathetic tropes. To exhibit 'refined feeling' was culturally valorised as a literary motif and to sob over such tales would be evidence of one's own sensibility and moral correctness. This was accompanied nevertheless by scepticism of its modishness as well as with

its alignments with higher social echelons. As a contained aesthetic experience, sentiment could be all too easily commodified for the consumption
of spectators merely wishing to indulge in its pleasures. When writing for
the Edinburgh periodical *The Lounger*, Henry Mackenzie himself attacks
the literary 'species called the Sentimental' that encouraged in readers
a 'sickly sort of refinement' (cited in Mullan 1988: 128). As a trained
Edinburgh lawyer, Mackenzie is suspicious of the sentiments that could be
fostered by such novels. Yet although he and others attacked the excesses
of sensibility in rendering readers unable or unwilling to operate successfully in ordinary life, they still believe that such novels represent the ideals
of refinement or delicacy that befit an advanced society. As John Mullan
argues in his account of eighteenth-century sensibility, Harley's admirable
sensibility was the 'fantasy' rather than the 'practice of a complex urban
society' (118).

Increasingly understood thus as an affective privilege, sentimentality
shifts in meaning rather significantly in the direction of a 'sickly' or cloying
moral posturing of a cultured but ethically compromised elite. Even
David Hume eventually set limits on the 'sympathy' initially celebrated
in his *Treatise*. Mullan, for instance, notes how 'warm sentiment' becomes
aligned in Hume's later work with aesthetic experience, a ('peculiarly literary capacity' or 'the great charm of poetry'), thus setting constraints
on the political efficacy of sentiment and its ethics (43). Put differently,
'sympathy' no longer constitutes a politics as such, as it can no longer be
guaranteed by Hume beyond the formal parameters of the artwork and
its immediate reception. The shifts in Hume's discourse demonstrate a
sympathy that is thus compromised by issues of aesthetic pleasure and
subjectivity. Sentimentality comes to invoke the discrepancy between an
idealised or aestheticised benevolence and the realities of social existence
that seem inimical to it. The philosophy of Adam Smith, Hume's friend
and admirer, can be similarly examined in terms of sentimentalisms's
marginalisation as a viable 'practice', not least once moral sentiment is
framed as an affect that must be regulated by the cold judgement of the
'impartial spectator' (Smith 2007: 184) of Smith's *The Theory of Moral
Sentiments*, published in 1759. Such a 'spectator', representing 'dignity',
'honour', and 'unalterable laws' (ibid.) observes the subject and enforces
a dispassionate behaviour. This behaviour, Smith argues, is different from
the behaviour informed by the subject's other perceptions of reality, one
that is based on 'his natural, his untaught and undisciplined feelings', in
relation to which Smith accords the spectator moral authority (ibid.).

It is here that we reach an impasse in the celebration of an individual
ethics as grounds for a politics. The off-hand cautions of Shaftesbury and

Hume against the 'extremes' of feeling take centre-stage for Smith and urge him and those who would follow him to heed Hobbes' advice and once again subjugate the passions to the necessities of social and political life. Indeed, according to the literary scholar Michael Bell, it is precisely with this loss of faith in the power of individual goodwill that sentimentalism attains its modern connotations. Thus, 'once the social order comes to be seen as a complex impersonal process changeable only by collective political will, then any appeal to individual feeling begins to seem necessarily, structurally, sentimental' (Bell 2000: 120). Whether through the 'impersonal' processes of new economic theory or the mass political movements in America and France at the end of the eighteenth century, hopes for the personified Enlightenment subject is eclipsed here by faith in collective will, declarations of rights, and scientifically approved means of distributing wealth. To limit one's faith to that of the individual subject's sensibility becomes a sentimental fantasy.[3]

Similarly, in France, the term 'sensiblerie' is coined in the 1780s to refer to a false or affected language of sympathetic gestures. The poet Mercier, in 1799, claims thus:

Some time before the Revolution, people of fashion had adopted a certain sentimental philosophy ('une certain philosophie sentimentale') which was the art of dispensing with being virtuous. This philosophy had its jargon, its sensibility, its accent, even its gestures.[4]

In Britain, the same concept comes to be termed 'sentimentality'.[5] 'Sentimental' becomes effectively a brand name for a genre, with the term itself appearing in many titles, most paradigmatically Laurence Sterne's *A Sentimental Journey through France and Italy* (1768). Many imitations follow Sterne's novel with titles such as *The Delicate Distress* (1757), *Excessive Sensibility* (1787), and *The Curse of Sentiment* (1787). Trading on displays of pathos that are presented in fleetingly episodic form, the sentimental narrative modifies classical tragedy for the purpose of intensified emotion. Raymond Williams argues thus in *Modern Tragedy* that scenes of suffering are given a particular moral dimension in eighteenth-century tragic forms, wherein the 'tragic catastrophe . . . moves its spectators to moral recognition and resolution' (as in *Clarissa*) or 'can be avoided altogether, by a change of heart' (1966: 31). Williams is notably critical of the often 'static' forms of morality represented in works from the period and the 'merely dogmatic' representation of 'good and evil'. As 'repentance and redemption' become the driving forces of eighteenth-century narrative, Williams is critical not of the period's 'moral emphasis' per se, but the rigidity with which morality comes to be represented and understood (ibid.).

Regarded increasingly as self-indulgent, excessive, and shallow, sensibility and the novel of sentiment become parodied by such writers as Jane Austen as early as 1790 with *Love and Freindship* [*sic*]. The novella provides a brief but incisive glimpse at the conformism and amorality of gentility and a form of subjectivity that applauds one's own sentimentalism as a model of conduct.[6] Arguably the most 'modern' responses to sentimentality would be manifest in texts where an ironic distance is inscribed in relation to its tropes. Particularly subtle in such regards would be Sterne's approach to the sentimental, where 'sympathy' and weeping are bracketed as social practices deployed for a variety of rhetorical and self-interested purposes by self-conscious characters. In *Sentimental Journey*, Yorick's account of his encounter with Madame de L*** contains clues that this narrator is motivated by multiple impulses towards her, both sexual and sympathetic, insisting on his own 'benevolence' while simultaneously alluding humorously to his lust. The fictional narrators of *A Sentimental Journey* (1768), and *Tristram Shandy* (1767), exhibit ironic self-consciousness towards their own accounts, demonstrating awareness of their own contradictory desires and thereby nuancing, if not effacing, the moralistic discourses that surround the sentimental novel. Sterne provides neither a model of conduct in his protagonists nor are they objects of simple satire. In this, the novel demonstrates what John Mullan refers to as a 'sociality' (1988: 67), both on the part of the author's ironic mode of address and a character's self-knowledge, aspects of which echo the concept of 'excess' in film theory discussed in later chapters.

Nineteenth-century Melodrama and the 'Puritan-Democratic Worldview'

Sentimentalism therefore becomes increasingly suspect in its alignments with hackneyed 'static' tropes and the pleasurable tears they could elicit in reader and/or audience. Such tropes as the imperilled moral hero or heroine and the struggle to overcome villainy would nevertheless of course be heavily reproduced in the visual and non-visual melodramas of the following century and beyond. This is owing in no small part to the discrepancies between critical and popular modes of reception, wherein the practice of reading 'for the sentiment' persisted as a dominant protocol aligned with bourgeois-liberal Christianised values of sacrifice, virtue, and redemption. To explain its continued popularity, sentimentality has indeed been profitably understood as a structure of feeling that shared affective contours with a distinctly Western, and particularly, American mode of cultural politics. M. W. Disher's work on nineteenth-century theatre, for instance, is often cited for its delineation of 'Virtue Triumphant'. Thus:

> Even in gaffs and saloons, melodrama so strongly insisted on the sure reward to be bestowed in this life upon the law-abiding that sociologists now see in this a Machiavellian plot to keep democracy servile to Church and State . . . There is no parting the two strains, moral and political, in the imagination of the nineteenth-century masses. They are hopelessly entangled. Democracy shaped its own entertainments at a time when the vogue of Virtue Triumphant was at its height and they took their pattern from it . . . Here are Virtue Triumphant's attendant errors: confusion between sacred and profane, between worldly and spiritual advancement, between self-interest and self-sacrifice. (cited in Elsaesser 1985: 188)

This passage contains many, if not all, the key symptoms afforded by a particular strain of the melodramatic tradition in nineteenth-century theatre. Fuelled by a logic of 'Virtue Triumphant', melodrama is aligned here with the 'moral and political' imagination of the period, an ideology of servility before 'Church' and 'State'. In a similar vein to Williams' critique of the 'static' dogmatisms of 'modern tragedy', Disher's argument revolves around what Elsaesser, in a footnote to his seminal essay on the 'sophisticated melodrama' (Elsaesser 1985: 167), terms the 'puritan-democratic worldview' (188) a constellation of affects that renew the aesthetics of the pre-revolutionary sentimental novel. Posed as a key antecedent to the cinema, melodrama is situated by Elsaesser as the 'record of the struggle of a morally and emotionally emancipated bourgeois consciousness against the remnants of feudalism' (168). Central to such stories are tropes of 'innocence persecuted and virtue rewarded', which Elsaesser aligns with a political championing of the 'claims of the individual in an absolutist society' (168). Sentimentality is framed in particular here as a stylistic development of the melodrama that strains for moral legibility. Thus:

> Whereas the pre-revolutionary melodramas had often ended tragically, those of the Restoration had happy endings, they reconciled the suffering individual to his social position, by affirming an 'open' society, where everything was possible. Over and over again, the victory of the 'good' citizen over 'evil' aristocrats, lecherous clergymen and the even more conventional villains drawn from the lumpenpoletariat, was re-enacted in sentimental spectacles full of tears and high moral tones. (Elsaesser 1985: 169)

The embedded presence of the sentimental, within or alongside melodrama, functions then in complex ways. It harks back to a pre-revolutionary defence of the bourgeois individual and the latter's inherent virtue as a humanist category. However, it is also implicated in the ideological simplifications of melodrama as it evolved into a dominant form of popular entertainment. 'Full of tears and high moral tones' designates indeed the two central registers of the sentimental established above. The two combine crucially by 'affirming an "open" society', a consoling reification of the status quo and 'social position' over a more tragic articulation of social conflict and its losses.

I dwell here on Elsaesser's essay because of its cautious and astute foregrounding of the sentimental period as a significant precursor to Hollywood cinema and the melodramatic tradition. Embedded within melodrama, the sentimental is clearly invoked by the 'high moral tones' of bourgeois discourse that Elsaesser equates, in his discussion of the Hollywood 'family melodrama', with the 'incurably naive moral and emotional idealism in the American psyche' (182). The sentimental became associated with an epistemology of affirmation and legibility, allowing the structures of the present and the past to be valorised through conservative appeals to 'position' and status quo – a 'happy ending' less in literal but ideological terms, where a 'feelgood' message is imparted in relation to the intensity and moral legibility of the world represented. Emotion, specifically weeping, is often vital of course to the sentimental as defined, but it is qualified by a fundamental distrust of any easy alliance between cognition and emotion. In as much as melodramatic emotions may speak of potentially subversive truths that are not articulated linguistically, they are also signified in sentimental spectacle, where they can rather more problematically serve as the rhetorical gloss of false ideology, misguidedly or even deliberately signalling a moral authority that is inadequate in critical terms.

Melodrama often indeed contends with sentimentalism as the generic label for such forms of representation, and both terms are often employed for similarly pejorative ends in relation to similar artistic devices. Just as the 'sentimental' is often used to implicitly convey condemnation of its own excess, melodrama has also traditionally been vilified in terms of a story being 'overly melodramatic' (Williams 2002: 10–11). The fields of meaning for the sentimental and the melodramatic also often exceed associations with any particular textual genre, lending both terms a vagueness that can sometimes undermine their claims to useful meaning. It should be emphasised, however, that the two words possess different genealogies and attributes, despite the fact that they are representing traditions that overlap at various discursive and aesthetic levels. For instance, Lea Jacobs, in her account of the decline of a 'sentimental' cinema in 1920s Hollywood, notes that sentimentality and melodrama 'are not the same despite the fact that many melodramas are sentimental. The literature of sentiment predates melodrama, and there are melodramatic traditions that are not sentimental' (2008: 277). Jacobs goes on indeed to find 'sensationalism' as the chief distinguishing feature between the two forms, citing research on various publications of the early twentieth-century film industry that apply the label 'melodrama' in relation to the combination of action, spectacle, and special effects that came to characterise so much Hollywood cinema. This 'sensationalist' aesthetics corresponds less with the didactic and maudlin 'sentimental' genres and more with a tradition of 'blood and thunder' melodrama as it developed in nineteenth-century theatres, which certainly by the middle of that century had come to predominate, and was marked by increased investment in elaborate stage mechanics and scenographic naturalism, features that, of course, would be replicated by the spectacle and historical verisimilitude of film genres like the Western, gangster film, or epic of the following century.[7]

Melodrama in the narrower sense of its being concerned chiefly with pathos, family, children, and virtuous sacrifice (its more sentimental variants) has certainly not been forgotten, however, least of all by scholars in film studies who have sought to analyse the politics of 'melodrama' from the standpoint of a variety of identity-driven debates as covered in the introduction. Following on from the championing of melodrama as a 'women's genre' by feminist critics in the 1970s and 1980s, and following Elsaesser's work, Steve Neale also identified sentimental antecedents to melodrama and its affective registers in cultures as diverse as the *drame* of Diderot's poetics and 'The Cult of True Womanhood' of the nineteenth century discussed below (1993: 75). The moralistic ideas and feelings transmitted by the sentimental comedy or melodrama remain to this day recognisable as instances of 'sentiment' (such as in the homely, folksy *It's a Wonderful Life* viewed on Christmas Eve to cite an appropriately clichéd example).

Indeed, the sentimental can in some ways be considered the ideological core of melodrama with its insistence on 'Virtue Triumphant' and the bourgeois idealisation of virtuous suffering. In France, melodrama's roots stemmed from the 'unlicensed' arts of pantomime, acrobatics, and musical theatre, art-forms associated with a greater emphasis on spectacle, visuality, gesture, and music.[8] Licensing laws allowed the spoken word only in properly licensed theatres while unlicensed venues initially relied on dumb-show and musical accompaniment to accompany narrative. Music here thus takes on a heightened role in relation to entrances, exits, and other narrative climaxes. The use of facial and bodily gesture became in turn essential skills for actors, who had to convey emotions without the aid of the spoken word, engendering a style of acting that would clearly find continuities in the notorious gesturality of the silent cinema. These founding properties of melodrama, at its purest a non-literary form, predisposed it to a close affinity with the expression of intense human emotion. While the spoken word of the legitimate theatre allowed for emotional restraint and theatrical *decorum* to be maintained (both in terms of acting and thematics), melodrama traded on the raw emotions of desperate, imperilled characters. Melodrama's key conflicts, as with the sentimental novel, revolved around the virtuous poor and an emergent bourgeois class, oppressed and pursued by villainous aristocrats, and later, rich industrialists.[9] Just as Richardson's heroines resorted to tears of despair as the last available response to their ordeals at the hands of rich masters, so virtue came to be associated with the victimised heroes of a cruel and oppressive Britain or France. Sensational turns of narrative, such as twins-separated-at-birth (for example, adaptations of Dumas' *The Corsican Brothers* (1844)), mistaken or disguised identities, love triangles, and stage-fights provided grist to the emotional mill. Sir Richard Steele's *The Conscious Lovers* (1731), for instance, sees the hero thwarted from marrying his love (the orphan Indiana) owing to their social disparity, only for it to be revealed at the play's climax that her father is alive and had the social position after all to be suitable for marriage. The play's morally unambiguous characters, didactic address, and emphasis on a tearful reunion scene between father and daughter came to exemplify the features of 'Sentimental Comedy', with 'comedy' indicating more the genre's light-heartedness and optimism than any intended laughter from the audience. In fact, Steele prioritised the genre's 'sentimental' elements over any comedic aspects when he commended this kind of drama as eliciting a 'joy too exquisite for laughter' (1971: 299), revealing a disdain (widespread by that time) for the licentious wit of an earlier generation's comic theatre and its cynicism towards respectable society.

A puritan veneration of benevolence, its 'high moral tones', was manifest then in the melodrama from an early stage, a didacticism that sought to excite the virtuous emotions of pathos and sympathy. Associated particularly in France with such dramatists as Guilbert de Pixérécourt, in Germany with August von Kotzebue, and in America with Dion Boucicault, melodrama's simple allocation of moral greatness to one set of characters and moral baseness to another became a structure that provided moral clarity, Peter Brooks argues, to a public that had come to find such certainties scarce in their own society. Poetic justice, where the good are recognised and rewarded while villains are found out and punished, fulfilled bourgeois fantasies of individual freedom and social mobility. The aesthetics of melodrama contrasted most particularly with the more intellectual modes of address that characterised the 'neo-classical' theatre of dramatists like Corneille, Racine, and Molière. Long associated with a tradition of courtly entertainment of the seventeenth century, and aligned too with the linguistic sophistication of Dryden and Pope, neo-classical theatre concerned itself with great aristocratic heroes, most often of the ancient world. Tragedy and comic satire were its chief forms and its rhetoric was thought to accord with the 'age of reason' and Enlightenment principles of order and rationality.[10] Its audience was diffuse but famously also incorporated the royal court and the king himself in France.[11]

This American Life

In contrast then to the courtly wit of neo-classical theatre and its cynical bracketing of non-conformism and authority, the melodrama promoted fantasies of individual mobility, romance, and familial contentment. In relation to sentimentalism specifically, the melodrama insisted on the possibility of an ethics grounded not in an analytical or intellectual apprehension of the world but in a sensitivity to everyday phenomena and things. It is this intimacy with the world, and its anticipation of film, that Stanley Cavell identifies specifically in the writings of the nineteenth-century American writers Ralph Waldo Emerson and Henry David Thoreau when he describes their privileging of the 'everyday, the near, the low, the familiar' (1992: 150). As part of a larger project of using the work of such writers to negotiate the Continental and Anglo-American philosophical traditions, Cavell refers in particular to Emerson's listing of everyday phenomena ('the meal in the firkin; the milk in the pan; the ballad in the street; the news of the boat; the glance of the eye') as examples of a proto-cinematic philosophy that brings the subject closer to 'ultimate reason' (149). In contrast to the Kantian emphasis on 'pure reason' and its connotations of an abstracted ineffability, experiences of the everyday and the 'near' are invested with 'sublime' possibility by virtue of their vital materiality. As with Hume's privileging of the subject's attention to the 'smallest concerns of his friend', an attention to the minutiae of life are re-asserted here as grounds for a 'perfectionist' philosophy that emphasises aesthetic experience. While Emerson's emphasis would be on everyday *things* in contrast to Hume's *friend*, the two nevertheless share clear concerns about the subject's intimate relation with the world, a concern that prefigures many of the positions taken by realist or phenomenology-influenced film theorists in the following century.

Indeed, for the present discussion, the writings of Emerson and Thoreau emerge as important examples of an American Transcendentalist tradition that Cavell would come to draw on increasingly in his own film theory, which in turn is now widely situated as an 'ethics'-based corrective to film theory's analytic distance from its object (see Frey and Choi 2013: 2–5). Understood in terms of a materialist 'perfectionism' that responds to the existential-scepticism of tragedy, such writers pose our intuition of the 'familiar' as a vital corrective to more 'pragmatist' approaches. Where the wit of courtly satire, for instance, foregrounded characters imprisoned by social hierarchy and the pragmatic survival strategy (and attitude) it fosters, both film and melodrama insist on affirmative statements of being and becoming. Linked certainly to the ideology of the American Dream in its attention to the individual's developmental trajectory, Transcendentalism's attachments to the 'sublime' nevertheless broaden its scope, allowing for an intuition-based ethics that is disinterested and heterodox. While the 'puritan–democratic worldview' is often aligned with what Raymond Williams referred to as a 'static' form of morality, the Transcendentalist position allows for the more fluid category of the ethical. The two perspectives are nevertheless inter-twined in the American imaginary and its privileging of nature and political freedom, intersecting with Rousseau's idealisation of the pastoral and its remove from civilisation.

It is through this fantasy of an everyday, even domestic, sublime and its implicit 'cheerfulness', as Nietzsche would note of Emerson's phi-losophy (Rhu 2010: 551), that the sentimentality of American culture can be conceived, linked moreover to bourgeois ideals of individual freedom, virtue and the embrace of nature. This fantasy also came, however, to define a culture deemed intellectually inadequate in the eyes of various critics as the nineteenth century drew on, eventually prompting a strident modernist critique of its embeddedness in liberal-bourgeois and feminis-ing principles. The American poet and philosopher George Santayana in 1911, for instance, attributes America's inadequate literary and intellectual culture to 'A Genteel Tradition' that he describes in explicitly gendered terms. Thus:

> The American Will inhabits the sky-scraper; the American Intellect inhabits the colonial mansion. The one is the sphere of the American man; the other, at least pre-dominantly, of the American woman. The one is all aggressive enterprise; the other is all genteel tradition. (Santayana 1967: 40)

While Santayana may chiefly have had in mind the New England high culture (poetry, prose, and philosophy) based on the privileged, distanced sentiments of a comfortable upper-middle class, his indictment of the American intellect as a feminised sensibility extends these flaws to a wider national psychology. Ruled, to his mind, by anachronistic pieties and the optimism of the founding fathers of a bygone era, he elsewhere describes

American poetry as 'grandmotherly in that sedate spectacled wonder with which it gazed at this terrible world and said how beautiful and interesting it all was' (1967: 73). While the male world of laissez-faire capitalism excluded any ethical design from its culture, its cloistered intelligentsia is framed here in terms of a privileged liberal elite, one removed, physically and logically, from the American dynamism of free enterprise. The romantic 'wonder' of such a tradition was deemed ill-founded and incompatible with the realities of a modern life that exemplified, as a growing number of pre-war intellectuals were coming to believe, urban degradation and alienation as much as human progress and equality, as echoed by such writers as Van Wyck Brooks (*America's Coming-of-Age*, 1915) and later, Malcolm Cowley (*After the Genteel Tradition*, 1937).[12]

Ann Douglas' influential study on the nineteenth century's 'feminization of American culture' is similarly critical of American gentility, identifying influences as diverse as Calvinism (as does Santayana), the sermons of protestant churchmen and the ascendency of women novelists, such as Harriet Beecher Stowe, as contributing factors. This gendering of the culture according to writers ranging from Santayana to Douglas is perhaps the most remarkable feature of this model, and provides a useful entry-point for considering the history of sentimentality as a specifically gendered category. Barbara Welter explained, for instance, in a classic article on the era's 'Cult of True Womanhood' how pamphlets, magazines, and books of the early to mid-nineteenth century persisted in the valorisation of a sentimental ideal of femininity emanating from the eighteenth century; the 'cult' is posited in such respects as an ideology that permeated the 'Victorian' gender consciousness with its four 'cardinal virtues' of 'piety, purity, submissiveness and domesticity' (1966: 152). Emphasising the woman's domestic and motherly role and subordinate status to her husband, the cult expounded a moral idealism with regard to women as a function of anxieties surrounding a male-dominated world of industry and enterprise, from which they were to be shielded in physical and psychological terms. As long as women were prevented from reading the 'wrong' kinds of literature or engaging in overly intellectual pursuits,[13] the 'cult' ensured that women would nevertheless remain a naïve, yet crucially moral, anchor for family, husbands, and the world. Welter explains, citing a pamphleteer, Mrs Gilman, that a woman was deemed quite able to handle a man's abrasiveness because:

in her heart she knew she was right and so could afford to be forgiving, even a trifle condescending. 'Men are not unreasonable,' averred Mrs. Gilman. 'Their difficulties lie in not understanding the moral and physical nature of our sex. They

often wound through ignorance, and are surprised at having offended.' Wives were
advised to do their best to reform men, but if they couldn't, to give up gracefully. 'If
any habit of his annoyed me, I spoke of it once or twice, calmly, then bore it quietly.'
(Welter 1966: 160)

So where women were advised to remain stoical, unfazed repositories of
virtue, men were expected to blunder through life in a struggle for wealth,
power, and sustenance for their families. Ethics was best left at home,
where it could be indulged in by an impractical sex, shielded from the
cruelties of a utilitarian world. Similar ideologies would come to apply to
children, as childhood similarly became removed from the sphere of work
as child labour laws were reformed and the urban bourgeois class grew. As
children became more sheltered in the family home, their symbolic value
changed from a monetary order to a sentimental one, becoming endowed
with the values of innocence, virtue, and unworldliness, as exemplified by
the Little Nells and Tiny Tims of Victorian literature. If the Artful Dodger
was the archetype of the child-adult streetwise survivor in Dickensian
London, Oliver Twist was his Utopian double: uncorrupted, innocent,
and ultimately permitted, through a melodramatic *deus ex machina*, to rise
above the cruelties of lower-class life and live the life of a child.[14]

'Victorian' Tastes

That social critique of the late nineteenth century equated a blinkered
bourgeois humanism with the feminine should come as no surprise given
the implicitly masculinist imperatives of debunking the apparent effemi-
nacies of Victorian society. Governed by similar observations in Britain,
the critic Lytton Strachey would set himself the task of knocking revered
establishment figures of the Victorian era off their pedestals in his 'Eminent
Victorians' of 1918. His biographical account of Florence Nightingale
provides evidence of the autocratic, single-minded arrogance of an upper-
class pillar of Victorian society as opposed to the meek and compassionate 'lady of the lamp' who ceaselessly nursed the soldiers at the Crimea.
Examining a representation of Nightingale that had traded on sentimental
notions of the virtuous maiden's unalloyed benevolence, Strachey presents
her flaws to call attention to the 'Victorian' vice of idealisation of women,
and its distortions of reality. Associated with other Bloomsbury group
stalwarts such as Virginia Woolf and Sir Leslie Stephen, Strachey's ideas
of modernisation and political reform applied equally to changing the
ossified literature and ideology inherited from the previous century as it
did to political action.

Even within the nineteenth century, though, when Oscar Wilde wrote that 'one must have a heart of stone to read the death of Little Nell without laughing', a sceptical self-consciousness with regard to the sentimental reception of Victorian melodrama was clearly in evidence. Recognising the trope of the dying, innocent child as an opportunity for Victorians to feel righteous indignation at the world's wrongs, Wilde detaches himself from 'reading for sentiment', condemning the entire practice as comically anachronistic. Nell's death, treated now as an artifice of literature where once treated by the aforementioned New Yorkers as a virtually real event, one gets the sense in Wilde's quote that, for a certain readership, any original experience of sentiment had worn thin and its tropes become laughably clichéd.[15] George Bernard Shaw expresses a similar disdain for the Manichaeism of Dickens' earlier novels, such as where a fragile Nell represented the ideals of moral perfection crushed by the machinations of heartless profiteers and sadists. In his 1912 preface to *Hard Times*, for instance, a novel noted as indicative of Dickens' turn to 'serious' social critique, Shaw commends Dickens' muting of his earlier novels' melodrama:

> You must therefore resign yourself, if you are reading Dickens's books in the order in which they were written, to bid adieu now to the light-hearted and only occasionally indignant Dickens of the earlier books, and get such entertainment as you can from him now that the occasional indignation has spread and deepened into a passionate revolt against the whole industrial order of the modern world. Here you will find no more villains and heroes, but only oppressors and victims, oppressing and suffering in spite of themselves, driven by a huge machinery which grinds to pieces the people it should nourish and ennoble, and having for its directors the basest and most foolish of us instead of the noblest and most farsighted. (Shaw 2001: 383)

Shaw notes in the above that the Dickens of mild social satire, or more commonly the application of poetic justice with regards to flawed individuals or 'individual delinquencies', has given way to a much more profound condemnation of the whole 'order' that underlies British life. Using such language as 'industrial', 'machinery', and 'directors', Shaw highlights the institutions of the nineteenth-century's unfettered industrial development as the root cause of systemic failure, and Dickens' chief targets. With the hindsight of the late nineteenth-/early twentieth-century movements for social emancipation, Shaw sees Dickens' shift from melodrama to social realism as analogous to British society's own increasingly developed awareness of its social degradation and reliance on systemic exploitation in that same century. Applauding *Hard Times* for its scathing depiction of a fully realised industrial town and its endemic oppression of workers, Shaw argues that the nineteenth century saw a 'Great Conversion', from a belief in the greatness of empire and British civilisation of the century's first half to the disillusion and calls for social reform of the latter half – a transition from the optimistic, imperial history of Macauley to the social critique of William Morris. Similar to the critiques of Marx, Carlyle, Ruskin, and Carpenter, Shaw sees the advent of Socialism as the key corollary of Dickens' abandonment of sentiment, comparing *The Old Curiosity Shop* and *Hard Times* as follows:

> *The Old Curiosity Shop* was written to amuse you, entertain you, touch you; and it succeeded. *Hard Times* was written to make you uncomfortable; and it will make you uncomfortable (and serve you right) though it will perhaps interest you more, and certainly leave a deeper scar on you, than any two of its forerunners. (Shaw 2001: 383)

Claiming a greater difficulty for the reader of Dickens' more biting commentaries, Shaw, as a playwright himself, equates the sentimental tragedy of *Old Curiosity Shop* with a popular, entertainment function that *Hard Times* eschews.[16] Art's more noble purpose is now to provide social critique of a corrupt society that urgently needs reform, no longer simply a guide to virtuous conduct transmitted to the reader as moral instruction. However, he is still aware of the popularity of melodrama and the 'simple pleasure' it elicits in the reader. He opposes the appeals of the sentimental to those of a more critical order, likening the former to the attractions of the 'merry-go-round' and the latter to a 'battle', with the former always still drawing 'a bigger crowd'.[17]

Equating the simple pleasures of melodrama with those of mass taste, Shaw therefore comes to employ a binary of high art/low art that has long endured in the twentieth century and beyond, where the 'crowd' is thought to resist the radical messages and meanings of socially critical art in favour of the consoling optimism of sentimental melodrama. Although he deems a novel like *Hard Times* as 'no less attractive' than popular melodrama, he is clearly conscious of its attracting a more radical and select group for its readership than for the latter, one that has already accepted the doctrines of a Carlyle or a Morris, if not perhaps a Marx. The period of critical indictment of Victorian society that began with critics of the late nineteenth century came to dominate elite intellectual and literary spheres, yet was structured around concerns for the emancipation of the common man or proletariat through a more accurate or 'realistic' representation of the world's ills and injustices.[18]

Victorianism and the Cinema

Sentimentalism emerges in European and American culture then as a cluster of discourses that negotiate the West's pioneering of industrial modernity, bourgeois individualism, and the free-market. Alongside the context of the skyscraper and the proliferation of an urban pragmatism is posed a genteel nostalgia for frail moral certainties and the pastoral or domestic spaces of a feminised ethics. This dichotomy is one that is highly significant to the discussion that follows in relation to cinema's emergence, for it is precisely in film's negotiation of these spaces and discourses that the medium gained both its popular success and its critical power. In her account of cinema's 'Decline of Sentiment' in the 1920s, for instance, Lea Jacobs focuses specifically on 'sentiment' as a taste category that diminished in popularity as the film industry came to attract more urbane audiences. She thus describes the 'sentimental' film as a distinct style that could be contrasted with various Hollywood popular genres that came to prominence in the 1920s, including the 'sophisticated comedy', the 'male adventure story', the 'seduction plot', and the 'romantic drama' (2008: 7). With an attendant rise in such thematics as poverty, urban alienation, or greed in such films, such a movement represents for Jacobs an end to more moralistic or idealistic modes of address – as prefigured for her by 'literary works that had the cock-eyed optimism to posit a morally comprehensible universe' (ibid.). Marked rather by 'the emergence of a preference for a laconic and understated style' (275), a more naturalistic cinema is evidenced for Jacobs by decreases in inter-titles and other mechanisms that facilitated a moralising discourse, as well as more overt depictions of sex, more slang, and recourse to more elliptical or opaque modes of narration.

Although taking care not to generalise across all films of the 1920s period and earlier, Jacobs identifies the sentimental as a category that permeated the US social context leading up to the 1920s, arguing:

> The films most frequently criticised for being old-fashioned and cloyingly sentimental were identified with rural and suburban audiences. Naïve taste, at least as the trade press understood it, was certainly not restricted to women's genres. It favoured stories about firemen and policemen as well as stories about dying babies. It included a predilection for 'hoke' slapstick and 'hoke' pathos, delivered to quote *Variety*, 'with more force than grace'. (Jacobs 2008: 271)

The sentimental emerges here then as a mode of address aligned with particular suburban or rural reception contexts. 'Naïve' or conservative tastes of specific audiences are identified that seek the reification of traditional 'familiar' structures of law and order, and obvious models of virtuous suffering and redemption. Once again, the sentimental is equated here with the exposition of honest, everyday characters and their imperilment, in the service of representing a morally comprehensible universe, or by extension to invoke nostalgia for a time antecedent to a contemporary, disarrayed modernity.

Notwithstanding Jacob's analysis of its 'decline', therefore, Hollywood sentimentality is acknowledged as a very significant and formative taste category in relation to US audiences prior to the 1920s. As recent scholarship about early cinema and pre-cinema corroborates, such a category was vital to ensuring the success of the great twentieth century art-form, given the vulgarity it was initially deemed to embody by more middle-class sectors of US society in the early twentieth century. Lee Grieveson shows, for instance, how mainstream American cinema developed in the early twentieth century in relation to a matrix of 'legislative and reform activism' that shaped the kind of medium it would become by the time of its classical period from the mid-teens (2004: 4). Charting its transition from funfair side-show to its emergence as a mainstream entertainment, Grieveson (see also Gunning 2004) shows how the movie business had to assuage middle-class anxieties surrounding the licentious activities taking place on-screen and off, by specifically catering to 'notions of domesticity and gentility' (27) inherited from the mid-nineteenth century and defended by various institutional groups like the People's Institute and the National Board of Censorship.[19]

The curtailment of cinema's 'unseemly' or 'vulgar' elements, both on-screen and in its exhibition contexts, constitutes indeed a highly significant point of departure for identifying sentimentalism as a key taste category informing the development of Hollywood cinema in its early period. Grieveson argues specifically that Hollywood cinema emerged from a balancing act between commercial priorities and social requirements that it educate or morally instruct. Melodrama and its common recourse to sentimental propriety brokered such a compromise effectively and lucratively, attracting audiences increasingly composed of middle-class individuals and groups who sought alternative social spaces to the saloon, brothel, and nickelodeon. While intellectual traditions like 'naturalism' (as described in detail by Jacobs) had already gained significant ground in relation to the 'higher' cultures of the novel and theatre, their effect would not be felt so markedly in Hollywood until as late as the 1920s, allowing the early cinema to reproduce the theatrical melodrama and its signature 'high moral tones' of the previous century. As Chapter 3 demonstrates, the evocation of sentimental responses in relation to the films of Chaplin or Griffiths were highly significant factors in the success of those film-makers over others, despite the realist or modernist elements of their work more often highlighted by discussions of early cinema and its aesthetics. The valorisation of family and the virtuous man or woman, the innocence of childhood, and the abandonment or reformation of vice were borrowed wholesale from the previous century's melodramatic traditions, for these tropes were recognised as the principal formulae for creating popular but respectable entertainment at the time.

However, if the emergent classical cinema was initially thought of as failing to respond to more contemporary tastes for naturalism or intellectual sophistication, such criteria are of course themselves made problematic by their reproduction of gendered aesthetic binaries and their often covert dismissal of 'feminine' emotions in the name of bourgeois gentility. Indeed, an ongoing question in what follows below relates to the possibility of understanding the sentimental, and its importance to film, in terms that reorient or recuperate our understanding of the 'domesticity and gentility' with which it has become in many ways synonymous. More specifically, I seek to account for a more pluralistic account of the ways in which film's sentimentalism would be conceived, particularly in relation to the classical film theory of such figures as Eisenstein, Vertov, Balàzs, and Bazin. This would of course incorporate its standard historical alignments with melodrama and middle-class taste categories, but it will also seek to broaden the possibilities engendered by the sentimental problematic itself, as already examined in relation to the philosophy of Hume, Rousseau, Smith, Emerson, and Thoreau. The discussion will seek in particular to chart the aesthetics and critical reception of cinema in relation to the transformations and traumas of urban modernity and the role it would come to play in reorienting the alienated spectator.

Notes

1. Samuel Johnson's ironic term for how Richardson's novels should be read, exasperated as he was by their repetitive storyline: 'Why, sir, if you were to read Richardson for the story, your impatience would be so much fretted that you would hang yourself. But you must read him for the sentiment, and consider the story as only giving occasion to the sentiment.' In James Boswell, *The Life of Samuel Johnson*, Ware: Wordsworth Editions, 2008, p. 341.
2. Actors are criticised for gesticulating excessively in order to please those in the audience who are too dull to appreciate the subtleties of a tragic plot. See Aristotle, *Poetics*, London: Nick Hern, 1999, pp. 40–2.
3. The new emphasis on impartiality and disinterest are taken up too, of course, by Immanuel Kant, whose theoretical continuities with the writings of Hume and Smith is widely established. See Michael Frazer, *The Enlightenment of*

Sympathy: Justice and the Moral Sentiments in the Eighteenth Century and Today, New York: Oxford University Press, 2010. Recent studies of the period's philosophy pose Kant indeed as a key figure of continuity and departure with sentimentalist doctrines, wherein Smith's 'impartial spectator' serves as a forerunner to Kant's insistence on the universality of moral reason (or 'duty'), and the inadequacy of the subject's benevolent 'inclinations'.

4. Louis-Sébastien Mercier cited in R. F. Brissenden, *Virtue in Distress: Studies in the Novel of Sentiment from Richardson to Sade*, London: Macmillan, 1974.

5. In his philological study of the word 'sentimental' in the eighteenth century (1951), Erik Erametsa describes how a major turning point for the term can be located in the publication of Sterne's *A Sentimental Journey through France and Italy*, a novel that wittily equivocates on the virtues and shortcomings of its protagonist's self-conscious desire for sympathetic (and sexual) interactions with other characters.

6. Austen's novella parodies the epistolary sentimental style, targeting especially the self-congratulatory rhetoric of the novel's protagonist, Laura. The latter, for instance, eulogises the dead in the fashion of *Clarissa* and Goethe's *The Sorrows of Young Werther* (1989 [1774]), the latter foregrounded as a novel one would have read in order to learn the codes of a refined, but morally vacuous, gentility.

7. For detailed accounts of the transposition of theatrical melodrama's conventions to the early cinema, see Frank Rahill, *The World of Melodrama*, University Park, PA: Pennsylvania State University Press, 1967; Ben Singer, *Melodrama and Modernity: Early Sensational Cinema and its Contexts*, New York: Columbia University Press, 2001; Ben Brewster and Lea Jacobs, *Theatre to Cinema: Stage Pictorialism and the Early Feature Film*, New York: Oxford University Press, 1998.

8. For general accounts of key productions and the central thematics of nineteenth-century theatrical melodrama, see David Grimsted, *Melodrama Unveiled: American Theater and Culture, 1800–1850*, Chicago: University of Chicago Press, 1968; Robert Heilman, *Tragedy and Melodrama: Versions of Experience*, Seattle: University of Washington Press, 1968; Frank Rahill, *The World of Melodrama*, University Park, PA: Pennsylvania State University Press, 1967.

9. Dickens' work provides perhaps the best examples of the substitution of industrialists or capitalists for roles initially applicable to aristocrats, such as Josiah Bounderby in *Hard Times* or Ebenezer Scrooge in *A Christmas Carol*.

10. See M. H. Abrams' entry on the 'Neo-Classic and Romantic' for a useful cursory distinction between the two traditions, in *A Glossary of Literary Terms*, G. G. Harpham (ed.), Boston: Heinle & Heinle, 1999. The 'Neoclassic' recognises a 'cosmic order' that dictates a given 'natural hierarchy' in life that sets certain limits on the subject's freedom. A certain 'avoidance of extremes' characterised neo-classic aesthetics, and was extended therefore to excesses

of feeling in the subject, or perhaps more significantly for the present discussion, implied certain equivalences between emotions and aesthetic excess.

11. The 'wit' of Molière's comedies encapsulated the neo-classical ideal through the playwright's mockery of characters who reject the logic and reason deemed to be the foundation of enlightened society, in the name of their own egoism. In *Bourgeois Gentleman*, for instance, Molière satirises a man with newly acquired wealth who wishes to pass himself off in aristocratic society. His comical failure to do so owing to continuous gaffes and embarrassments spoke of society's intolerance and rejection of the individual who attempted to break out of his social class. Likewise, *The Misanthrope* conveys the story of a man whose moral extremism leads him to reject social graces and genteel affectations despite his desire to gain the love of a woman within that society. His failure to do so, and his eventual retreat to a desert island away from society, once again signals the intractability of social convention and the need to temper one's own emotions of disgust or boredom towards that society if one wishes to survive.

12. H. L. Mencken's *Prejudices* (2006 [1920]) is another key work in this regard. In more recent literary theory, the 'sentimental power' of such works as *Uncle Tom's Cabin* (Stowe, Harriet Beecher, *Uncle Tom's Cabin*, London: CRW Publishing, 2004 [1852]) and nineteenth-century sentimental culture have since been re-evaluated and celebrated, notably by Jane Tompkins. See Jane Tompkins, *Sensational Designs: The Cultural Work of American Fiction, 1790–1860*, New York: Oxford University Press, 1985, pp. 122–46. A more recent and less evaluative account is provided by Lauren Berlant in a historicisation of sentimentality and its associations with female identity, aesthetics, and feminised ideas of justice (see 'The Subject of True Feeling: Pain, Privacy and Politics', in Jodi Dean (ed.), *Cultural Studies and Political Theory*, Ithaca, NY: Cornell University Press, 2000, pp. 42–62, and *The Female Complaint: The Unfinished Business of Sentimentality in American Culture*, New York: Duke University Press, 2008.

13. Ibid. This indeed extended to their reading habits, in which novels were to be treated with caution as opposed to works of 'religious biography', and other literary forms that did not interfere 'with serious piety'. Constructions of a literature intended for women through an exclusive attention to sentimental tropes of domesticity or the family has continued to shape much critical discourse and has been challenged in only more recent re-assessments of the period. Like the eighteenth century's 'novel of sentiment', a body of scholarship has labelled this period of nineteenth-century American literature with the generic descriptor of the 'sentimental', opposing its peddling to mass/feminine tastes to the work of the great Romantic novelists such as Hawthorne, Emerson, or Melville. See Herbert Ross Brown, *The Sentimental Novel in America, 1789–1860*, New York: Pageant Books, 1959 [c.1940]; Fred Lewis Pattee, *The Feminine Fifties*. New York: D. Appleton-Century Company, 1940; Ann Douglas, *The Feminization of American Culture*, New York: Knopf, 1978.

14. Thorough accounts of transformations in the social valence of children and their increased idealisation in the nineteenth century are provided in Henry Jenkins, 'Introduction: Childhood Innocence and Other Modern Myths,' in Henry Jenkins (ed.), *The Children's Culture Reader*, New York: New York University Press, 1998, pp. 1–37; Mary Lynn Stevens Heininger, 'Children, Childhood, and Change in America, 1820–1920,' in Mary Lynn Stevens Heininger et al. (eds), *A Century of Childhood, 1820–1920*, Rochester, NY: Margaret Woodbury Strong Museum, 1984, pp. 1–32; Viviana A. Zelizer, *Pricing the Priceless Child: The Changing Social Value of Children*, New York: Basic Books, 1985.

15. Wilde's famous aphorisms included two quips on sentimentality:

> 'A sentimentalist is simply one who desires to have the luxury of an emotion without paying for it.' (Oscar Wilde, *The Picture of Dorian Gray and Other Writings*, New York: Simon & Schuster, 2005, p. 348.)
> 'Sentimentality is merely the bank holiday of cynicism.' (Oscar Wilde, *Selected Letters*, Rupert Hart-Davis (ed.), Oxford: Oxford University Press, 1979, p. 501.)

16. F. R. Leavis had praise only for *Hard Times* in 'The Great Tradition', claiming its superiority over all of Dickens' other novels, and considered it the only work that justified Dickens' inclusion in the canon of English literature. Dickens was also targeted in 1930 by Aldous Huxley for alleged lapses into sentimentality in the latter's *Vulgarity in Literature*. See Aldous Huxley, *Vulgarity in Literature: Digressions from a Theme*, 1st edn, London: Chatto and Windus, 1930.

17. Shaw also applauded the plays of Ibsen for the same reasons, for such work also target the staid and oppressive conditions of Victorian domestic life as determinants of marital dissatisfaction and failure, such as in *A Doll's House* or *Hedda Gabler*.

18. Jacobs charts the emergence of literary 'naturalism' in early twentieth-century America as a key precursor to its manifestations in the Hollywood cinema of the 1920s, which she argues demonstrates an overall 'Decline of Sentiment'. See also Henry May, *The End of American Innocence: A Study of the First Years of Our Own Time, 1912–1917*, Oxford: Oxford University Press, 1959. To give a wider sense of its manifestations in world theatre in late nineteenth/early twentieth century and for a penetrating critique of naturalism, see Raymond Williams, *Drama from Ibsen to Brecht*, New York: Oxford University Press, 1969.

19. See also Russell Merritt's account of the rise in social prestige of early cinema in 'Nickelodeon Theaters, 1905–1914: Building an Audience for the Movies', in Tino Balio (ed.), *The American Film Industry*, Madison: University of Wisconsion Press, 1976, pp. 83–102. Tom Gunning surveys the rise of a morally respectable cinema in America over the course of six years (1903 to 1909) in 'From the Opium Den to the Theater of Morality: Moral Discourse

and the Film in Early American Cinema', in Lee Greiveson and Peter Krämer (eds), *The Silent Cinema Reader*, New York: Routledge, 2004, pp. 145–54. See also William Uricchio and Roberta E. Pearson, *Reframing Culture: The Case of the Vitagraph Quality Films*, Princeton: Princeton University Press, 1993.

CHAPTER 2

Sentimental Aesthetics and Classical Film Theory

Whether understood in terms of the uniquely American unconscious at play in the classical Hollywood vernacular, or the Rousseauian validation of figures untainted by social order, cinema has continuously negotiated the traditions it inherits from the sentimental period, with its own unique set of formal conventions and constraints. A crucial emphasis for what follows below is a thoroughgoing attention to the formal dimensions of the medium within which sentiment has been supposed, at different times, to have been both ubiquitised and utterly dismantled, depending on the governing rubric at hand. Core to these debates rests the place of US culture and Hollywood in the formation of the melodramatic 'mode' introduced above, and the complex strands of influence that this may entail. Thus, in his 1943 essay 'Dickens, Griffith and Film Today', the Soviet film-maker and theorist Sergei Eisenstein argues:

> In order to understand Griffith, one must visualise an America made up of more than visions of speeding automobiles, speeding trains, racing ticker tape, inexorable conveyor belts. One is obliged to comprehend the second side of America – America the traditional, the patriarchal, the provincial. And then you will be considerably less astonished by this link between Griffith and Dickens. (Eisenstein 1977: 198)

Thus, in the latter stages of his life and career, Eisenstein observes a key division in American culture, two 'faces of America' that contribute equally and vitally to the national psyche. 'Super-Dynamic America' represents the nation's pioneering of new technologies as essential components of a fully rationalised modernity, typified by 'speeding trains', Griffith's cinema, and a pervasively kinetic culture.[1] 'Small Town America' conversely represents the pastoralism, traditionalism, and sentimentality of a nation that hangs back from such visions of the contemporary, one that is more content with established social structures and ensconced in a hegemony of bourgeois, Victorian, middle-class values. Eisenstein poses Charles Dickens and D. W. Griffith as exponents of both the modernity *and* sentimentality of their respective cultures, yet applied to their work, the dynamic 'parallel action' of cross-cutting scenes (theorised as a precursor to Soviet-montage) is largely valorised over the sympathetic depiction of liberal bourgeois characters, the unredeemed victimhood of a lower class, and a confused scheme of 'virtue rewarded'. Griffith's 'classical' style is deemed by Eisenstein both vital to cinema history yet necessarily inferior ideologically. A modernism in cinematic technique is compromised or undermined by a 'way down East' attitude of middle-class morals and manners, or what he further down critiques as a 'sentimental humanism' (233).

Eisenstein's valorisation of cinema's technological dynamism accords in various ways then with a Soviet and modernist project of revolutionary innovation in the service of transforming an unjust bourgeois world. His scepticism towards America's pastoralism is evident too, for instance, in his allusions to a New York apartment in the same essay, a passage that expands upon his approval of a Western culture that has adopted modern, rationalised technologies over the nostalgic objects of its past. He describes here a 'good old provincialism . . . nestling in clusters around fireplaces, furnished with soft grandfather chairs and the lace doilies that shroud the wonders of modern technique: refrigerators, washing-machines, radios' (197). A clear scepticism is evident here as to the function of these kitsch objects, specifically with regards to their serving any other purpose than to 'shroud' the innovations of current technology. Where the refrigerator or washing-machine signify utility and function, the fireplaces and doilies represent the outdated kitsch of people's private dwellings. While the machines belong in a futurist everywhere, the kitsch objects are rooted in the nostalgic spaces of the past – at best, decorative and, at worst, ideologically corrupting. Revealed here, too, however, is Eisenstein's uncertainty as to the clear demarcation between these two Americas, to the extent that the 'provincialism' of kitsch ominously pervades an apartment in what was regarded as the foremost urbanised city of the world.[2] What remains in much of Eisenstein's writing indeed is a residual fascination with Western culture as a totality, evinced by a recognition that cementing the connection between Dickens and Griffith involves considerations of both their technical innovation along with their place in a historically humanist or liberal tradition.

Eisenstein's varied and fragmented responses to American culture manifest thus a central tension between the (foreign) intellectual's disdain for the US cinema's alleged subordination to commercial priorities, a cult of the star (or individual), and its concomitant aesthetic of sentimentalism, and an infatuated admiration for its films and the big players that he would

meet while visiting New York and California. This ambivalence on the part
of Eisenstein as to cinema's excessive, conservative, pathetic, or humanist
tendencies, is central, I would suggest, to comprehending the sentimental
tradition as it persisted in the cinematic age of the early to mid-twentieth
century. While early theories of the cinema were closely aligned, as with
Eisenstein, with a formalist attention to cinema's capacity for manipulating reality, the realities of mass audiences who remained in thrall to
human stories, characters, and 'virtue triumphant' would also be integral
to the theoretical models propounded by figures like Eisenstein, Balázs,
and Bazin. I suggest indeed that theorisation of cinema's unique affectivity involved for many theorists a firm understanding of the medium's
negotiation of older traditions and art-forms. Moreover, I argue below that
some of the best-known film theorists of that era realised the centrality of
melodrama despite considerable adherences to the austere radicalism of
the high modernist moment.

A key question in this debate, as in previous eras, concerned thus the
role that cinema could or should play in transformations of subjectivity.
The sentimental, as in previous centuries, comes to denote a model of
spectatorship for a complacent subject or class that resists the radical
potentials of art as a device for change, and art's sometime complicity with
such a model. Pathos would be experienced in the reception of sentimental
art without any concomitant change in the subject's moral treatment of
the world, the latter assumed as a first priority for any substantive political
change. Yet at the crux of such arguments, as we have seen, is a theory that
still bestows importance to agency, or more philosophically, *free will* at the
level of the subject. While sentimental art was deemed to allow, or indeed
encourage, the subject to feel the pleasures of sympathy or virtue without
earning it (that is, without altering consciousness), superior art could
transform the subject politically or ethically, prompting him or her to exert
a significant influence upon the social sphere within which s/he interacts.
The cinema arrives at a moment, however, when this notion itself has
come into question as a naïvely 'humanist' position. Determining whether
a work of art is sentimental becomes redundant if the teleology of an
ethical subject is itself inadequate. This problematic of an ethical subject
extends to the moral individuals, families, or social groups depicted within
the novel, the play, or the film themselves, the idealisation of whom comes
to be deemed anachronistic and once again the indulgence of a cosseted
middle class.

An important strand of modernism, therefore, posits technology as
the only hope for humankind in modernity, where an alienated subject
has become an insignificant element operating within larger structures

of knowledge and power. Only as part of a larger critical mass does the subject recover any significance. The novelty of cinema gives cause for such euphoric exclamations as to its central role to social change – a grand new medium put to the service of a grand narrative of collectivism. A writer like Walter Benjamin in 1927 posits the importance of cinema in its deployment as a 'collectivist' technology, in what could be deemed a dry run for his famous Artwork essay of 1935 (Benjamin 1999). He deems nothing less than the technological innovation of film itself a 'violent fissure' in 'art's development', a 'new region of consciousness' that is revolutionarily autonomous from its application by man, because

> the important, elementary moments of progress in art are novelties neither of content nor of form; the revolution in technique precedes both. (Benjamin 1995: 626)

As a formalist position that equates a paradigm shift in technology with the redemption of the 'mass' or 'proletariat', Benjamin's claim necessarily overlooks the individual, either as the creator or the crucial subject of film. The 'individual' only becomes significant as a test-case of the larger social and ideological structures that govern his/her behaviour. Apartments or 'furnished rooms' also feature significantly in this essay, as in Eisenstein's above, except here they are not the repositories of new technologies admixed ambiguously with regressive kitsch but the 'hopelessly sad' reminders of individual, atomised (bourgeois) existence that need to be 'exploded' by the cinema's reconfiguration of space and time. An 'old world of incarceration' is transformed to a technologised utopia of collectivist rationality and freedom. If socialists from the nineteenth century like G. B. Shaw regarded the cinema as a potentially useful vehicle for socialist ideas and themes, Benjamin advances technology itself as the messianic saviour of such aims, excluding man entirely from the project of his own redemption.

And yet, film theory was formulated in a world that seemed far from ready to abandon 'regions of consciousness' that had been inherited from long traditions of the sentimental or realist novel, the melodrama, the 'well-made play', and the classical Hollywood film. The ascendency of Hollywood clearly attests to the popularity of sentimental tastes, wherein the 'mass' could still be addressed as individual subjects with unique experiences, desires, thoughts, and beliefs. Sympathy or empathy with characters (identification) remained a key attraction of a cinema that accentuated what other art-forms had already delivered on a grand scale. The famous montage sequences of Eisenstein's *Battleship Potemkin*, a film applauded by Benjamin, would be inconceivable without the crucial reaction shots of particular individuals, caught up in the joys and agonies of a crushed prole-tarian uprising. In a similar vein, much as though Benjamin celebrates the destruction of alienated bourgeois existence through the explosive force of cinema, one is moved as much by his description of those atomised, solitary lives as much as by his revolutionary desire for filmic perception to transcend it. One must recognise that at least in a pervasively philosophical sense, sentimentalism is manifest in both cinematic practice and theory. This should lead us to question what the political stakes were of such ruptures within the 'hopelessly sad' life of the subject, if the capacity for pathos would be itself exploded in Utopian efforts to efface the subject.

Early British Film Theory: *Close-Up*

The writers of the early British film journal *Close-Up* (active from 1927 to 1933) wrote extensively on the cutting edge of cinematic praxis of the period. Unashamedly avant-gardist in their aims, the contributors were preoccupied heavily with questions of form and spectatorship, and advanced a radical aesthetics that in many ways stood in opposition to the mainstream, commercial cinemas of Hollywood and Europe. Mired in clichés and formulae, commercial cinema is aligned in various articles with a sentimentalism that indulges the spectator's attachments and moral allegiance to characters, as opposed to work that foregrounds formal inno-vation. A canon comprising Eisenstein's *Battleship Potemkin*, G. W. Pabst's *The Joyless Street*, and Paul Wegener's *The Student of Prague*, among others, is praised by the magazine's founding editor Kenneth Macpherson as exhibiting 'pure form, every single attribute of photographic art, mira-cles to work in tone and tone depths, light, geometry, design, sculpture . . . pure abstraction all of it' (see Marcus 2007: 347).

It is often indeed as 'pure abstraction' then that cinema promises here to deliver the world in a simplified, legible state. One of *Close-Up*'s most fre-quent writers, H. D., writes analogously of the spectator's 'inner speech', a code that resonates with the abstractions of the modernist film in its paring down of reality. Her comparison of film with hieroglyph, as in Eisenstein's writings in reference to Japanese ideographic writing, out-lines cinema's affinities for juxtaposition and montage in the service of a universal language of cinema. She thus describes the figure of a woman from the Russian film *Expiation* as 'a hieroglyph, that spells almost visibly some message of cryptic symbolism. Her gestures are magnificent. If this is Russian, then I am Russian' (Donald, Friedberg and Marcus 1998: 126). In a way that is 'psychic, compelling, in a way destructive' the realism of such imagery is reflected on by H. D. here in terms of a more radical identificatory procedure to that offered by a bourgeois aesthetics of the 'beautiful' or the picturesque. While commercial cinema was limited by its inclusion, for H. D., of non-essential elements, or the 'too extraneous underbrush of tangled detail' (111), she focuses on the cinema as an ideal of 'artistic restraint' (113), filtering out all superfluities. Aligning cinema with the simplicity of 'light', she argues for a 'classic' aesthetic that para-doxically befits modernity through its avoidance of 'exaggeration', 'elabo-rate material', or 'waste' (112).

Such claims regarding the specificity and purity of cinematic art correspond with the formalist theory of such figures as Rudolph Arnheim, who would also claim virtue for the cinema in its deviance from the sub-ject's unmediated perception of the world, amidst a suspicion of the cin-ema's mimeticism. Arnheim echoes writers like H. D., for instance, when he claims:

> There is serious danger that the filmmaker will rest content with such shapeless reproduction. In order that the film artist may create a work of art it is important that he consciously stress the peculiarities of his medium. This, however, should be done in such a manner that the character of the objects represented should not thereby be destroyed but rather strengthened, concentrated, and interpreted. (Arnheim 1957: 35)

Emphasising a role for cinema that stresses its enhancement or interpre-tation of reality, Arnheim rehearses a formalist 'specificity thesis' as to the unique role that any art-form must play in order to constitute itself as real art.[3] With editing, the cinema justifies its claim as art through its manipulation of a reality that arrives at the lens in 'shapeless' form, that is, without any as yet artistic design. Reality becomes the raw material that needs to be worked on, much as rock is chipped away at by the sculptor to create a new artistic object.

A 'shapeless' modes of representation is thus the target here for various formalist positions of this era, and as with Eisenstein and other Soviets discussed below (some of whose writings were translated and published in *Close-Up*), Hollywood is positioned as the paradigm of this non-essentialised cinema. Hollywood's particular rehearsal of clichés inherited from non-cinematic traditions is aligned with the camera's unfiltered reg-istration of raw reality. The magazine's chief financial backer and con-tributor Bryher writes disdainfully, for instance, of a Hollywood that 'can produce kitsch magnificently but cannot produce art' (28). She therefore imagines *Potemkin*'s remake in Hollywood, for instance, in terms of a heroine's survival through love for an 'old father-mother-grandparent', 'love at first sight' between hero and heroine, and a marriage that serves as a happy ending witnessed by great crowds including 'children with doves' (29). Hollywood's 'atrocious domestic and wild west dramas' are similarly dismissed by Macpherson for their recourse to the upbeat and formulaic. Film emerging from the European movements of German Expressionism and Soviet Montage, by contrast, promise something different for these writers. Macpherson describes Expressionism in terms of its 'curious details, watchfulness, harking at claustrophobia' (36), aspects of which he aligns with the 'REAL.'

This universalistic aesthetic, pared-down of sentimentalised cultural particulars, finds a theoretical counterpart for other *Close-Up* writers in Freud's theory of dreams. The psychoanalyst Hanns Sachs (who served as analyst for several of the *Close-Up* contributors and wrote for the journal) theorises commercial cinema as a body of work that largely fails to engage with the unconscious in such direct ways as H. D.'s cinema of 'restraint'. Sachs thus describes the predictability of the kitsch film's emotional itinerary as follows:

> Owing to the skill with which the distribution of the emotions is anticipated, the public are indeed saved a good deal of worry, including that of choice, but at the same time the free development of the emotions is restricted; the possibility of lifting them by degrees out of the unconscious and letting them have free play is done away with. The process must have the minimum of psychic activity and must never be arrested. (Donald, Friedberg and Marcus 1998: 266)

Commercial cinema is argued here then to not so much ignore unconscious desire and fantasy but rather inhibits its coming to consciousness. While 'lifting' emotions to consciousness requires the 'development' or 'psychic activity' elicited by the hieroglyphic aesthetic praised by H. D., kitsch keeps the spectator mired in conscious thought despite the possibilities of the film-viewing process. Kitsch comes of a failure to follow Pound's modernist imperative to 'make it new' and instead conveys the same as what already resides in a collective conscious. Deprived of the richness of the visual world by a sentimental gloss, the spectator of kitsch thus maintains (and complacently enjoys) the self-perpetuating emotional models to which he or she is accustomed while remaining unexposed to transformative data.

Aligning the 'plainly legible signposts' of the formulaic film with a pandering to the 'dullest intelligence' (266), Sachs unfortunately also here signals some of the elitist undercurrents of *Close-Up*'s aesthetics, and, of course, of high modernist aesthetics more broadly conceived. Anticipating Roland Barthes' theory of the 'writerly' versus 'readerly' text, the unconscious is posed by Sachs here as a repository of emotions that require 'development' through the film's activation of creative, 'writerly' processes. Film fulfils this function by paradoxically becoming what H. D. terms a 'cryptic symbolism', requiring a spectator's 'intelligence' in order to decipher meaning.

While *Close-Up* theory rests therefore on prescriptions for a universally cinematic language, the sentimental film is critiqued somewhat paradoxically on the grounds that it is excessively easy to understand, or too 'readerly' in Barthes' terms. Disturbed by the passivity of cinematic spectatorship at the time, Macpherson elsewhere, for instance, deploys 'dope' in relation to commercial cinema's lack of 'real consideration of problems, artistic, or sociological' (326), Emotions are likewise posed as problematic in relation to the creative process of film-viewing, as indicated in Bryher's praise for Eisenstein's *October*:

> Perhaps it is because its entire appeal is to the intellect – not to the emotions solely, but to the brain, which is beyond emotion – the super or over-conscious, that is habitually so starved. (Donald, Friedberg and Marcus 2007: 339)

An intellectual engagement with film is valorised here then as a process that sits almost necessarily in tension with 'emotions'. The universal language thesis that informs much of this writing privileges a linguistic paradigm of comprehension and cognition over a more affective model. Commercial cinema is critiqued certainly for its own *language* of virtue and individualism, but implicated too in these critiques is cinema's excessive reliance on antecedent arts, where melodrama and its sentimental foregrounding of the bourgeois, ethical subject is positioned as a regrettable dominant of mainstream cinema. Cinema's capacity to resonate with the subject's 'inner speech' is meanwhile positioned as a mode of understanding that must be evacuated of kitsch and the superfluous materials of the everyday.

Eisenstein and Dickens

The Soviet films of the time would be revered above all by the *Close-Up* milieu because, compared to the commercial cinemas of America, Britain, and other European countries, such films were deemed to foreground the essential properties of cinematic art, in relation to which the spectator is posed as a vital intellectual force. The British Board of Film Classification's (BBFC's) strict regulation of Russian cinema in the UK, bitterly opposed by writers like Macpherson and Bryher, revealed in their view the conjoined political biases and philistinism of censor and film industry. Representing for them the best film-makers of the era for their 'intellectual' principles

of film-making, such figures as Eisenstein, Kuleshov, Vertov, or Pudovkin
would meanwhile be positioned antithetically to the cinemas of Hollywood
and other Western European countries.

Eisenstein's theory is notable, however, for its nuancing of such nation-
based oppositions, as exemplified perhaps by his discussion of 'pre-
logical, sensuous thinking' in his autobiography (*IM* 1983: 211). This
phrase, used in reference to 'pre-lingual' cultures such as the Aztecs or
the Toltecs, shows Eisenstein as a thinker who presciently regards film
as a medium that communicates in a radically different order to that of
the written or spoken word. Both pre-linguistic yet radically infused with
meaning, the power of the cinematic image is acknowledged here in terms
of its affective as much as analytic dimensions. Of course, Eisenstein's
films, such as *The Strike* and *Battleship Potemkin*, are widely understood to
have foregrounded 'montage' as the basis of an 'intellectual' cinema that
almost necessarily privileges thought over emotion. Eisenstein's writing is
nevertheless highly nuanced in its approach to sentimental or humanist
principles.

Comparisons between Eisenstein and his contemporary Dziga Vertov,
for instance, yield some useful insights as to their different aesthetic
agendas. While Vertov's practice demonstrates similar commitments
as Eisenstein to editing and poetics, his theory explicitly proclaims the
primacy of a realist aesthetic diametrically opposed to bourgeois forms. As
a newsreel and documentary film-maker, Vertov coins the term 'Cine-Eye'
as the chief metaphor for a body of work that aims to depict the 'life caught
unawares', an aesthetic he would consider opposed to the 'film-drama'
and the 'bourgeois fairy-tale scripts' (1984: 65) of capitalist society. Vertov
is quite explicit in his favouring of electricity and machines over human
agency, aligning his project with the transformation of a 'bumbling citizen
through the poetry of the machine to the perfect electric man' (8). With
the movie camera serving as a 'mechanical eye', a superior reality is outlined here by Vertov, one no longer reliant on the alleged 'fiction' or 'psy-
chologism' of bourgeois literature and theatre. In the polemical manifesto
of 1922, moreover, Vertov invites the reader to 'flee,'

> the sweet embraces of the romance
> the poison of the psychological novel
> the clutches of the theatre of adultery
> to turn your back on music (Vertov 1984: 7)

Insisting that 'man' as such falls short of the 'precision' of machines
(a 'stopwatch' is given as example), Vertov advocates man's temporary
exclusion 'as a subject fit for film'. This logic fuels Vertov's criticism of

Eisenstein's *Strike* and *Battleship Potemkin*, which for Vertov represented the continuance of the 'acted film' and so remained antithetical to Kino-eye aesthetics (see 58–60).

Despite beginnings in the theatre and his adoption of a notionally narrative cinema, Eisenstein's montage aesthetics at first consideration conforms to imperatives very much akin to Vertov's theory, similarly seeking to differentiate the Soviet cinema from its predecessors through the forceful constructions of filmic meaning.[4] His critique of the ideology of the individual, for instance, would extend to problematising the valorisation of the 'star', not only as hero of the bourgeois drama but also in terms of artistic contributions to the film-making process. In reference to the bourgeois West, Eisenstein would remark that 'someone has to be the "star." *One* person. Yesterday it was the actor. This time let's say it's the cameraman. Tomorrow it will be the lighting technician' (1998: 68). Opposing such systems to Soviet collectivity and equality, Eisenstein here emphasises 'unity' as the aesthetic horizon of Soviet montage, whereby the individual heroic character is effaced by the proletarian mass. Applied to film form specifically, the shot is analogously endowed with complete meaning only through its juxtaposition with other shots and cinematic effects. Indeed, at least in Eisenstein's initial films, it is rare for central protagonists to emerge with which to identify emotionally, as a spectator may have done in relation to linear narratives and focalised protagonists in Hollywood cinema. Eisenstein's use of 'montage' gains authority ostensibly in relation to the formalist celebration of film's capacity for abstraction and intellect, as with Vertov and other formalist film-makers.

Eisenstein's examination of D. W. Griffith in 'Griffith, Dickens and Film Today' reveals, however, a tension between formalist and what Dudley Andrew terms 'organicist' (65) impulses in Eisenstein's thought. Written in 1944, Eisenstein had already by this point made *The General Line* (also known as *Old and New*), *Alexander Nevsky*, and *Ivan the Terrible*, all works that saw him compromise with the Socialist Realist School's demands for character, plot, focalised heroes, and moral legibility, in an effort to assuage charges of formalism from his contemporaries. He thus comes to argue that Griffith inherits a tradition of narrative construction from Dickens that was to be admired both for the evocative characters he creates and for the parallel editing and cross-cutting between scenes. Discussing the scene that sees Oliver Twist leave his well-to-do grandfather's house on an errand only to be abducted by Nancy, Fagin, and Bill Sykes – Eisenstein analyses the sequence as the narrative switches between the abductors (now with Oliver) and Brownlow as he waits in vain for Oliver's return. For Eisenstein, the oscillation between 'storylines' enhances the emotional impact of the narrative overall, whereby 'one (the waiting gentlemen) emotionally heightens the tension and drama of the other (the capture of Oliver)'. This leads Eisenstein to construct Dickens as cinematic *avant la lettre*, alluding to the latter's mastery of melodrama in the novel as a key factor to Griffith's success in the cinema. Eisenstein accounts for Dickens' and cinema's successes as follows:

> What were the novels of Dickens for his contemporaries, for his readers? There is one answer: they bore the same relation to them that the film bears to the same strata in our time. They compelled the reader to live with the same passions. They appealed to the same good and sentimental elements as does the film (at least on the surface); they alike shudder before vice, they alike mill the extraordinary, the unusual, the fantastic, from boring, prosaic and everyday existence. (Eisenstein 1977: 206)

In this passage, Dickens' employment of 'parallel action' inspires the same technique in Griffith's films and thereby achieves the same levels of success with their respective publics. We see here Eisenstein's clear recognition of cinema's melodramatic roots and its evident popularity as mass culture. Yet his qualification 'at least on the surface' provides an insight as to how the Dickens/Griffith style is deemed to differ from Soviet montage at least theoretically. For while Eisenstein recognises the popularity of the liberal-humanist aims of representing virtue triumphing over vice, there is a sense to which such aims have become anachronistic or at least limited in relation to the modernist-socialist ambitions for film. Eisenstein thus expresses surprise, in a footnote, that 'as late as 1944' Griffith maintained the above aims as the 'chief social function of filmmaking' (ibid.).

While melodrama may for Eisenstein have defined the Dickens/Griffith axis of story construction, Eisenstein affirms his own innovations in film technique as serving more explicitly political objectives. While he regards both figures as precursors to the 'montage' that inspires him and his Soviet colleagues, Griffith is argued to have reached a 'standstill' with 'parallel action'. Eisenstein furthermore applies this status of standstill to Griffith's politics. Thus:

> In social attitudes Griffith was always a liberal, never departing far from the sweet sentimental humanism of the good old gentlemen and sweet old ladies of Victorian England, just as Dickens loved to picture them. His tender hearted film morals go no higher than a level of Christian accusation of human injustice and nowhere in his film is there sounded a protest against social injustice. (Eisenstein 1977: 233–4)

Asserting Griffith's status as an artist of the 'bourgeois world', Eisenstein is ambivalent about the pioneer film-maker's sentimentality, failings he aligns moreover with the racism of *Birth of a Nation* or the Manichean metaphysics of *Intolerance*. What then follows in the article is a complex discussion of the differences between American and Soviet technique where political ideology is centralised as a determinative factor of cinematic style. He argues that Soviet ideology facilitates 'qualitative' innovations in technique that most expressly problematise American pretences at 'objectivity'. In order to achieve full political expressivity, 'montage' is argued here to have required a more 'full, conscious, completed' use, entailing above all the shaping of filmic reality as opposed to the passive registration of bourgeois truism. While 'parallel action' signifies here the seeds of a more dynamic cinema, it remains mired in a social and aesthetic conservatism, unable to be 'freed from narrow commercial tasks'. Thus:

> Griffith's cinema does not know this type of montage construction. His close-ups create atmosphere, outline traits of the characters, alternate in dialogues of the leading characters, and close-ups of the chaser and the chased speed up the tempo of the chase. But Griffith at all times remains on the level of *representation* and *objectivity* and nowhere does he try through the *juxtaposition* of shots to shape *import* and *image*. (Eisenstein 1977: 240; emphasis in the original)

In the name of 'import' then, Eisenstein advances Soviet montage as a technique that breaks down the bourgeois values sustained by Griffith's films. A chief binary in this argument is that of 'rich' and 'poor', a hierarchy that for Eisenstein dictates the formal parameters of Griffith's approach. While he recognises the centrality of the binary to melodrama, he rejects what he deems Griffith's 'dualistic picture of the world', which, for both him and Dickens, prevent their 'moving beyond these divisions'. The 'parallel' structure is argued to work differently in Soviet cinema, where via the application of Hegelian/Marxist dialectics in shot composition and editing, the meanings of the image are re-synthesised.

Eisenstein's chief criticisms of Griffith's cinema come to centre then on the complacency with which the American film-maker uncritically reproduces his world, and thereby evades a more interventionist aesthetics. This, for Eisenstein, defies Marxian imperatives to change history rather than merely understand it. Where Soviet cinema synthesised meaning in accordance with revolutionarily principles, American cinema problematically reproduced the stagnant subjectivities of bourgeois society. In relation to the nexus of 'Small Town America' and 'Super-Dynamic America', Eisenstein's attitude is ultimately thus one of caution. The dynamism of the crowds, stock-market, traffic, and skyscrapers of New York are analogised with the 'dizzying action' of Griffith's set pieces and the montage of his own epics. Its embeddedness in American individualist ideology limits it, however, to the addressing of individual destinies ('human injustice') as opposed to deeper political change ('social injustice'). Nowhere is this more evident, for instance, than in Eisenstein's 'intimate' description of the (for him) memorable passers-by and 'bit-characters' of Griffith's *Intolerance* and its marked contrast with his repudiations elsewhere of Hollywood's 'star' ideology. While the star upheld ideologies of individuality, Eisenstein predictably reserves his praise for characters who 'seem to have run straight from life onto the screen' (199).

There is clear recognition in Eisenstein's writing, in other words, that the human constitutes a vital component of cinema despite the imperatives of an impersonal dynamism in form. Much revisionist scholarship on Eisenstein testifies indeed to this complex approach to identification and affect. The critic Peter Wollen notes a tension, for instance, between the constructivist, semiotic montage theory of the early Eisenstein and the Wagnerian 'synesthesia' (44) of his later writings.[5] Eisenstein uses terms such as 'ecstasy', 'pathos', and even the 'pathetic' in his later writings (Eisenstein 2004: 6–9), while maintaining distinctions between character engagement and 'action'. 'If we wish the spectator to experience a maximum emotional upsurge, to send him into ecstasy', he argues,

> we must offer him a suitable 'formula' which will eventually excite the desirable emotions in him.
> The simple method is to present on the screen a human being in the state of ecstasy, that is, a character who is gripped by some emotion, who is 'beside himself'.
> A more complicated and effective method is the realization of the main condition of a work of pathos – constant qualitative changes in the action – not through the medium of one character, but through the entire environment. In other words, when everything around him is also 'beside itself'. A classical example of this method is the storm raging in the breast of King Lear and everywhere around him in nature. (Eisenstein 2004: 7)

If this passage rehearses Eisenstein's preferred site of cinematic affect as the 'super-dynamic' and the 'environment', it should also alert us to the distance between Eisenstein's modernism and the 'simple method' of the sentimental. While the latter method of course works with partial success, there is more than a suggestion here that character 'ecstasy' must necessarily be accompanied, and is largely justified, by the larger movements captured by film. While a contemporary director such as Steven Spielberg would no doubt agree with such a claim when one considers his investment in the great spectacle of his films, key ideological differences remain between the two film-makers that may account for the sentimental charges made against the latter's work (discussed in detail in Ch. 5). If the modernist politicism of Eisenstein's epic work has traditionally removed him from such criticisms, this is precisely what is considered lacking in Spielbergian 'ecstasy', despite key aesthetic parallels between the two.

André Bazin

For André Bazin, the importance of cinema was to be gauged by the extent to which the medium could capture reality *without* modification, and the human struggles for freedom captured by the post-war Italian neorealist cinema exemplified the spirit with which such reality should be conveyed. Much of the revered contemporary cinema of Bazin's day had reached an aesthetic impasse for him, owing to what he deemed a disrespectful distortion of pro-filmic reality in favour of fabricated, ideologically inflected myth, divorced from a more authentic historical reality.[6] One kind of cinematic sentimentality for Bazin, as for others, would be implicated in such dissociations between image and reality, the production of the 'imaginary' as opposed to the 'real'. While modernists would generally advocate greater intervention on the part of the medium between these two elements, Bazin notoriously seeks to collapse them. In this respect, Italian neorealism was deemed to deliver the gritty realities of post-war Italian life through an aesthetic that necessarily eliminated the stylistic excesses of Soviet modernism or the overly stylised classicism of Hollywood and French cinemas. However, the virtues of neorealism for Bazin were also bound up with the 'love' of the auteur for characters oppressed by harsh social conditions. In as much as a sympathetic engagement with such characters becomes a vital key to the political relevance of these films, a cultural humanism emerges in Bazin's theory that conflicts with certain high modernist assumptions concerning cinematic spectatorship.

An example of how montage and the sentimental are implicated with one another in Bazin's theory is manifest in his critique of Jean Tourane's *Une Fée pas comme les autres* where live footage of animals is subjected to editing, voiceover, and narrative in the service of anthropomorphised spectacle. While Bazin is careful not to denounce what he considers a human predisposition for the anthropomorphic, he claims that Tourane operates at its 'lowest level' owing to his reliance on 'trick' and 'illusion'. A key problem of creating such stories comes down to a question of ontology:

> The apparent action and the meaning we attribute to it do not exist, to all intents and purposes, prior to the assembling of the film, not even in the form of fragmented scenes out of which the setups are generally composed. I will go further and say that, in the circumstances, the use of montage was not just one way of making this film, it was the *only* way. (Bazin 2005: 44; emphasis in the original)

In accordance with his theory concerning the ontological essence of cinema, Bazin proposes here that if a film evidences the distortion of pro-filmic reality to the extent that it cannot exist without such distortion, such a film constitutes a fatal deviation from reality. He disdainfully affirms elsewhere that Tourane's 'naïve ambition' is to achieve little more than 'to make Disney pictures with live animals' (43), suggesting that, as with Disney's animal characters, a spectator is tricked into anthropomorphic identification by an illusory cinema divorced from reality.

It is worth emphasising here that Bazin's critique aims not to attack the sentimental spectator but the film-maker who seeks to exploit the former's capacity for anthropomorphic perception. With the article concerning itself with children's literature and film generally, Bazin outlines a theory of best practice that necessitates respect for the authenticity of the image while not entirely abandoning basic cinematic devices – the 'imaginary' is a cinematic constant, but, for Bazin, it must also 'include what is real' (47). Authenticity becomes the guarantee that the spectator is engaged with a reality that lends itself to the spectator's imaginary even prior to its capture by the camera, with cinema enhancing that process as opposed to creating it through excessive trickery. Unlike the 'zoomorphism' (45) of Tourane's animals, Bazin praises Lamorrisse's 'red balloon' tale, as the story allows itself to remain a 'pure creation of the mind' (46). In other words, Bazin claims that the spectator has a predisposition for a senti-mental engagement with the image while nevertheless maintaining that its abuse all too often results from cheap simulations of that otherwise imaginative process.

Bazin applies a similar logic to his analysis of neorealism itself, where the sentimental once more pertains to sympathetic and imaginative engagements with 'realist' narrative yet remains a danger of cinema's excessive emotional engagement as a consequence of excessively visible editing style. In this context, Bazin discusses narrative construction in De Sica's *Umberto D*. In as much as the film could be argued to use melodra-matic conventions, Bazin paraphrases the criticisms of other critics who see the film as a '"populist" melodrama with social pretensions' (1972: 80). However, unlike such critics, Bazin notes the reductiveness of accusa-tions of the film's sentimentality. He argues that a central concern of their critique rests on how the film's evocation of 'pity' in the spectator arises out of the manipulation of plot developments in relation to an ostensibly pathetic central protagonist (that is, the hero's unmistakeable suffering is shown to be causally related to mistreatment by cruel antagonists). In as much as the film concerns itself with the protagonist's loneliness and poverty (a retired, penniless pensioner, and his faithful dog), Bazin agrees that the film belongs to a tradition of melodrama. He claims, however, that the film does not accentuate 'pathos' for its own sake, preferring instead to convey events in the protagonist's life, some of which are pitiable (being thrown out of his flat owing to rent arrears) and others that are not (his comic stay in hospital owing to a harmless angina). Thus, for Bazin, the film conveys man's downfall due to the 'the lack of fellow-feeling that characterises' the 'middle-class' (81) and succeeds in producing a variety of emotions in the spectator rather than an exclusive 'pity.' Bazin counters the critics by applauding the film's emotional eclecticism – an important attribute of neorealism, and, as we have seen, of melodrama generally.

Bazin goes on to bracket the above discussion (and his own contributions to it) as a 'lapsing back into traditional critical concepts' (81), that is, dramatic construction. With narrative and character constituting the two main factors of such analysis, Bazin claims an exclusive attention to the 'dramatic' as superfluous to the true aims of *Umberto D* (and film generally). Thus, he writes:

> If one assumes some distance from the story and can still see in it a dramatic patterning, some general development in character, a single general trend in its component events, this is only after the fact. The narrative unit is not the episode, the event, the sudden turn of events, or the character of its protagonists; it is the succession of concrete instants of life, no one of which can be said to be more important than the other, for their ontological equality destroys drama at its very basis. (Bazin 1972: 81)

Bazin in the above applauds the film not for its plot or its characters then but for the fidelity with which it captures the reality of the depicted events. If the dramatic elements of *Umberto D* are still manifest to the spectator (or to the critic who is ready to claim sentimentality), Bazin concludes that such attributes, shared with theatrical and novelistic forms, come secondary to the film's more unique achievement of 'ontological equality'. This latter attribute has little to do with the construction of story in dramatic terms, and refers more to the success with which the film conveys 'concrete instants of life'. Whether pity is still evoked by the film becomes a secondary concern, trumped by the necessity of maintaining a style that is unencumbered by the 'dramatic' concerns of more conventional narratives. Describing a scene that dwells on the young maid waking up and going about her chores, Bazin asserts that such mundane moments are free of an 'art of ellipsis' that 'organises the facts in accord with the general dramatic direction to which it forces them to submit' (81). Drama becomes implicated as a simplistic rendering of reality, a 'construction' that must be minimised in order that 'life might in this perfect mirror be visible poetry, be the self into which film finally changes it' (82).

For Bazin, then, it is not so much the emotions generated by 'drama' that are attacked but, as with the Tourane's animated films, the means by which they would be elicited by styles of cinematic rhetoric that deform reality to an excessive level. As Dudley Andrew notes, Bazin's notorious claim that cinema 'is also a language' rests on the notion of what Bazin considers its more significant attribute of indexicality, an attribute deemed distinct from its linguistic function, both in terms of its modernist and Hollywood dialects (2005: 16). While cinema's linguistic function risks its manipulation by oppressive, repressive, or sentimental ideologies, respect for the indexical reality of the image serves for Bazin as a stylistic priority that defends the medium from the dangers of abstraction. In these respects, Bazin's realism remains as austere towards dramatic categories as the formalists, still favouring the conveyance of a politically vital reality to the 'lapsing back' towards anachronistic forms. Whether the sentimental signifies emotion shown by characters within narrative, or those evoked in spectators becomes a question belonging to another aesthetic debate in relation to media that still rely existentially on abstraction, unlike the cinema.

While the 'dramatic' seems repudiated by both camps, therefore, Bazin's emphasis on the cinema's photographic ontology leads him to a greater acceptance of sentiment than the formalists. His preference for an unmanipulated pro-filmic reality leaves the affect inherent in such phenomena available to the spectator as long as it stems from a faithful, unimpeded deployment of cinematography. Moreover, more than any of the theorists so far discussed, Bazin's rhetoric in praise of neorealist films is suffused with references to the sentimental values of their directors. In another article in praise of De Sica, Bazin applauds the 'love' and sense of 'poetry' evoked by such films as *Bicycle Thieves* or *Miracle in Milan*, virtues that he deems constitutive of a proper auteur. Posing a humanism of 'courtly and discreet gentleness' or 'liberal generosity' (2005: 70) as key to the neorealism of De Sica and other Italian directors, Bazin positions them within a long line of humanist directors that includes Vigo, Flaherty, Renoir, and most especially, Chaplin. All the above, for Bazin, exercise the 'tenderness' or 'sentimental affection' (72) required of a cinematic auteur. Noting, for instance, that if Chaplin's work were transposed into cinema, 'it would tend to lapse into sentimentality' (72), he nevertheless poses just such aspects of the director's work as testament to the latter's artistry and a chief attribute of the cinema itself. Writing of a 'quality of presence', the 'radiation of tenderness' or 'an intense sense of the human presence' in the work of such auteurs, Bazin affirms a distinctly humanist set of elements as crucial to cinematic representation. He confirms most explicitly

Chaplin's place in this cinematic sentimental tradition in the following description of the latter's oeuvre, for instance:

> cruelty is not excluded from his world; on the contrary, it has a necessary and dialectic relationship to love, as is evident from *Monsieur Verdoux*. Charlie is goodness itself, projected onto the world. He is ready to love everything, but the world does not always respond. (Bazin 1971: 72–3)

While the above clearly confirms Bazin's approval of a sentimental aesthetic, what remains problematic is how such humanism is posed in relation to Bazin's more hard-edged notion of neorealism as an abandonment of the contrived, melodramatic tendencies suggested by an 'art of ellipsis'. A qualified answer can be offered by observing that while such a sentimental aesthetic as 'virtue in distress' is made central here, and historicised as an important cinematic tradition, Bazin retains a certain catholicity as to the kinds of emotion that should inspire such work and to those such work should evoke. As with *Umberto D*, sympathy remains a complex of thoughts and emotions available to auteur and spectator, in contrast to a singular pity for its protagonist. Instead, Bazin advocates a spectatorship characterised by a 'dialectic' between subjectivity (feeling 'love' for realistic characters) and objectivity (the witnessing 'cruelty' as well as its causes and consequences). In a discussion of Antonioni's *Cronaca di un amore*, for instance, he notes the film's 'expensive sets' and 'melodramatic narrative' but praises the realism of the film's characters, such that the Italian director:

> builds all his effects on their way of life, their way of crying, of walking, of laughing. They are caught in the maze of the plot like laboratory rats being sent through a labyrinth. (Bazin 1971: 67)

Bazin's praise here underlines the importance of human emotion to this film, yet also implies an engagement with human behaviour aligned with the realism of scientific observation. Given that 'crying' or 'laughing' are inevitable manifestations of human emotion captured by the camera, they must not be excluded from the realist film, for such emotions guarantee the authenticity of the human activities represented. In advocating a quasi-scientific model of sympathy, however, Bazin's neorealism remains a generous and courtly practice that cannot be too emotionally involved with its subjects. For De Sica, too, Bazin commends in the auteur-director a detached kind of sympathy rather than empathy in relation to character:

> [B]ut the affection De Sica feels for his creatures is no threat to them, there is nothing threatening or abusive about it. It is courtly and discreet gentleness, a liberal

generosity, and it demands nothing in return. There is no admixture of pity in it even
for the poorest or the most wretched, because pity does violence to the dignity of the
man who is its object. It is a burden on his conscience. (Bazin 1971: 70)

Bazin's praise of De Sica's approach here rehearses a key problem of the
sentimental, for while his language evokes the key virtues of sentiment, his
message enforces an identificatory process of sympathetic detachment over
one of empathy, the necessity of understanding over and above emotional
contagion between spectator and character. The cinema permits a 'gentle'
examination of the world motivated by 'affection', 'love', or 'poetry', yet
its best practice for Bazin stops short of permitting the 'violence' of pity.
Bazin's outline of De Sica's 'love' is suggestive of the sensibility an auteur
must feel in relation to the humanity depicted in his films, yet it must also
be a virtue that restrains the impulse to manipulate the spectator's perspective towards excessively empathic reactions, which all too often arise
for Bazin from styles of narrative that overly abstract from the reality of
depicted events.

As much as Bazin deems the representation of real, hostile conditions,
and an uncaring society a vital task of neorealism, his praise for central
characters repeatedly, as we have seen, emphasises the necessity of conveying a well-meaning benevolence. Although the spectator should not
be entreated to 'pity' such put-upon heroes as Chaplin's tramp, *Umberto
D*, or Ricci from *Bicycle Thieves*, Bazin's praise for the underdog as a
necessary rhetorical weapon for change seems implicit in his essay on De
Sica. Bazin is nevertheless cautious about an overly idealising framing of
the hero. The sympathy one should have for virtuous characters becomes
nuanced, for instance, by comments such as those that follow his discussion of Chaplin's 'goodness,' where he compares the latter to De Sica.

Chaplin also chooses his cast carefully but always with an eye to himself and to
putting his character in a better light. We find in De Sica the humanity of Chaplin,
but shared with the world at large. (Bazin 1971: 73)

As opposed to Chaplin's having 'an eye to himself', Bazin suggests De
Sica's preference for a virtue that is shared by humanity at large, albeit one
that may be exemplified by pathetic protagonists like the tramp. Because
Bazin implies that the underdog courts an excessive sympathy when
singled out as an idealised symbol of benevolence, Bazin prefers De Sica's
Miracle in Milan with its depiction of an entire group of homeless people
divested of their homes and living a poor but honest life in a shanty town.
Emphasising the mass as opposed to the individual, this film resembles
Eisenstein's own epics of mass struggle, their shift away from the virtuous

hero. Bazin's argument places value on such a shift and reveals his caution with regard to a hero who is overly idealised above other characters.

Béla Balázs

If Bazin expresses caution as to the idealisation of a moral hero, the stakes are raised by the theory of Béla Balázs, for whom truth is revealed above all by the cinema's attention to the human face and its affinity for conveying the narrative trajectory of a hero. In many ways, Balázs' theory complements Bazin's in its emphasis on cinema's affinity for revealing and explaining the complexities of human nature, yet for Balázs, a shift of focus away from the individual threatens to destabilise that capacity. Balázs' emphasis remains on the expressivity of man as distinct from the abstract, anti-imitative models of the modernist avant-gardes or the human behaviour captured by the 'objective' documentary. Nevertheless, his discussion of cinema's representation of the human is communicated once more in scientific terms, qualifying the extent to which the spectator's engagement with the individual can be idealised or sentimental.

Balázs has often been considered a modernist or formalist owing largely to the period and location within which he wrote (1920s Weimar Germany) and a recurrent emphasis on cinema's necessary transformations of pro-filmic reality. Recent scholarship, however, has problematised easy categorisation of the theorist in either the formalist or realist camps, along with other theorists such as Epstein, Vertov, and Kracauer.[7] While Balázs' admiration of the close-up suggests a modernist's attention to editing, his invocations of cinematic humanism require a realist's focus on the referent. The revelation of life's hidden details, particularly the nuances of human emotion and gesture, become cinema's special vocation for Balázs, producing a modern human subject attuned to visual signs of emotion. Balázs' humanist metaphor for the aesthetic he perceives as central to cinema is encapsulated by the title of *Theory of the Film*'s most well-known sections on the close-up, 'The Face of Things'. Asserting that normal human perception leads us to 'skim over the teeming substance of life', Balázs argues that the camera 'has uncovered that cell-life of the vital issues in which all great events are ultimately conceived' (Balázs and Bone 1952: 55). The face here serves as metaphor for the anthropomorphised significance of film, a benchmark for the richness that the close-up is able to convey.

Balázs' discussion of children and animals as cinema's newly found objects extends this deep concern with cinema's ability to reveal authentic aspects of the world. While arguing that their representation forged a new style rather than a language of cinema, he writes of both with an almost mystical attachment to the authenticity of their gesture. While adults could be 'stage-managed' to act in pre-determined ways, Balázs writes of the autonomy of children and animals from what he describes elsewhere as 'severe rules that govern grammar' that he considered to potentially govern gesture or expression. When children act in films, Balázs argues:

> This is not acting – it is a natural manifestation of youthful consciousness and it can be observed not only in the human young but in the young of other species as well. It is a transposition such as occurs in dreams, or in a trance. (Balázs and Bone 1952: 80)

While facial expression and gestures are already rich in 'polyphony' for Balázs, children or animals are positioned in the above as guarantors of an emotional realism in their freedom from convention. While Balázs avoids praise for the realism of non-actors over actors (he prefers the close-ups of such film actors as Asta Nielsen or Renée Maria Falconetti to the supposedly objective expressions of non-actors), his descriptions of the fairy-tale-like otherness of children, animals, and native savages suggest a latent fascination with the 'inaccessible nature and inaccessible fairy-land' connoted by them. If such passages undermine his own distinction between a filmic style and a filmic language, his thesis gains strength in its overall veneration of a curious spectator enthralled by cinema's delivery of a 'microphysiognomy' that is beyond linguistic constraints.

What emerges in Balázs' thought, therefore, is the saliency of physiognomy and gesture, created by the tensions of dramatic action (narrative) and, relatedly, freedom from a kind of emotional barrenness, as applied either to dispassionate film-makers, insensitive spectators, and, indeed, untrained actors. With such sub-titles as 'Education in Physiognomics' or 'Sound Explaining Pictures', the aims of *Theory of the Film* accord with a humanistic goal of better understanding between people via film's affinity for revealing subjectivity. Responding to Soviet methods of creating images of mismatched emotional reactions (his example is the use of a mother's reaction to her child's pram overturned inserted by Eisenstein as the reaction shot of a woman facing the barrel of a gun), Balázs writes:

> This method is always a deception; it is rendered possible only by the fact that our physiognomic culture is not as yet sufficiently sensitive to be able to differentiate between terrors induced by different causes . . . The close-up which has made us so sensitive to the naturalness of a facial expression will sooner or later develop our sensitivity further, so that we shall be able to discern in a facial expression its cause as well as its nature. (Balázs and Bone 1952: 79)

Balázs here goes some way in expressing here not only his disdain for the 'fanatics of "naturalness"', but also makes salient his aim of allowing cinema to educate the spectator in a new cinematic lingua franca of human emotion. The stakes of this endeavour are couched in the necessity of averting the kinds of cruelty that emanate, for Balázs, in the Soviet directors' narrow-minded inattention to emotional nuance. Such disregard for the integrity of human emotion in favour of its role in a supposedly superior synthesis of meaning grated Balázs in terms that vary between the ontological (mismatched actual and represented emotions), humanitarian (the directors' emotional callousness), and educational (the spectators' exploited ignorance of the sham owing to a lamentable insensitivity to emotion). If emotional meanings could be correctly depicted and then adduced by newly sensitised subjects, Balázs implies that the cinema constitutes man's best hope for mutual understanding. As a universalised language of human emotion and gesture, cinema promises to emancipate man from the 'severe rules' of abstracted meaning that prevented the emergence of a truly popular art. Thus, he argues:

> it will probably be the art of the film after all which may bring together the peoples and nations, make them accustomed to each other, and lead them to mutual understanding. The silent film is free of the isolating walls of language differences. If we look at and understand each other's faces and gestures, we not only understand, we also learn to feel each other's emotions. The gesture is not only the outward projection of emotion, it is also its initiator. (Balázs and Bone 1952: 44)

With language differences posing for Balázs, as for many other theorists, a great challenge to 'mutual understanding', cinema (especially silent cinema) directly addresses the spectator's conscious and unconscious. By revealing 'hidden' emotions, film would make visible to the spectator truths that had as yet remained occluded by surface appearances. With such descriptions as 'the hidden mainsprings of a life which we had thought we already knew so well' (55), Balázs insists that cinema constitutes more than just a quantitative increase in perceptual information; it creates a qualitative change. Anticipating counter-arguments that the close-up may only show new details of pro-filmic objects as opposed to necessarily providing new meanings, Balázs justifies the semiotic value of the cinema's detailed scrutiny:

> The close-up may sometimes give the impression of a mere naturalist preoccupation with detail. But good close-ups radiate a tender human attitude in the contemplation of hidden things, a delicate solicitude, a gentle bending over the intimacies of life-in-the-miniature, a warm sensibility. Good close-ups are lyrical; it is the heart, not the eye, that has perceived them. (Balázs and Bone 1952: 56)

Balázs' sentimental language in the above passage reveals the underlying impulse in his theory to emphasise the role of human consciousness in the deployment of the close-up. While inadequate close-ups reveal little of extra significance, the good close-up is motivated by 'intimacies', whether on the part of the spectator or the film-maker. Anticipating Bazin's theory of the benevolent auteur, Balázs' theory of the close-up requires a concern for meaning founded in a 'tender human attitude' towards the world, as opposed to an appetite for increased detail for its own sake. Emotional investment suggests the film-maker's benevolent impulse to show the world in new ways; the 'mere naturalist' is posed meanwhile as a non-artistic cataloguer of visual facts in the name of a kind of dispassionate taxonomy.

One can see how Balázs' aesthetic dismay over both documentary and avant-garde practices derives then from this above formulation of detached film-making. He argues that the avant-garde seeks to represent nothing but 'absolute visuality' (159) or the 'poetry of things' (59) while the documentary seeks an objective and impartial registration of reality. Narrative remains for him, therefore, the key intermediary between excesses of the subjective and objective, particularly when bound by the necessity of representing a 'hero'. The mass epics of Eisenstein, the Vertovian documentary, or the 'abstract' avant-garde film all abandon, for Balázs, this necessary 'individualisation' in favour of an aesthetic of 'the natural or the logical', with the following consequences:

> The trouble was that if an artist renounces individualisation, what he achieves is not something of universal validity; it is on the contrary, complete disintegration. (Balázs and Bone 1952: 161)

Balázs condemns the subordination of narrative and the presentation of 'human destinies' to what he deems elitist styles because it comes at the cost of comprehensibility and coherence. Only by treating the 'fable' or 'story' as 'a closed entity' (that is, an adherent to narrative form) could the film-maker hope to give best expression to filmed material. The 'hero' provides for Balázs the ideal emotional anchor for the registration of ongoing changes in narrative, without which the film risks 'disintegration'. If these prejudices reveal Balázs' somewhat conservative conception of film's ideal practice in his valorisation of narrative over other representative modes, they nevertheless emphasise his humanist concerns. Problematically overlooking the constructed nature of narrative itself, 'dramatic action' catalyses the 'face of things' for Balázs compared to the avant-garde's exclusive attention to form or the documentary's fetishisation of objectivity or naturalism. As distinct from the latter practice, for instance, Balázs commends the use of trained, experienced actors over the non-actors of documentary precisely because the former were for him better able to convey the nuances of facial and gestural emotion. While using non-actors would bring an apparent 'objectivity' to the film, the richness of human expression and its 'polyphony' is lost without the actor's ability to create physiognomic or bodily meanings.

Nevertheless, despite his emphasis on the 'intimacies' of good film-making, Balázs' model of spectatorship, as with Bazin's metaphor of a 'maze', is also likened to the accuracy of scientific observation. Thus, in cinema's depiction of family drama:

> The micro-tragedies in the peace and quiet of ordinary families were shown as deadly battles, just as the microscope shows the fierce struggles of micro-organisms in a drop of water. (Balázs and Bone 1952: 85)

If the above suggests, as with Bazin, the possibility of the scientist's vantage point and an implicit emotional impartiality, the two writers both share an enthusiasm for human conflict as the preferred object of analysis. While Balázs is far less concerned with the ontological realism with which such human conflict is staged, there is a shared consensus as to the need for the cinema's dispassionate scrutiny of human behaviour. The implication for both theorists is the possibility of representing 'fierce struggles' and the darker side of human nature as much as morally exemplary behaviour. Despite the 'warm sensibility' with which Balázs encourages our encounter with life up close, he writes of what we may find in terms of a moral realism, such as in his description of film's rooting out of a 'capable liar':

> In vain does his mouth smile ever so sweetly the lobe of his ear, the side of a nostril shown in isolated magnification reveal the hidden coarseness and cruelty. (Balázs and Bone 1952: 75)

If cinema's truthfulness must necessarily convey the moral baseness of the human condition, such as in the lies, cruelty, and coarseness of superficially moral characters, Balázs endows cinema with the moral imperative of revealing it and enabling the spectator to exercise superior discrimination, in relation to on-screen and off-screen characters. With this level of realism guaranteed by the cinema, Balázs is more than content to permit such a model as 'virtue in distress' as a legitimate characteristic of the narrative hero. A scorned sentimental trope in other art-forms often owing to the one-dimensionality with which the object of sympathy is drawn, pathos for Balázs lends itself to cinema's vivid analysis and thereby facilitates moral legibility. Chaplin, for instance, becomes a paradigm for Balázs of the heroic individual thwarted by an 'inhuman society', his 'golden-hearted' nature in no way diminished by the clarity with which the cinema delivers the tramp as 'shiftless, blundering' and even 'cunning' (285).

With such characters as Chaplin's tramp serving as moral anchors for narrative action, the melodramatic 'mode' becomes, as Linda Williams has suggested, a deeply embedded presence of Hollywood storytelling, with 'action' and 'pathos' contributing in equal measure to the resolution of conflict between good and evil and the recognition of moral virtue. Cinema, with its affinity for the close-up, the human face, and an incomparable capacity to invoke an omniscient spectator through editing, becomes the medium of choice for melodrama's articulation of 'moral legibility'. Invoking the moral realism discussed by Bazin, Balázs, and others above, the subject represented by such figures as the tramp remains a potent signifier of humanity victimised by 'mechanisation and capitalism', the plucky hero who asserts his right to life despite the status of perpetual misfit, played for Balázs with a 'melancholy optimism' that 'expresses the opposition of all of us to an inhuman order of society' (ibid.).

In short, therefore, the sentimental persists as a contested aesthetic discourse surrounding the cinema as it emerged as a dominant medium in the early-to-mid-twentieth century. Despite, or in many ways owing to, the repudiations of kitsch, mass, or bourgeois tastes or simplistic character engagements that informed the critiques analysed above, the sentimental comes to represent much of what a certain hard-edged set of modernisms, formalisms, and realisms sought to problematise and transform. At the same time, the philosophical ideals that motivate such critiques are time and again shown to be rather less than inimical to sentimental values of universal communication, sympathy for those oppressed by economic disparities, and the significance of art's humanist function. If, as a practice, the sentimental and its reproduction in the cinema were, or indeed are, all too often considered to devalue such ideals for the sake of cheap, unearned emotion, and/or bourgeois entertainment, it is important to bear in mind the extent to which it retained critical importance for theorists of this era as a distinct affective category.

Notes

1. Ben Singer identifies this alignment of cinema and other dynamic features of modern, urban experience as an important strand of 'culturalist' film theory that posits a causal or correlative relationship between such phenomena and transformations in human perception. David Bordwell has critiqued some of

the central assumptions of this 'modernity thesis'. See Ben Singer, *Melodrama and Modernity: Early Sensational Cinema and its Contexts*, New York: Columbia University Press, 2001, Ch. 4; David Bordwell, *On the History of Film Style*, Cambridge, MA: Harvard University Press, 1997, pp. 140–9.

2. Writing on the perceptual 'trick' of the New York skyscraper, Eisenstein finds the provincial America of private dwellings to be also inscribed in them, enough to find them 'cosy, domestic, small-town'. See Eisenstein, Sergei, *Film Form*, J. Leyda (trans.), New York: Harcourt Brace, 1972 [1949], p. 197.
3. For a critique of the assumptions underlying the 'specificity thesis', see Noël Carroll, 'The Specificity Thesis', in L. Braudy, M. Cohen, and G. Mast (eds), *Film Theory and Criticism: Introductory Readings*, 5th edn, New York: Oxford University Press, 1998, pp. 322–8.
4. While Eisenstein engaged in ongoing debates with Vertov as to the function and aesthetics of the new cinema, much of this conflict has been attributed to the fierce competition for funding and prestige in the Soviet Union of that era. See Annette Michelson's introduction to *Kino-Eye: The Writings of Dziga Vertov*, p. xlvi-l.
5. Wollen argues that while Eisenstein's introduction of 'sound and colour' seemed for 1970s film theory to be explained as a mere compromise with Stalinist demands, he highlights Eisenstein's continuous theoretical attention to film's polyphonic or synaesthetic attributes, and his commitment to 'real bodies and real movement'.
6. As Dudley Andrew argues, while prior film theory held film up as a painterly 'frame' that invites the artist to create, film for Bazin now served as a 'window' on to the world, offering thus a much needed re-engagement with social and political reality. See *The Major Film Theories*, Oxford: Oxford University Press, 1976.
7. See Malcolm Turvey's critique of Dudley Andrew's categorisation of Balázs as a formalist in 'Balázs: Realist or Modernist', *October* 115 (winter 2006), pp. 77–87.

CHAPTER 3

The Sentimental Chaplin:
Comedy and Classical Narrative

In a scene from Richard Attenborough's *Chaplin*, a 1992 biopic of the early film-maker and star, an elderly Chaplin (Robert Downey Jr) recounts to his biographer (Anthony Hopkins) his invention of the tramp character that would bring him so much success in the early days of Hollywood. The sequence begins with the younger Chaplin's entrance into the wardrobe at Hollywood's Sennet studios, his gaze immediately drawn to the hat that would become essential to the tramp's costume. In a heavily stylised preliminary sequence, the hat, towards which an entranced Chaplin advances balletically, glows with a superimposed purple tint. Accompanied by a soundtrack of romantic strings and soft-focus camerawork, the scene is infused with conventions of the dream-sequence, gently mocking the reverential tone with which its off-screen author (the elderly Chaplin) feeds the mythology of the tramp's creation. Acknowledging the possibility of fabulation, the sequence draws attention to artifice, wherein the tramp's hat advances magically up the younger Chaplin's arm to his head, followed by the famous cane, that rattles in its holder for Chaplin's attention, and having done so, flies out to his hand.

This sequence ends abruptly when Chaplin's biographer accuses the elder Chaplin of couching the whole story in 'purple' prose (with an off-screen 'bullshit, and you know it'), to which the elder Chaplin complains, 'but the truth was so boring, George'. What follows then is the apparently real history of the tramp's creation, where Chaplin bumbles through the wardrobe (at doubled speed), trying on different items bearing little relation to the tramp's iconic costume. The soundtrack switches from romantic strings to the style of the silent film's chase-sequence or last-minute rescue, invoking the frantic and chaotic pace of a Hollywood wardrobe department, the predominance of work and effort over magic and enchantment. This shift serves as a realist disavowal of the elder Chaplin's story, countering the sentimentalism of his myth-making. Corroborating indeed its parodic tendencies, it is here that comedy comes to dominate, invoking what Henry Jenkins coins an 'anarchistic comedy' and its constitution of 'an alternative set of social and artistic norms' (1992: 24) to classical Hollywood norms. Its mixture of parody and homage constitutes, in other words, a mode of address that privileges disorder and irony. The normativity of biography and its sentimental fabulations are targeted, wherein Chaplin is framed and gently mocked as the master melodramatist that can't help sentimentalising his own story.

What is all the more telling in this complex sequence, however, is how the affective tone of the sequence shifts gear once again before it is through. So potent is the myth of creative genius (despite the salience of parody and homage up to this point) that the middle, 'realist' portion of this sequence ends with a return to the sentimental mode with which it began, except with irony now dispensed with entirely. As a now fully costumed Chaplin-as-tramp selects his oversized shoes from the basket, the leitmotif of gentle strings returns as Chaplin gingerly picks up the shoes and ponders their excessive significance in relation to the tramp's iconicity, once again privileging the spectator's knowledge of their import and re-introducing the theme of their magically ordained rightness. Looking into his reflection as a near finished-product in an off-screen mirror, Chaplin slowly smiles, his recognition of himself-as-icon invoking destiny and foreknowledge that negates the comedy of the sequence's earlier recourse to parody and slapstick realism. Selecting then a small moustache and, having stumbled upon the shoes, adopting the tramp's walk (like at the climax of *The Tramp* (1915), away from camera and in silhouette), Chaplin is now 'Chaplin'. Like the sequence in Hitchcock's *Vertigo* (1958) that sees Judy return to Scotty's (and the spectator's) exact vision of Madeleine on the day of her death, the tramp is finally here permitted its status as a mythical fetish object, one belonging to the image culture of Hollywood.

As much as though Attenborough's biopic of Chaplin thus deploys comedy to mock and disavow the 'bullshit' of biography and mythologisation, *Chaplin* remains committed to telling the story of a comic genius within the melodramatic parameters it inherits from one of its great pioneers. Despite its nods at the vicissitudes and indeterminacies of creative labour, the sentimental elements of the sequence come to dominate in their invocation of iconicity, individual genius, and destiny over chance and chaos. With the film having stumbled into a 'boring' comic sequence, owing to a self-conscious acknowledgement and disparagement of its own myth-making, comedy ultimately gives way to sentiment in order to complete the re-construction of the fetish object. As in the famous psychoanalytic dictum of fetishistic disavowal, 'I know very well, but nevertheless,'[1] the ironic realism of comedy is offset here by the catharsis of recognition.

The younger Chaplin senses the rightness of the tramp, just as the spectator of *Chaplin* must feel, as much as understand, the genesis of such an
icon. *Chaplin* thus both appeases the 'hip' irony of a contemporary cinematic spectatorship while retaining the affect of a reverential biopic and
its concomitant recourse to sentimentalism; it wants us to believe that the
tramp was intentional, a product of genius, 'meant to be'.

   This chapter seeks analogously to explore the tensions between comedy
and sentiment in Hollywood's early and classical periods as affects that
contend for dominance in the Hollywood film. It focuses on the career of
Chaplin's tramp figure in particular, as a figure of profound ambivalence
as to the development and success of sentimentalism as a taste category
in early feature film-making. Just as the sequence described above shifts
between two distinct structures of affect (the comedic and the sentimental), I examine how Chaplin's modifications of the tramp character correlate with the coming to prominence of sentimentality in the classical
Hollywood period, addressing both its superseding slapstick humour and
its legacy in classical Hollywood cinema. With the tramp re-crafted by
Chaplin himself into a figure of sentiment and pathos to complement the
slapstick and violence of his early shorts, the discussion charts this shift in
relation to anxieties surrounding ideas of 'Virtue Triumphant' in modernity, where sentiment emerges as the moral feeling of a 'gentleman' who
can no longer secure a place in a newly middle-class dominated society.
Brought in line with the theme of the virtuous soul, whose sentiments
are too rarefied and whose capital insubstantial, the tramp instantiates
indeed a unique reconciliation of sentimental and modernist values, fuel-
ling intense critical speculation in relation to his own import and that of
the cinema at the time of his reception.

The Gentleman Tramp

Any discussion of Chaplin's sentiment must begin with a consideration
of Chaplin's films in relation to the cinema's established accommodation
of the tastes of the desirable (lucrative), middle-class audiences of the
1910s and 1920s. Chaplin began his cinematic career under the direction of Mack Sennet at Keystone studios in 1914 and appeared continually
as the tramp, an ideal character for the slapstick talents he had honed in the
London music halls. Amidst growing fame, he gradually gained increased
control over the direction of his films and in the following years signed new
contracts with Essenay and then Mutual as both central performer and
director for the many shorts produced during the rest of the 1910s. Such a
high level of control over production has been considered a chief factor in

how the tramp figure became subject to 'refinement', particularly once at Mutual. It has been well established by Chaplin biographers and critics in relation to Chaplin's Keystone/Essenay/Mutual period (the many shorts that preceded his first feature, *The Kid*, in 1921 for First National) that a key development occurs in Chaplin's tramp persona from the thieving, lecherous, and rather violent tramp of the Keystone and early-Essenay period to the well-meaning yet romantically vulnerable loner of his later shorts and features (see Maland 1989: 14–24; Woal and Kowall Woal 1994: 3–15). If the slapstick antics, chase-scenes, and kickabout humour are never eliminated from Chaplin's oeuvre, films from as early on as *The Vagabond* (1916, Mutual), *The Bank* (1915, Mutual), and *The Immigrant* (1917, Mutual) incorporate parallel narratives of romance and unrequited love with Chaplin's leading lady (played by Edna Purviance) that allow the films to invoke pathos alongside comedy.

A brief consideration of a Keystone film illustrates the extent to which Chaplin's archetypal character began as a notably unsentimental protagonist. In *Twenty Minutes of Love* (1914, Keystone), for instance, the tramp (wearing an uncharacteristically sneering facial expression and puffing on a cigarette) enters a park and observes a romantic couple embracing on a park bench. Finding their behaviour laughably ridiculous, Chaplin mimics their facial expressions and embraces and kisses the tree he's standing next to as a parody of their courtship. When the couple seem not to notice and carry on what they're doing, the tramp's face turns back to one of envious menace before approaching them to disrupt their behaviour more effectively. While this last facial expression certainly confirms Chaplin's displeasure at their coupling (a vital element of the 'sad loner' persona that would remain integral to the character), it is his recourse to parody and then to direct confrontation that overshadows, or indeed effaces, the pathos of his character. Moreover, the remainder of the film charts a rather Hobbesian matrix of relationships between its characters, where romantic attachment is shown to be predicated on material gain. Another couple in the park pause their embraces at the woman's request that the man produce a token of his love, which leads the latter to steal a pocket-watch from a man sleeping on a bench. The tramp intervenes in turn by stealing the pocket-watch off the thief in order to woo the latter's girlfriend by presenting her with a twice-stolen watch as though to give as a gift. Successfully won over by a gift from an entirely new suitor (the tramp), the woman's response further confirms the fickle conditions upon which a very cynically conceived 'love' is often founded. The film ends with all the characters fighting in the sea except the woman and the tramp, leading to both his victory over the other suitors and justifying the attitude of cynical envy with which he entered the film from the outset.

While in later films the tramp's childish attempts and failures at romance would be deeply related to the tramp's perpetual alienation from social relationships (and a clear source of pathos), this early film delivers a scheme of romance and a code of practice that differs markedly from the genteel, sentimental tradition. However, where *Twenty Minutes of Love* allows everyone to behave irresponsibly and rewards the tramp as the most cunning of them all, such competitive and ruthless instincts are suppressed in favour of moral protocol in later films. The tramp comes to emerge as a more complex subject who *knows* how to behave socially, yet whose instincts, and seemingly ineradicable identity of outsider, tragically disrupts any easy insertion into bourgeois subjectivity. In *The Tramp*, much as though the tramp is attracted to working on a farm as a means of wooing the farmer's daughter with whom he initially finds favour (by rescuing her from thieves), his incompetence and ineptitude for the work prefigure his ultimate rejection by her. As a social outcast, the tramp is unemployable, struggling with his desires for continued freedom that sit in tension with desires for social belonging. When the girl's fiancé emerges in the last section of the film, quashing all chances of romance between her and the tramp, it is with knowing resignation that the tramp famously walks away from the camera, disappointed with how the world has rejected him once again yet determined nevertheless to keep trying. From the ruthless individual among other ruthless individuals in *Twenty Minutes of Love* to the confused victim of a middle-class respectability that he both desires and rejects, the tramp now becomes the plucky loner and outsider. Rather than simply lower-class, the tramp becomes a figure existing outside the class system entirely, a status that has always gone hand in hand with notions of moral sensibility and its demarcation of sensitive subjects from other, more worldly, people.

In such respects, Chaplin's appeals to bourgeois standards of respectability becomes highly ambiguous, for the sensibility valorised in the tramp figure fails to correlate with bourgeois subjectivity any more than with that of the working class. Indeed, Chaplin's films rarely confirm middle-class values of hard work or a place of one's own, the latter rather more often represented as impediments to the tramp's symbolisation of freedom, the latter invested more than any perhaps in the joys of flânerie, spatial interstitiality, and plain luck.[2] Such an 'outsider' subjectivity enhances the critical insights of such films, as a function of the spectator's engagement with a figure who only partially ascribes to the codes of all established class categories. If working-class labour conflicts with the tramp's aspirations to gentlemanly comfort and freedom, middle-class status remains elusive and dependent on one's capital or that of one's family, neither of which the 'outsider' possesses nor strives too hard to attain. The pathos of failure is thus always offset by the tramp's invocation of freedom and moral independence.

In order to appeal to as many sectors of his potential audience as possible, Chaplin thus succeeded in diversifying the tramp's identity, with increased attention to character realism and pathos. If slapstick (in the films of Chaplin and others) invoked the anarchistic spirit of the underdog who boisterously rejects any insertion into social belonging, it did so at the risk of remaining fundamentally at odds with the spectator's complex desires for freedom and belonging. Such comic fantasies of lawlessness were, of course, hugely appealing to audiences, including the middle class. They nevertheless rely on discrepancies between cinematic and actual world that come to precipitate accusations of vulgarity, considerations that Chaplin's sentimental turn seems to redress quite directly. Chaplin's augmentation of pathos and romance in his films can be seen indeed as a widening of the terms of identification, or in Murray Smith's terms, character 'engagement'.[3] Such a transition arguably forged greater alliances between his films and the requirements of a more 'genteel' middle-class audience who was similarly won over to the cinema through the latter's appropriation of the 'legitimate' theatre's classical narrative.

Charles Maland similarly finds in his detailed study of Chaplin's career and varied reception that the 'refining' of the tramp from the amoral slapstick outlaw to the pathos-driven romantic lead was a matter of maximising audiences. This was achieved by accommodating the tastes of middle-class constituencies that were feared to be excluded by the Keystone films. Maland argues thus that it is the pathetic romance that becomes central to most of these later shorts and subsequent feature films. Acknowledging Chaplin's awareness and appeasement of the 'Genteel Tradition' outlined by George Santayana in the nineteenth century, Maland argues that such themes of unrequited love and the virtuous do-gooder spurned by the world come to invoke morally 'serious' connotations:

> Although in later films Chaplin handles his romantic relationships and pathos more effectively, it is important to reiterate here that Chaplin's romances increased his appeal to men who had been rejected in love because of inadequate wealth, prestige or power; to women who admired his tender and nurturing spirit; and to viewers with genteel sensibilities for whom the romance helped to 'negate' the vulgarity that worried them. (Maland 1989: 23)[4]

It would appear, in fact, that Chaplin's shift in emphasis echoes, rather than abandons, the vaudeville tradition, which was far more eclectic in its repertoire than knockabout comedy alone, both within and between acts. Associations with an exclusively lower-class audience were continuously addressed by vaudeville managers through the employment of stars, or adaptations of shows from the 'legitimate' theatre of classical drama. Henry Jenkins has accounted, for instance, for how the sentimental operated alongside, rather than antithetically to, slapstick comedy in his discussion of early twentieth century vaudeville theatre (see Jenkins 1992: 81–5). While vaudeville is celebrated for the great comedians of cinema that learned their craft in the chaotic atmosphere of the variety circuit (including, of course, Chaplin, not to mention Buster Keaton, Harold Lloyd, and Stan Laurel), Jenkins charts the period (from roughly 1907 to 1912) that sees the inclusion of 'dramatic sketches' or 'playlets' within the already highly varied billings. Discussing how actors who had been working on the 'legitimate stage' became employed to perform non-comic scenes, Jenkins shows thus that changes to the vaudeville roster signal vaudeville's coming to accommodate higher-class audiences while retaining melodrama or music-hall as its core elements. Such sketches were subject moreover to 'compression and intensification' (83) in order to fit the time-slots allocated to them. While such dramas may largely have been drawn from the 'realist' theatre, Jenkins shows how modifications would serve to create a 'series of emotionally intensified "moments" of drama' as opposed to the subtle, well-timed narrative sequencing of more naturalistic pieces. With the criteria for well-developed or 'rounded' characters a lesser priority, Jenkins continues that 'emphasis was placed' instead 'upon the performer's ability to move an audience toward an outward display of emotion, not toward the more thoughtful or contemplative reaction promoted by the legitimate theatre'.

Jenkins analysis shows, therefore, that despite the intermittent suspension of realism or naturalism in such vaudeville playlets, their underlying pathos and drama continued to be as 'popular' in the twentieth-century music hall as it was at the time of sentimental comedy or nineteenth-century melodrama.[5] Despite modifications between low and high theatres, easy distinctions between vaudeville as 'low affect' and the legitimate theatre as detached thought become flawed, for, at root, sentimentality was common to both aesthetic spheres. The tastes of a hypothetical middle-class, 'genteel' audience could not have been as monolithic as presumed, for even the 'legit' theatre itself was largely a sphere of sentimental affect, save for the more radically modernist plays of such innovators as Shaw, Chekhov, or Ibsen, for whom naïvely sentimental schemes of romance were more stridently excluded. By the standards of the legitimate theatre, the possible persistence of vulgarity in vaudeville was thus signified not by affect per se, but by the latter's 'intensification' and presumed divorce from naturalist standards of verisimilitude, as applicable to comedy as much as to pathos.

However, such aesthetic distinctions did not always coincide with moral ones. Maland provides evidence for certain moral constituencies *within* a broadly middle-class milieu, centred especially on church and other civic institutions, for whom the pre-classical cinema displayed vulgarity and immorality. Such objections had more to do with content and conditions of consumption than with form (Grieveson 2004). Intense affect was fine, indeed desirable, as long as the moral message (or sentiment) was appropriate. This is borne out by more recent studies that account for clear developments in the moral tenor of cinematic productions from the earliest cinematic era, 1906–7 to a pre-classical or classical period starting in the early 1910s. Tom Gunning shows, for instance, how the film industry took such protests seriously and itself set up a censorship board charged with validating the morality of new productions, as a means of accommodating such charges (Gunning 2004). Motivated, of course, by business interests and the fear of offending middle-class audiences, the film industry's efforts to refine its product constituted both public relations exercise and textual reality, and as Gunning shows, can be verified by key contrasts in films produced within as little as six years of each other.[6] Others have written on how similar social pressures contributed to the demise of the original nickelodeons and the rise of the movie theatre and the eventual 'Picture Palace'. The latter's emulation of the more highly regarded theatre is commonly explained as the forging of a more cultivated image for 'cinema' than that represented by the nickelodeon and its predominantly working-class, immigrant audiences; the curtailment of sleaziness, rowdy behaviour, and sexual license served thus as both on-screen and off-screen endeavour (see Merritt 1976).

If the period spanning 1908–9 constituted therefore for American cinema, as Gunning claims, a 'conscious movement into a realm of moral discourse' (2004: 146), the moral tensions signified by such a shift would have been well established by 1913–14, when Chaplin had just taken on directorial control of his films for the first time. The courting of 'high' critical tastes becomes a means of increasing audience attendance and maximising an already lucrative business in a fast-changing industry. Moreover, as Chaplin suspected early on, sentimental pathos (related to, but not an exclusive attribute of, the 'legit' theatre) could enhance one's own artistic credentials, as it was approved by bourgeois tastes in a way that slapstick, circus acts, and mime were less so.[7]

Cool Chaplin

Invoking fantasies of both belonging and escape from social convention, the tramp articulates thus both the desirable and problematic elements of American petty bourgeois identity, not least in terms of its constraints on the body. When the tramp meets Edna Purviance on board the sea-swept ship bound for New York in *The Immigrant*, taking her hand and offering her his seat with a courteous gesture of love-at-first-sight goodwill, he can't help but look at his hand to see if her dirty hand has left a residue on his, deflating the romance of the moment with comic effect. Likewise, as he leaves the ship's galley, smiling back at his new love interest, a barely concealed belch once again undermines his ability to remain within the ideal scheme of bourgeois romance. Posing the tramp here as a 'body of modernity' (2010), Tom Gunning writes of similar performative contradictions in films like *The Pawnshop* (1916, Mutual), where a poor old man's story of woe provokes such sympathetic tears on the tramp's part that he begins to spit out the crackers he was eating. Archetypal scenes of sympathy or bourgeois romance embodying established sentimental ideals of pity or love are here expressly undermined by the tramp's subordination to his body, a continuous puncturing of attempts to adhere to genteel standards of propriety and managed feeling.[8]

These particular subversions of sentiment abound in Chaplin's films, all foregrounding the foibles, neuroses, and indelicacies of the tramp's body in the face of a genteel protocol. It becomes an attribute of Chaplin's cinema that moreover becomes integral to the tramp's cultural value for many critics of the time. This praise is aligned with a European, particularly French, praise for the anarchic 'Charlot', as well as to the rise of what Henry Jenkins describes as the 'New Humor' (Jenkins 1992: 26) taking place in America itself. While Santayana and other literary naturalists had condemned the overly feminised aesthetic of the earlier century's 'genteel' literature, related thought situates comedy as a potent force of disruption in relation to the 'Genteel Tradition', analogous indeed with the modernist works of Conrad, Dreiser, or Joyce. More accessible to mass audiences than the anti-realist novel or symbolist poetry, the comic promised to re-orient the subject to the kinds of 'affective immediacy' outlined above. For Jenkins, a fundamental tension could be traced therefore between the 'New Humor' of gags, intense laughter, and bodily shock (vaudeville, slapstick cinema) and a 'thoughtful' comedy of kindly humour and moral sentiments (theatrical comedy), which he accounts for in terms of Pierre Bourdieu's sociological theory:

The working class of the country's expanding cities, for whom entertainment dollars were scarce and leisure time limited, placed a greater emphasis upon the 'use-value' of cultural experience, upon the amount of pleasure received per expenditure. The aesthetic choices of the working class, Bourdieu argues, often reflect a desire for 'maximum "effect" . . . at minimum cost, a formula which for bourgeois taste is the very definition of vulgarity.' Hunger for immediate gratification and intense stimulation grows from an insistence on the ultimate return on one's investment and a need for an immediate, though short-lived, release from the rigors of one's environment. (Jenkins 1992: 45)

If slapstick was structurally aligned therefore with the tastes of a 'working class' audience who hadn't the income nor the emotional aptitude for sentimental comedy owing to oppressive environmental and monetary conditions, what emerges is a mass audience whose tastes in comedy and much else would be divided along class lines. This division alone contributes in turn to how writers like Gilbert Seldes approach the 'lower' entertainments of Chaplin's ilk when he writes of the 'remorseless hostility of the genteel' that was threatening to 'corrupt the purity of slap-stick' (Seldes 1952: 4). Enamoured by the 'driving energy' (4) of slap-stick, there is here the clear disdain of the 'elite' intellectual for his own class's policing of the 'vulgar' in the name of a more tasteful comedy. In Seldes' inversion of received taste hierarchies, slapstick is superior in its disruption of 'genteel' sincerity and its moralistic standards.

Going back to some of the definitions for sentiment discussed in prior chapters, what seems at issue then are questions concerning how beliefs concerning the heroes of sentimental narrative influence their emotional claims on the spectator. A chief question that Chaplin in particular seems to invoke here concerns the extent to which the tramp is willing to countenance the troubles that he encounters. While, as Ben Singer explains about melodramatic pathos, 'We pity the perenially powerless who endure pain through no fault or action of their own' (2001: 56), where pity is invoked most forcefully alongside our recognition of an unwilling victim of circumstance, the tramp's suffering is more complex and ambiguous. For in as much as Chaplin's films give us grounds for seeing the tramp as partially complicit with his lot, as desiring his social annexation as much as having it foisted upon him, a specifically sentimental reception of him becomes an issue of critical belief and perspective. When the tramp is abandoned at the end of *The Tramp*, could his plucky gesture of resolve not instead be interpreted as the jouissance of renewed freedom for one that was perhaps better off anyway? The bodily gesture as he walks away from camera could be deemed a renewal of energy that visibly courses through the tramp's entire body as much as a stoical 'picking oneself up after a knock'. Where the latter concerns a pitiable subject re-enlivened by brave thoughts ('things aren't too bad', 'maybe its for the best', 'I'll live to fight another day'), the former gives greater prominence to the body itself, relieved of fetters and stress, reenergised without the intervention of bourgeois ideology.

Despite ambiguities concerning the tramp's victimisation, slapstick certainly seemed to certain critics of the time more explicitly irreverent and radical through its more comprehensive expunging of 'feminising' pathos. In order to be radical, the tramp had to be the irreverent and virile anarchist of the slapstick film, not the pathetic underdog that may or may not have been more accepting of his lot in the later films. Going by such rubrics, his power lay in disruption and irreverence, not in his humanisation as a romantic or pitiable subject.

Not for all modernist critics, however. Indeed, for various notable critics, it was the films of Chaplin's oeuvre that seemed the most reluctantly resigned to ideology that proved most inspirational. If we recall the comments of Béla Balázs, it is the extent to which the 'melancholy optimism' of the tramp 'expresses the opposition of all of us to an inhuman order of society' (Balázs and Bone 1952: 285) that Chaplin's rhetoric is deemed to succeed. The point of focus shifts from the tramp's embodiment of a virile defiance of anti-genteel subjectivity to the cultural work engendered by the tramp's signification of sentiment and oppressed subjectivity. When we turn to the reception of Chaplin in the Germany of the 1920s, we find a Chaplin thus that was celebrated by left-liberal intellectuals from a middle class that Chaplin had as yet failed to successfully attract through slapstick or sentiment. Joseph Garncarz, for instance, has shown how Chaplin's films did not poll so highly during this decade in Germany, and concludes that while popular with working-class audiences, 'the middle class did not like him' (2010: 291). Intellectuals who celebrated Chaplin therefore had less reason to isolate aesthetic superiority in a specific corpus of Chaplin films, unlike Seldes, for whom slapstick was applauded above all for embodying a working-class or popular voice.

Many of the writings of such figures as Walter Benjamin, Béla Balázs, and Siegfried Kracauer are also more immediately attuned to the pathetic elements of Chaplin's persona without condemnation of the tramp as a regressively sentimental figure. Balázs writes that Chaplin's creation:

is not the revolutionary image of the exploited factory worker or agricultural labourer, but that of a 'Lumpen-proletarian' who defends himself with charming cunning against the heartlessness of the rich and revenges himself by petty means. (Balázs and Bone 1952: 55)

Chaplin is understood here then and applauded far more as a sympathetic figure that can only counter his oppression by 'petty means', rather than as the rogue who takes down the bourgeoisie in a more effective, revolutionary fashion. What may be lost by accepting Chaplin as a figure of pathos (in terms of his not embodying the soldier-like role model for revolutionary action) is recuperated in the cultural work of the tramp as a figure of moral sympathy. Walter Benjamin was enthused by the 'laughter' that such a figure as the tramp could evoke in an international audience, commenting in 1929 that 'Chaplin has directed himself toward both the most international and most revolutionary affect of the masses – laughter' (1996: 331). However, humour is also bound up for Benjamin with the sad and demoralising realities of capitalist oppression. Thus, when he writes of the 'American farce' as an exemplar of an internationalist 'collective' cinema, the 'comical' takes on a portentous rather than escapist function. Thus:

> Such a film is comical, after all, only in that the laughter it inspires hovers over the abyss of horror. The reverse of a ridiculously unrestrained technique is the mortal precision of a fleet of naval vessels on manoeuvre, relentlessly captured in *Potemkin*. (Benjamin 1995: 626–7)

Where the 'New Humor' seems in Seldes' view to promise a different form of sociality that supersedes genteel decorum and ossified Victorian values, Benjamin poses laughter in ironic counterpoint to an 'abyss of horror'. Echoing Kracauer below, it is the 'abyss' that must be acknowledged as the chief affective catalyst of humour, slapstick or otherwise, wherein the spectacle of human suffering serves as a vital currency. Even for a Benjamin exhilarated by technology and Brechtian forms of critical spectatorship, Chaplin's sympathetic figure still serves radical purposes, through his affective embodiment of suffering. In a review of Chaplin's *The Circus* (1928, United Artists), for instance, Benjamin saves his scepticism for Chaplin's plans of making films on 'Napoleon' and 'Christ', deeming them 'giant screens behind which the great artist is hiding his weariness' (Arnham, Benjamin and Mackay 1996: 311) While the Chaplin of 1929, suffering from creative blockage or excessive compromise with the film industry, is criticised by Benjamin for turning his hands to the epic rendering of grand, historical, or religious figures (a genre identified and condemned here for its implicit recourse to reverential biography), Benjamin privileges Chaplin's earlier corpus (slapstick and sentiment combined) as Chaplin at his most unrestrained and radical.

The extent to which the tramp's comedy is judged by critics of the period as an anarchistic antidote to sentimentality is thus highly debatable, given the wide variance in critical response to the tramp throughout the modernist period. Siegfried Kracauer's responses to Chaplin's slapstick range in particular from a 'left-fordist' opposition to American capitalism and mass culture, to later critiques of the 'mass ornament' embodied by the Tiller Girls and urban movie-going (see Kracuaer 1995). In a 1926 review, Kracauer regards slapstick as a redemptive subversion of an American-led industrial, capitalist order, commenting:

> One has to hand this to the Americans: with slapstick films they have created a form that offers a counterweight to their reality: if in that reality they subject the world to an often unbearable discipline, the film in turn dismantles this self-imposed order quite forcefully. (cited in Hansen 1993: 462)

If the above already identifies aspects of American culture in terms of an emancipatory spirit, Kracauer is here unspecific as to the chief affect associated with this process of 'dismantling'. In a 1931 piece on Chaplin, however, Kracauer expands upon the full import of Chaplin's affective power as one that depends on more than his 'gags' alone. In a review of *City Lights* (1931, United Artists), he writes:

> Chaplin, a storyteller of the Dickens school, knows very well how gags and harmless clowning have to be used to reduce narrative tension, and uses them willingly. But then he always plunges again into that abyss where the Comic originates, and lays it bare. (Kracauer 1997: 117)

Chaplin's work is celebrated thus, like Benjamin, as a paradigm of the modern subject's encounter with the 'abyss', the climax of *City Lights* providing the 'most resonant' (117) of moments. Situated as the chief source of 'narrative tension', the melodrama of this sequence is privileged aesthetically over comic relief, and its sentiment becomes equated with the full disclosure of the film's socio-political meaning; Chaplin's 'display of facial expressions' in this sequence is now situated as 'among the most shattering achievements of his art' (117). While the 'clowning' of the tramp's slapstick become merely 'harmless', it must now for Kracauer be considered alongside more legible signifiers of struggle, exemplified in the pathos of Chaplin's face at the climax of *City Lights*. In such respects, Dickensian sentimentality, now deployed by Chaplin, once again seems far from antithetical to the transformative ideals of critical theory.

A Re-Victorianised Chaplin

Perceptions of the tramp as a 'radical' persona rested on more therefore than his inhabiting a working-class subjectivity or posing a virile challenge to bourgeois respectability. If the 'refining' of Chaplin introduced the tramp's desires for upward mobility, romantic love, and social belonging, it also reveals their emotional ironies, and intensifies the critical stakes of his outcast status. Before class, gender, or political persuasion, the tramp was human, fallible, and vulnerable. Seldes' implicit binary of masculine/working-class/popular/aggressive/subversive versus the genteel/feminine/middle-class/disingenuous comes radically unstuck in the light of these other critiques.

Yet if the sentiment/comedy binary unpacked in the above seems a somewhat vulgarised application of various modernist or Marxian principles, it nevertheless persists in subsequent critical perceptions of Chaplin's sentimentality, especially when compared to Buster Keaton. If Chaplin has seemed a 'cool' exponent of the Jazz age, urban modernity, and the 'New Objectivity', such a reputation itself is tempered by reappraisals and reconfigurations of Chaplin's classicism and melodrama, aspects of which are once again highlighted as anachronisms of his Victorian influences. The same modernist calls for formal innovation and medium reflexivity found auteur heroes from Brecht to Godard to Sirk, and in the case of silent film comedy itself, in Buster Keaton. Chaplin's sympathetic protagonist of classical cinema gives way to Keaton's 'deadpan' modernist. While certainly not championing the latter's work over the former's, Tom Gunning compares Chaplin's and Keaton's comedy by commenting that whereas 'Chaplin used film to create a startling intimacy with his audience, allowing them insight into his most private moments of romantic longing and disappointment (as in the final sequence of *City Lights*), Keaton's relation to the audience remained distanced' (1995: 15). Keaton's physiognomy becomes in Gunning's view bound up with a numbed acquiescence to, and accommodation of, modernity's traumas ('mechanical reproduction') as opposed to Chaplin's indignant or panicked opposition. Thus:

> If Chaplin's reaction to industrial production was one of Luddite destruction or anarchic hysteria, Keaton tried constantly to adjust his body to the new demands of systematic environments. These adjustments unmasked the absurdity of the system itself, its anxiety-causing, infantilising power. (Gunning 1995b: 14)

If Gunning accounts for Keaton's impassivity as a radically different, although by no means superior, affect experienced in relation to modernity, he nevertheless adds how such an attitude appealed to certain 'avant-garde' sensibilities in a way that Chaplin did not. Reflecting the 'nonconsciousness of the machine' (15), Keaton's response to technology, as 'one of victimisation and mastery of this inhumanely ordered environment', paradoxically promised a better solution to man's conflict with modern industry than Chaplin's defiant hysteria.

Keaton has often won out as the modernist player with cinematic form compared to Chaplin, whose apparent ease with the conventions of melodrama are foregrounded as grounds for dismissal within a strictly formalist aesthetics. While such Keaton films as *Sherlock Jr.* (1924) may be deemed to subvert the 'classical realism' of Hollywood cinema, Chaplin is considered innovative only at the level of individual performance: his cinematic value is constrained by the allegedly uncritical reproduction of melodramatic conventions. However, such evaluative comparisons tend to overlook the ideological work of the films themselves (as a function of their socio-historic conditions) in favour of a facile categorisation of the two comedians within separate aesthetic agendas, playing the modernist off against Victorian sentiment as a means of defining the terms of a new canon of cinematic modernism (that supersedes realism or melodrama). In such respects, as Henry Jenkins humorously notes, the classical canon of Chaplin, Griffith, and Ford taught in the film class of the 'liberal-humanist... .. .. Professor Oldman' are superseded by the Keaton, Godard, and Sirk films taught by the modernist 'Professor Youngman' (see Jenkins 1997: 30–3). Both rubrics, however, renew a binary of low art/high art, where the classical Chaplin becomes the sentimental storyteller, enforcing spectator sympathy at the expense of formal experimentalism. Consigned now to the status of 'eternal clown' or apolitical 'humanist', Chaplin becomes either the Victorian anachronism or even worse, the universal sign that foreshadows an omnipresent, sentimental Hollywood culture that dominates the globe and inhibits alternative practices and subjectivities.

Comedy and Classical Narrative

Contemporary commentators have thus responded to such dichotomies by foregrounding the cultural work of Chaplin's original films as texts of socio-historical and political importance, that contrast, moreover, with what Charles Musser deemed an 'ideological cleansing' (1988: 63) of the tramp image in more recent examples of contemporary image culture (specifically, the use of the tramp character in IBM television commercials of the 1980s). Critiquing the 'vague humanism' (62) of such recent appropriations of the tramp allows critics like Musser to defend Chaplin's original films in their foregrounding of class, poverty, and the bourgeois work ethic in urban modernity. Chaplin's films are framed by Musser indeed as 'social comedies' (62) that use the tramp as a figure of pathos and alternative subjectivity in a world of social conformism and economic depression.[9] As much as the pathos invoked by the tramp figure may appeal to genteel ideologies of victimisation and rewarded virtue, it serves equally to court the spectator's allegiance to positions of opposition or resistance.

Like the comments made by Benjamin and Kracauer, Chaplin's comedy is best understood here then in terms of its productive tensions with the representation of virtue and suffering, a negotiation that very much disrupts any easy sense to which comedy must by necessity operate autonomously of sentiment. Rather, and as remarked on by various scholars of early cinema comedy, Chaplin's features both emerge from, and amplify, a dominant tendency in Hollywood feature-film making towards a form of comedy that is, in the words of Steve Neale and Frank Krutnik, more 'hybridised' or 'combined with other components' (1990: 130). Lea Jacobs makes a similar point in her study of the way that Hollywood films of the 1920s underwent a 'Decline of Sentiment' (2008) in favour of genre diversification and stylistic sophistication. Her discussion of the 'Sophisticated Comedy' of 1930s Hollywood, for instance, foregrounds films that moved away from the 'hokum' of both slapstick and didactic melodrama in favour of the more naturalistic, less moralistic tone of films leading up to the screwball comedy. With careful attention to nuancing oppositions between sophisticated urban audiences and 'rural' tastes for a more overt moralising (through the use of didactic inter-titles, for example), Jacobs shows that shifts occur in the mid-20s towards the increased production of films that are more 'understated and restrained' (90) and that dealt with the more adult thematics of marital discord, infidelity, divorce, and remarriage.

Through such observations, Jacobs signals the extent to which what is tempting to call 'purer' forms of the comic (slapstick) and the sentimental (pathetic didacticism) become tempered by stylistic and narrative innovations. A particularly fruitful insight comes in Jacob's alignment of such 'modern' techniques with 'principles of storytelling and scenography . . . seen as typical of the classical Hollywood cinema' (125). Using Chaplin's *A Woman of Paris* (1923) as a major example and influence of such shifts, Chaplin's films emerge in particular as a vital antecedent to the classical style in their increasingly nuanced fusion of comic and pathetic elements. Sentimentalism, as a signifier of 'hokum' in its more obviously stylised and mannered deployments, is subject to a 'decline', but only on the condition that its stock tableaux and 'high moral tones' are understood to have been more effectively incorporated into the formal techniques of film narration itself, rather than abandoned as such.

The sophistication of this hybridisation thus becomes the norm of Hollywood cinema, wherein both comedy and pathos are invoked by increasingly subtle modes of narration and style. What comes of this decrease in hokey didacticism and gentility is a comedy that could be deployed in a far wider set of films to counter the classical cinema's affirmativity and moralism, for which the tramp's parapraxes and slips have remained paradigmatic. Consider a sequence, for instance, from John Ford's *Stagecoach* (1939), and its epitomisation of the sentimental comedy inaugurated by him and other pioneers like Griffith and Chaplin. The scene depicts the entrance into a saloon's main parlour of the prostitute Dallas, where her fellow male passengers have been awaiting news of a female passenger who has gone into labour (the respectable, middle-class Lucy Mallory). Carrying Lucy's newborn baby into the parlour from the rear, Dallas's entrance serves in the first instance as a key moment in the romance narrative between she and the outlaw character Ringo (John Wayne), wherein their romance is cemented through a series of silently shared looks at each other, communicated through alternating shot/reverse-shots. Ringo's solemn gaze at Dallas and her counter-look take place crucially while four other characters look on at the new baby, augmenting the visuality of the romance. The presence of the four male characters and their dialogue serves here as an important counter-point to Ringo and Dallas' intimacy; comedy is deployed as a tonal contrast to the genteel connotations of the parallel romance narrative. The sequence is carefully edited in the first instance to capture the all male group's reaction (as a four shot) to the arrival of Dallas and the newborn, who invokes, as Matthew Bernstein notes, an idealised iconography of 'Madonna and child'. While the others look on at the baby, it is Ringo who is isolated in his gaze at Dallas through the editing of a series of medium to extreme close-ups, intercut by her own looks back at him, captured in profile. At the level of sound, the dialogue is dominated by a comic interchange between the buffoonish stage-driver Buck and the whisky salesman Peacock, as an amazed Buck comically repeats the phrase 'Well I'll be god-darned!' three times before finally blowing a loud raspberry at the baby. At this, he is immediately reproached by Peacock ('Don't do that!'), for spoiling an otherwise solemn moment of reverence and wonder at the newborn's arrival.

The sequence as a whole is thus structured around key oppositions around which the comic and sentimental contend for dominance. The most salient is that between adult and child, literalised in the first instance by the recurring tableau of Dallas and Lucy's baby, but which is then conceptually segmented into the separate character units of the romantic couple and the all-male group of onlookers as the sequence proceeds. Ringo and Dallas take on the function of sentimental subjectivity in their relay of looks, with Dallas' self-conscious performance of motherhood and domesticated virtue counterposed by Ringo's assumption of the male that recognises virtue in a woman of ostensibly low-class status and reputation. This is contrasted by the formal and tonal segmentation of the four peripheral characters, who engage with the newborn child as onlookers (recalling again a nativity scene) and in Buck's case, regress to an imagined performance of infancy. The latter segment lends itself to the comedic in its inarticulate repetitions and hyperbolic regressions, the humour compounded by Buck's discrepancy from the decorum of reverential spectatorship, bodily restraint, and, perhaps most importantly, silence. Indeed, just as Ringo and Dallas's romance runs in parallel to the scene, their romance is naturalised by its silent harmony with the Christ-like tableau, its visuality implicitly privileged over the banal noise of the larger party, which in turn echoes the more formal privileging of the silent cinema over the talkie.

While Chaplin's 'body of modernity' would come therefore to be defined by his tramp's comic struggle to adhere to impossibly genteel codes of propriety and decorum, the sequence described above echoes such tensions between adult/child, silent/sound, stillness/movement, and mind/body. As a sequence that emphasises sentimental procedures of realisation and recognition on the part of the two leads, Chaplin's self-handicapping persona is split here between separate characters (or character units) and their correspondent regimes of meaning. The implications of this division, such that the sentimental is given precedence over the comic as a now externalised nuisance character(s), goes further in illustrating the extent to which narrative (so often allied to romance) is given priority as such over spectacle (comic or otherwise) in the classic narrative system of the studio era and beyond. As opposed to the impossible constraints posed by the body in relation to sentimental codes, and their perpetually comedic conflict in Chaplin's features, a hierarchy is established here between figures of romance and sentimental propriety and the comic relief of characters consigned to peripheral status.

The contrast between Chaplin and the scene from *Stagecoach* is usefully understood here by borrowing terms from Neale and Krutnik's discussions of Chaplin's slapstick, particularly in their differentiation between the 'blending' of comedy and gentility and allowing the former to 'undermine' the latter. Thus, they argue:

> Chaplin's solution was very much his own. It consisted not of blending, or seeking to blend, genteel and slapstick components, but of playing the one off against the other in order to highlight their differences. As David Robinson has pointed out, one of the commonest forms this strategy takes is that of using slapstick elements to undermine, or cut across, the genteel ones. (Neale and Krutnik 1990: 127)

The effect of Chaplin's fusion of slapstick and sentimental elements is thus clearly aligned in the above with an 'undermining', a process that allows Chaplin's 'sentiment' in the words of his biographer David Robinson, to be 'invariably saved from mawkishness by the comedy and the belligerence that always underlies his despair' (cited in Neale and Krutnik 1990: 128). The important point here concerns the differentiation between 'undermining' and a mere 'blending', wherein the latter process implicitly fails to privilege the subversive potentialities of the comic body. It is just such a 'blending' that seems more characteristic here of the *Stagecoach* scene examined above, particularly in its more 'classical' segmentation of romantic and comedic character units. This splitting of the Chaplinesque 'body' into discrete character units dampens the subversive negativity of the comic failure or parapraxis, at the same time as it forces the romance between Dallas and Ringo to be conveyed in a stylistically understated, subtler way.

Nevertheless, the above discussion goes some way in underscoring a classical Hollywood style comprised from an early stage by a particularly complex fusion of comic and pathetic elements, generating in turn the need for more sensitive modes of analysis, such as those required, for instance, in determining the difference between 'blending' and 'undermining' in any particular sequence. Indeed, the means by which classical narration is subject to nuance, irony, and stylisation here becomes vital with respect to the critical analysis of Hollywood films, where the comic as such becomes only one of various techniques or modes by which the spectator can be entreated to 'distance' herself from the text. Such indeed becomes a key issue for the tradition of political-modernism and 'affect theory' focused on in the next chapter, wherein the sentimental persists as a category mired in discourses of moral conduct and character virtue.

Notes

1. Translated from Octave Mannoni's oft-cited 'Je sais bien, mais quand même' in *Clefs pour l'imaginaire ou l'autre scène*, Paris: Éditions du Seuil, 1969, pp. 9–33.
2. While the flâneur has traditionally been discussed in terms of the urban space he/she surveys and takes enjoyment in, it is the tramp figure, epitomised by Chaplin but also invoked by such novels as Orwell's *Down and Out in Paris and London*, that nuances the concept to incorporate both urban and rural locations while maintaining its emphasis on indeterminate observation and social alterity. See George Orwell, *Down and Out in Paris and London*. London:

Penguin, 1999. See also Benjamin's celebrated account of Baudelaire's original concept in Walter Benjamin, *Charles Baudelaire: A Lyric Poet in the Era of High Capitalism*, Harry Zohn (trans.), London: Verso, 1983.

3. Smith's formulation nuances the much used concept of identification by both focusing on that which Christian Metz would refer to as 'secondary identification' (in *The Imaginary Signifier: Psychoanalysis and Cinema*, Ben Brewster (trans.), Bloomington: Indiana University Press, 1982, pp. 89–98), and underlining the importance of distinctions between a spectator's 'alignment' with on-screen characters and a more moral 'allegiance' with them. See Murray Smith, *Engaging Characters: Fiction, Emotion and the Cinema*, Oxford: Clarendon Press, 1995, pp. 73–109.

4. Maland also reveals that Chaplin, earning ever more directorial control of his films, nervously asked the writer Charles McGuirk what he thought of *The tramp*, admitting to having taken 'an awful chance' by incorporating a romantic plot for the first time. See Charles J. Maland, *Chaplin and American Culture: The Evolution of a Star Image*, Princeton: Princeton University Press, 1989, p. 23.

5. Indeed, in studies such as Bordwell, Staiger, and Thompsons's monumental work, *The Classical Hollywood Cinema: Film Style & Mode of Production to 1960*, the 'playlet' is cited as a direct influence on the first full-length narrative cinematic features, many of which had to similarly compress long novels or plays to fit the duration of standard features (perhaps most famously, Porter's 1903 version of *Uncle Tom's Cabin*). See David Bordwell, Janet Staiger and Kristin Thompson, *The Classical Hollywood Cinema: Film Style & Mode of Production to 1960*, New York: Columbia University Press, 1985, pp. 159–61.

6. Gunning's main example illustrates the contrast between a 1906 film that unashamedly depicts the enjoyments of an opium den to a later film about the reform of an alcoholic father for the sake of his family, demonstrating a discernible change in moral attitude with regards to issues of adult drug-use.

7. Chaplin's gamble with pathos can also be understood as a shift in the direction of what has been termed the 'classical Hollywood cinema' as it crystallised in the mid-1910s. In place of the trick films, chase-films, curiosities, and other shorts that made up the 'cinema of attractions' (and its theatrical cousin, vaudeville), longer films are produced (resulting in the standard feature length) and a set of editing techniques becomes established for a film practice that relies above all on continuities of narrative and character (see David Bordwell, Janet Staiger and Kristin Thompson, *The Classical Hollywood Cinema: Film Style & Mode of Production to 1960*, New York: Columbia University Press, 1985, note 10).

8. Another scene discussed by Gunning is in *The Idle Class* (1921, First National) that sees a rich drunkard of a husband learning that his wife abandoned him owing to his continued drinking and neglect of her. With his back facing camera and shaking from apparent sobs, he turns back to camera to reveal his movements to have been the effort to merely shake a cocktail, his face comically unmoved by the news.

9. Musser, underlining the extent to which Chaplin's films functioned as significant engagements with social reality, situates the tramp in terms of his accurate resemblance to real-life counterparts in early twentieth century society, despite the latter becoming more casual in dress as the century progressed.

CHAPTER 4

Affect, or Postmodern Sentimentalism

In the above chapters, sentimentalism has been examined as a concept or mode of considerable importance to classical and contemporary film theory and criticism, one that has undergone radical shifts in meaning and value in its history of deployment, while remaining in common usage to the present in both popular and critical discourse. The key development concerns its shift from a denotative to a connotative status, from a term that maps out a new philosophy of ethics driven by an optimum balance between 'reason' and the 'passions', to one that struggles to escape connotations of 'gross sentimentality' – the excessive affectivity of the subject, the abuses of idealisation, and the related problematic of kitsch. At the same time, our examination of the positions of various writers reveals a deep concern about emotion and subjectivity at the cinema, and an awareness of its conceptual negotiation of melodrama and the sentimental novel. For many of them, cinema is unparalleled in its capacity to move us, albeit owing to formal elements of the medium, and/or rhetorical patterns, that are not agreed upon.

Such fascination concerning the interplay of texts and emotion has more recently come centre stage with a more broadly renewed emphasis on the body, emotion, and 'affect' in the humanities. As with the film scholarship analysed above, the role of sentimentalism in this field of enquiry is highly contested, something that this chapter seeks to examine and elucidate from the standpoint of both critical theory and contemporary film theory, in order to highlight the significance of its rhetorical address to the reception of various post-classical films examined in the chapters to follow. 'Affect theory', or more commonly 'affect', and the approach to emotion and textuality it signifies, is grounded indeed in a revisionism concerning the 'depth model of truth' (Best and Marcus 2009: 10) inherited from various critical models inspired by Freud and Marx, particularly hermeneutics, where critical work is predicated on the revelation of hidden truths that lie behind the 'surface' of texts. With philosophers like Susan

Sontag, Michel Foucault, and Gilles Deleuze as its early proponents, the affective turn is marked by criticism of a 'hermeneutics of suspicion' in favour of taking such textual and cultural 'surfaces' seriously. It is in this post-Freudian, anti-humanist landscape that feeling emerges in particular as a key term of reference in its collapsing of subjective and objective regimes of meaning. As has been shown in relation to the sentimental, affect is inside and outside, on the surface and underneath, physiological and cognitive, and thus resonates with poststructuralist, or postmodern, approaches to textuality, surface, and liminality.

The discussion below seeks then to unpack the intersections of affect-oriented discourse and sentimentalism, prompted in no small part by this negotiation of sentimentalism with models of 'depth' and interiority. In previous chapters, sentimentalism has been shown to invoke both the superficial and the real, the genteel performance and the quintessence of virtue, as manifest in texts as diverse as Chaplin and his tramp's plucky frailty or De Sica's simple everymen. Sentimentalism's procedures can be 'equated', as Linda Williams admits in relation to melodrama, 'with the most egregious false consciousness' (61). At the same time, her discussions of sentimentalism and those of other critics examined above, are justified by their adherence to more contemporary theoretical approaches that rely far less on its dismissal, or interpretation of necessarily latent meanings, and more on the contextual or historical analysis of cultural objects as they become manifest in their lived reality. 'Affect' indeed carries much less 'baggage' than sentimentalism, owing to its closer alignments with a poststructuralist methodology that foregrounds the validity of 'surface readings' and contextual phenomena. While sentimentalism is problematic because of its attachment to the classical, knowable subject and the suspicion of emotions that efface such realities, 'affect' announces a more fluid and deconstructive approach to emotion that accepts sentimentalism as a vital phenomenon of everyday experience that can nevertheless sometimes be ideologically compromised. Sara Ahmed, for instance, argues in support of a 'Cultural Politics of Emotion' that displaces emotion from its usual signification of an individual's interiority and privacy, and shifts focus towards more group-based, although still emotion-driven phenomena like racism and nationalism. Collapsing such an 'inside/outside' dichotomy allows Ahmed, and similar studies, to focus on how emotions are 'produced' in relation to particular socio-cultural objects, and how such objects come to be invested in emotionally by mass publics, such as in her example of the extreme patriotic sentiments of the British National Front and its membership. The critical project announced here is one that examines how '"feelings" become "fetishes", qualities that seem to

reside in objects, only through an erasure of the history of their production and circulation' (2004: 11). Emotions, in other words, are positioned
as more than unknowable, hidden phenomena, explainable only through
the revelation of personal, private histories, but also as social, visible, and
constructed processes whose connections with various institutional and
cultural norms and practices can be revealed and examined.

To be sure, the contemporary focus on 'affect' by recent scholarship in
cultural studies emerges from an intellectual project that remains sceptical
of sentimentalism and the part it can often play in the orchestration of such
'fetishes' as nation, women, the family, or heterosexuality, wherein 'emotions can attach us to the very conditions of our subordination' (ibid.).
Critical attention to the perils of sentimentalisation is highly salient, for
instance, in studies that deal specifically with the virtue-oriented rhetoric
of melodrama in a variety of socio-cultural texts and contexts. such as
in studies by Linda Williams, Lauren Berlant, and the political scientist
Elizabeth Anker, all of whom centralise the melodramatic imaginary as
a problematic dominant of American cultural politics. Whether in terms
of the historical treatment of race (Williams 2002), the essentialisation of
female identity and nationality (Berlant 2008), or even the legitimation of
Western foreign policy in relation to the terrorism of the last thirty years
(Anker 2014), such studies engage in the critical unpacking of sentimentalism in relation to 'good' and 'bad' objects. Anker notes, for instance, in
explaining the rationale for the US-led wars in Iraq and Afghanistan, that
the US's melodramatic culture promotes 'a specific type of citizenship, in
which the felt experience of being an American comprises not only persecuted innocence and empathetic connection with other Americans' suffering but also the express demand to legitimate state power' (4). 'Virtue
in distress', in other words, is recognised by Anker here as a discourse that
all too often serves nationalistic power to the detriment of more nuanced
or reflective modes of engagement with the Other, reducing such negotiations to an 'us versus them' schema. Sentimentalising nation through the
self-adoption of victimhood and persecuted innocence is posed merely as
the recto here to the verso of a defensive unilateralism in foreign policy.

Sentimentalism enjoys indeed a renewed scrutiny alongside such
excavations of the melodramatic imaginary and its intersections with
emotion-based rhetoric. Sentimental affect is framed by such work, as
with the chapters above, as a mode of significant complexity, particularly
in terms of its ambiguous function of allowing virtue to become both
'legible' (Brooks 1976: 42) and fetishised. Of crucial importance to much
of this work is the avoidance of merely equating sentimentality with false
ideological consciousness, while engaging with its tropes and modes as

popular, although often still highly politicised, forms of rhetorical address. It has become important in all such instances to be clear about what kinds of critical distance, or better, 'disinterest', are advocated by such affect-oriented approaches, something the discussion below reinforces in its analysis of postmodern emotion and film, with particular focus on camp and its ambivalent processing of classical Hollywood tropes. This chapter looks first, however, to voices from an earlier era of cultural theory that seem most aligned with the 'mandarin' mentality as it has come to be known, of those critics most condemnatory of 'mass' culture, as exemplified by figures like Theodor Adorno and Bertolt Brecht. It seeks to make sense of how far such critics were willing to go with regards to the bracketing or quarantine of sentimental affectivity in the name of modernist detachment. This lays the groundwork, or better, a kind of baseline, for examining the philosophy surrounding films that very overtly re-negotiate the sentimental tradition in contemporary American cinema, where the ugliness and bodily excesses of socio-historical reality must go hand in hand with the prettified, decorous, or optimistic patterning of the sentimental. The category of 'camp' is foregrounded in particular by this and the following chapters as a highly emotive, although not particularly sincere, mode of spectatorship in such regards, an aesthetic characterised by its ambivalence and playfulness about sentimentalism and its rhetorical style. The work of postmodern auteurs like Quentin Tarantino and Lars von Trier will be shown in such regards to be phenomenologically different from the sentimental mode of classical Hollywood cinema, while still fundamentally linked to its ideological underpinnings, even in their apparent rejection or critique of its rhetoric.

Condemnation and Critique

If the sentimental began as a term representing the ambitions of Enlightenment thinkers to found ethics in a renewed formulation of emotion or 'moral sense', critical undercurrents running alongside them and certainly following them have continually sought to expose the fallacies of sentimentalism in practice. If the popular grief at Little Nell's death was the test and the badge of Victorian moral subjectivity, Oscar Wilde's ironic suggestion of 'laughter' in its place serves as a frustrated appeal for a playful mode of reception that should be anything but sentimental, pointing the way to the subversive humour (discussed in Chapter 3) that may take down an insipidly genteel melancholia.[1] Another aspect of this camp aloofness about sentimentalism, however, would be the elitist privileging of high-modernist art categories that we find with writers like

Adorno and Horkheimer, and that has been deemed by many commentators to be integral to the 'ideological stoicism' (Plantinga 1997: 373) of contemporary film theory. Critics of political-modernist tendencies in film theory often indeed target the Frankfurt School and its privileging of the avant-gardes as a key determinant of orthodox film theory's distaste for narrative cinema, a problem that many scholars now equate specifically with the inertia of moving beyond a cinema-as-illusion, or delusion, hypothesis. Richard Rushton argues, for instance, that film studies has 'perhaps unwittingly – relied on a logic of representation; it has shut films off as a deficient and secondary mode of reality' (2010: 3). Confined to the category of 'illusion', films for Rushton are thus still approached in reductionist terms by most contemporary strands of film scholarship, only to be recuperated in the name of various legitimated research paradigms, from historicism and culturalism to Deleuzian or Neo-Lacanian paradigms.

As part of the 'Culture Industry', cinema is judged negatively as what Adorno elsewhere terms a 'dependent art' (Adorno and Benjamin 2001: 130), dependent that is on the capitalist system of banks, electric companies, and film companies that collude in producing 'entertainment' that reifies the existing conditions of production in favour of an upper class cushioned by wealth and capital. The subject of capitalist ideology under this rubric emerges furthermore as a passive recipient of mass culture, whose expectations and desires are determined and limited by capitalist commodification. Structuring desire and identity in accordance with the commodity, an authentic, self-conscious subject becomes antithetical to templates determined by the mass culture. 'Personality', Adorno and Horkheimer conclude, for instance, at the end of the 'Cultural Industry', 'means hardly more than dazzling white teeth and freedom from body odor and emotions' (Horkheimer and Adorno 2002: 136) .[23]

Emotions, within the 'Cultural Industry' rubric, are thus also often hopelessly moulded by processes of illusion and misrecognition, under full control of the capitalist culture that channels which form they will take through displacement on to commodity forms. A critique of 'Virtue in Distress' is manifest, for instance, in their criticism of Hollywood cartoons, wherein their violence is argued to habituate the spectator to his own victimised existence in modern, industrial society. Accustoming the subject to the 'new tempo' of modern life and its attendant 'breaking down of all individual resistance', Adorno and Horkheimer account for the 'thrashing' of Donald Duck in reference to the sado-masochistic desires of an audience who must 'learn to take their own punishment' (Horkheimer and Adorno 2002: 110). Virtue in distress here becomes a means of conditioning the subject to the unjust violence of capitalist society, wherein identification functions as the sado-masochistic pleasure of, (a) violence perpetrated on a commodified, aestheticised other, distanced from the spectator as an image-commodity and (b) confirming the subject's place in that same system of oppression.

Adorno's partial solution to this politically regressive mechanisation of society lies thus with the 'autonomous' artwork and its attention to modernist fragmentation, disunity, and self-reflexivity. Kafka's prose and Schoenberg's music, in their deviations from traditional art's alleged pretensions to 'harmony' or 'totality', represent for Adorno the only hopes for art, through their negation of its original, allegedly naïve purposes. In giving the lie to what Adorno elsewhere terms 'the totality of a rounded temporal experience' (1983: 265), autonomous art would differ radically from dependent art through its modernist rejection of 'mimesis', which is dismissed in Adorno's thought as the mere imitation of existing forms inscribed by capitalist logic. It is here that Adorno's thought rehearses ideas shared by Walter Benjamin, but about which the two forcefully debated in correspondence, often coming to divergent conclusions. While both theorists were deeply concerned with the consequences of 'mechanical reproduction' (with cinema posed by Benjamin as a prime example), it is Adorno's theory that most forcefully maintains the wholesale inadequacy of mass culture for revolutionary purposes. Benjamin's Artwork essay is by contrast more optimistic about 'mechanical reproduction' and its destruction of 'aura'. In his *One-Way Street* of 1928, Benjamin applauds a new 'sentimentality . . . restored to health and liberated in American style' (1996: 476) when referring to the new subjectivity engendered by the wall advertisements and cinema of an Americanised culture. It would be the disintegration of auratic distance promised by mass cultural media that for Benjamin could result in such affect precisely owing to technology's reintegration of subject and object.

Writing of a transformation such that 'people whom nothing moves or touches any longer learn to cry again', Benjamin therefore theorises the emancipatory potential of mass media in specifically affective terms. While, as expanded on by Susan Buck-Morss, the commodified world or image 'anaesthetises' the subject to the world's oppressive realities (the factory, war, commodity culture) cinema offers to resensitise the subject to a world alienated by technology.[4] Mickey Mouse, a quintessential product of modernity, is interpreted by Benjamin here in terms of an uncanny, Utopian fusion of the technological and the human, a process differentiated from the sado-masochism of Adorno's 'culture industry'.[5] Adorno's response is to question the assumption of film's absence of aura. In a letter responding to his reading of a draft of Benjamin's Artwork essay, a Disney character becomes chief evidence of the 'highly suspect degree' to which film displays an 'aural character':

> Your attack on Werfel gave me great pleasure. But if you consider Mickey Mouse instead, the situation is much more complex, and the serious question arises as to whether the reproduction on the part of each individual really does constitute that a priori you claim it to be, or whether this act of reproduction precisely belongs instead to precisely that 'naïve realism', concerning the bourgeois nature of which we found ourselves in complete agreement in Paris. (Adorno and Benjamin 2001: 130–1)

Posing Mickey Mouse as paradigm of the 'naïve realism' that sustains a ritualistic, 'auratic' reception of film (that Benjamin wishes to eliminate from the experience of art), Adorno denies film's capacity for transforming subjectivity. In some ways guilty of the same cultural conservatism as the more right-wing intellectual figures of the day in his seemingly outright dismissal of the medium, his scepticism oscillates in this letter between a repudiation of film in general and a more focused attention on what are posed as its more sentimental variants. While Mickey Mouse may have served as the epitome for Adorno of film's affinity for naïve realism, for reasons analogous to those in reference to Donald Duck, it is an ostensible indictment of film's mimetic anthropomorphism that motivates his critique here. Such an aesthetic cannot remain confined to Disney or the cartoon, for Adorno's wider critique implicates 'naive realism' as a more pervasive force of ideology in film generally. Elsewhere in his letter, it is the semblance of 'technicality' that must be proved by film in order to escape the charge of ideological reification, echoing the formalist positions of Eisenstein or Balázs. For instance, commenting on his visit to the film studios at Neubabelsberg, he bemoans the lack of 'technicality' in the feature film (formal devices of close-up, montage) in favour of a 'reality' that is 'everywhere *constructed* with an infantile mimeticism and then "photographed"' (131; emphasis in the original). As long as film maintained its imitative relation to the world as a cover for its ideological operations, it could never for Adorno engage in the aesthetic negation deemed necessary for revolutionary change.

Despite this dismissal of 'dependent art', Adorno was nevertheless far from Utopian about 'autonomous' high-culture, specifically owing to its necessary mechanism of negation with regards to mimetic art. Elsewhere in his letter to Benjamin, he refers to the (dependent) 'cinema' and the (autonomous) 'great work of art' as 'torn halves of an integral freedom, to which however they do not add up' (Adorno and Benjamin 2001: 130). Autonomous art is limited by its being defined by its logical negation of mechanical reproducibility, an exclusivity forged by its relation to capitalism and thus compromised and constrained by the necessity of its own structural autonomy. While both 'bear the stigmata of capitalism' and 'contain elements of change', the impossibility of their aesthetic reintegration becomes a problem for both forms. While mass culture provides the legibility and reproducibility of mimetic representation, the latter's exclusion by modern art dooms it to another kind of non-meaning, particularly in terms of its exclusivity from the wider public sphere of mass consumption.[6] Benjamin would echo such sentiments in his own writings as precisely those problems that pertain to the aura of the 'unique' work of art that 'autonomous' art only served to reproduce. As the 'hidden' holy object of ancient religious practice represents for Benjamin a foundational logic of auratic experience, Adorno's 'autonomous' art is similarly argued to assert 'cult value' as opposed to dismantling the sustained aura that remains in its reception. In both instances, the ritualistic elements of their reception inhibit the revolutionary destruction of bourgeois aesthetic value that technologies of mechanical reproduction threaten promisingly to subvert. As a 'theology of art', Benjamin critiques the reception of 'unique' art, as manifest for him in the 'cult of beauty' and 'l'art pour 'l'art'. Characterised by a 'distance' that traditionally separates bourgeois spectator and aesthetic object, an auratic experience serves to sustain the aesthetic object as sentimental 'myth', with the analogous ideological force of the commodity.

Conversely, film's penetration of this aesthetic 'distance' would for Benjamin allow for a materialist dissection of previously obscured realities. He advocates a radical aesthetic experience of the moving-image as something more akin to the scientific analysis of 'hidden' realities, in a manner very similar, and some argue indebted, to Balázs' theory of the 'face of things' (see Marcus 2007: 242). Benjamin makes explicit, however, that film's capacity to unlock such secrets constitutes a radical bid for freedom under conditions that he and Adorno agree are governed by the perceptual dominance of the commodity and its complicity with the oppression of the labour class. The freedom to 'calmly and adventurously go travelling' at the cinema would be aligned with its promise to 'burst this prison world asunder' (1999: 229), referring unmistakably to the conditions of bourgeois capitalism and the structures of perception and memory dictated by it. Asserting that 'the camera introduces us to unconscious optics as does psychoanalysis to unconscious impulses' (238), Benjamin influentially suggests an analogy between the subject's attainment of self-knowingness in psychoanalysis and the demystification of material reality through film's unique scientific dissection. Like other theorists discussed above, Benjamin was enthralled by the close-up and slow-motion in their capacity to yield hidden truths from 'familiar objects', while montage promised to reconstitute the world's image as never before. The revolutionary potential of film would come with the 'shock' with which such 'technicality' altered the spectator's consciousness as distinct from the contemplation required by bourgeois art, such as painting. Contrasting the two art-forms, Benjamin argues that the 'painting invites the spectator to contemplation' because, 'before it the spectator can abandon himself to his associations. Before the movie frame he cannot do so. No sooner has his eye grasped a scene than it is already changed' (230).

With contemplation of the object connoting too much of the auratic experience, the 'shock' of the moving-image would thus for Benjamin entail disrupted cognition, with the spectator confronted with an ongoing stream of new images. Through the techniques of image juxtaposition, enlargement, and so forth 'shock' would alter perception by forcing the spectator to experience reality in a qualitatively different way. While bourgeois contemplation poses man's capacity to arrive at a rational, ethical subjectivity through perception of the beautiful or the good (or even nothing at all), Benjamin obliges a confrontation between man and the material world that is unprecedentedly aestheticised by technology, and made superior in the following terms:

> For the tasks which face the human apparatus of perception at the turning points of history cannot be solved by optical means, that is, by contemplation, alone. They are mastered gradually by habit, under the guidance of tactile appropriation.
> The distracted person, too, can form habits. (Benjamin 1999: 233)

Benjamin in the above suggests a radical potential in film's 'tactile' address through its enforcement of 'habit' as opposed to the cognitive activity of contemplation. In place of cognition, film forces a necessarily 'distracted' subject to engage in filmic reality in order that critical consciousness becomes a second-nature response rather than one arrived at through contemplation by the bourgeois subject. If the latter is deemed to be mired still in the data of the ideologically self-evident and cannot arrive at truly revolutionary consciousness, the 'distracted' masses could yet be capable of such consciousness precisely by being open to the effects of mass technology as 'tactile appropriation' (233). Free of the bourgeois subject's sentimental reverence for cognition as contemplation, the subject of mass culture is thus considered more porous to film's revelation of political realities.

Benjamin nevertheless still deems capitalist ideology to have permeated existing film culture of the era in irredeemable ways. He rehearses similar objections to the sentimentality of a naïvely realist commercial cinema as other writers discussed above, including Adorno. Cinematic conventions that reinsert 'aura' into a potentially revolutionary medium would need to be eliminated in order to facilitate film's higher purpose. The 'cult of the movie star' is thus seen as a conservative response to the 'shrivelling of the aura' in successfully reintroducing the 'phoney spell of a commodity' (231) to film spectatorship. Commodity and the film 'personality' conspire in Benjamin's view to render cinema into an object of contemplation, reasserting the dominance of bourgeois aesthetics in a mass medium. Benjamin equally perceives 'cult value' in the 'human countenance' as manifest in the portraiture of early photography. By employing photography (and implicitly film) as a means of retaining the 'aura' of 'loved ones, absent or dead', Benjamin suggests the undermining of the true purposes of these technologies in favour of their employment in the maintenance of 'myth' or 'magic', all of which served to sustain the dominance of the commodity. Commending the evidentiary quality of Atget's photos of empty Parisian streets, Benjamin clearly favours the use of the new technologies for their evocation of 'hidden political significance' as opposed to their affinity for the anthropomorphic and its sentimental valences.

In these respects, Benjamin's Artwork essay reveals the influence of Bertolt Brecht, whose own writings and theatrical technique would similarly assert the primacy of political materialism over the emotional manipulation of the era's bourgeois theatre. With 'defamiliarisation' or making strange (*verfremden*) posited as the principal aesthetic imperative of this radicalised, didactic art, 'empathy' with characters is considered a regressive mode of reception that impedes the critical activation of the spectator. In 'What is Epic Theatre?' Benjamin commends Brecht's use of 'interruption' and 'gesture' as a means of breaking up the illusion of naturalistic drama. Corresponding with his idea of the deployment of 'shocks', Benjamin compares the gestures of the 'epic drama' specifically with the 'images on a film strip' such that:

> The songs, the captions, the gestural conventions differentiate the scenes. As a result, intervals occur which tend to destroy illusion. These intervals paralyse the audience's readiness for empathy. Their purpose is to enable the spectator to adopt a critical attitude (towards the represented behaviour of the play's characters and towards the way in which behaviour is represented). (Benjamin 1973: 21)

So Brecht and Benjamin discourage the play's capacity for illusion and absorption in the name of activating the spectator's critical consciousness. While an auratic, illusionistic theatre reproduced the conditions of oppression through its seamless attention to narrative, identification, and catharsis, 'epic theatre' would call attention to the artifice of such conventions. 'Empathy with the hero' here is discouraged in favour of 'astonishment' with regards to the 'circumstances within which he has his being' (18). To 'uncover those conditions' (18) through which characters are represented attains more importance than the narrative conditions within which they are depicted. In such respects the actor in Brechtian theatre is encouraged to emerge out of character at certain moments in order to break the illusion of reality, just as an aesthetics of 'shock' would aim via the cinema to reveal the constructed nature of 'familiar' experience.

Benjamin and Brecht's overall aim of making 'what is shown on the stage unsensational' (xiii) corresponds with minimising the sentimental aspects of 'dramatic' theatre through strategies of estrangement. The application of 'making strange' would focus on the necessities of changing aesthetic reception. Unlike Eisenstein's cinema, where thought becomes an attribute of intellectual montage itself, Brecht's work aims to allow the spectator to think owing to the play's incompleteness and emotional distancing. Benjamin thereby opposes 'the use of theatre to dominate the masses by manipulating their reflexes and sensations' with a theatre where audiences are constituted by 'collectives freely choosing their positions' (10). By calling on the otherwise passive spectator to process deliberately interrupted, elliptical, and incomplete information, Benjamin advocates once again the critical training of a subject whose perceptions of socio-political realities outside of the theatre are qualitatively transformed by an ongoing exposure to non-auratic art.

A tension in Benjamin's work is manifest therefore between his messianic valorisation of film technology per se and his responses to an auratic cinema that surrounded him. If film destroys 'aura' as the very condition of its mechanical reproducibility, Benjamin faces the problem of the sentimental-as-auratic elements that continue to be reproduced within cinema. While Adorno and Horkheimer saw this as reason to condemn the entire medium in the 'Culture Industry', Benjamin's emphasis on film's potential for progressive perceptual transformation suggests a shift towards questions of self-reflexivity that have been echoed by many more recent theories in film and media studies. Whether through the uncanny 'technicity' of Mickey Mouse or the Brechtian disruptions of narrative and character identification, film's potential is aligned with a sentimentalism of eclectic affect that deviates significantly from the anthropocentric-humanist model. As noted in the previous chapter, this new mode of engagement is nothing if not affective, an emotionalism that rejects the stoicism of the 'Culture Industry' model in favour of less constrained modes of feeling.

Postmodern Emotions

Indeed, it is very much an emphasis on film's conflation of high and low art registers, and an acknowledgement of its complex sentimentalism that has dominated postmodern discourses surrounding film and its spectatorship. The critical category of 'affect' emerges perhaps most forcefully in its definitive shift away from the critically aloof attitude and towards an embrace of eclecticism and surface in film that mirrors a post-structuralist foregrounding of fragmented meaning and intertextuality. In place of an an austerely modernist attachment to apparatus, institution, experimentation, and non-realist forms, postmodern pastiche brackets the sentimental trope within a larger polysemic stream, allowing the sentimental its own internal integrity while juxtaposed alongside a multitude of other generic tropes. As noted in Chapter 3, Chaplin's slapstick persona coexists and is emotionally intensified by the pathetic moments of weakness, frailty, and plucky resolve that resonated with the social conditions of his era. Equally, the Hollywood 'blockbuster' may overwhelm the spectator with high-octane special effects and kinetics, yet recourse to the sentimental has been noted as an equally key ingredient to this particularly post-classical of genres. As Barry Langford notes, a genre that incorporates output ranging from Spielberg to Simpson and Bruckheimer has become a 'New Hollywood' dominant not only through 'high-concept' genre hybridity, cross-media cooptability, and generic self-consciousness, but also through an adherence and revitalisation of Hollywood's melodramatic tradition. Langford argues therefore that as

> ultra-modern – even postmodern – as in so many ways the action blockbuster obviously is, it also manifests abiding continuities with and through the history of Hollywood genre. In its combination of visual spectacle, sensational episodic storylines, performative and presentational excess, and starkly simplified, personalised narratives, the action blockbuster is umbilically linked to the foundational melodramatic tradition of Hollywood film. (Langford 2005: 236)

Post-classical film is marked indeed both by a contemporaneity and reflexivity that foregrounds the cinematic apparatus as capitalist commodity and marketing vehicle, while nevertheless time and again revealing its continuities with its 'domestic/pathetic melodramatic traditions'. If a certain modernism's streamlined rupture with the past is negated by such continuities, the sentimental becomes once again a legitimate player within a thoroughly inclusive postmodern aesthetic.

Or does it? Indeed, what is postmodernism and its underlying philosophy of emotion? Moreover, what place (if any) does sentimentality have in a postmodern cultural landscape now apparently characterised by the collapse of high/low categories of taste and an appreciation for sentimentalism that can only be enjoyed ironically as kitsch? As many commentators have noted, postmodernism does not chronologically (and for some even theoretically) supersede its supposed predecessor (as modernism was wished to do, in relation to its own forbears), but represents precisely the impossibilities of such a 'paradigm shift', despite its 'post'-ness. Whether put in terms of Lyotard's relegation of 'grand narratives' (Lyotard 1984: 15),[7] Baudrillard's 'simulacra',[8] the slow and agonised falling out of favour with Western Marxist discourse, or Foucault's related insistence on 'Power' as the pervasive play of ideology and dominance without a metaphysical centre,[9] the postmodern questions the possibilities of a radically achieved purity of the political-modernist project in favour of a disillusioned but celebratory carnival of omnipresent representation and 'différance'.[10] Where the progressive, 'writerly' text promised to jolt the reader or spectator into a new, rather sobering recognition of the political Real, the postmodern text is one above all of 'shallowness', demystifying the ideology of an ultimate totality or referent (or the 'meta-subject' in Hegelian terms[11]) in favour of the perpetual deferral of meaning and a delirious calculus of images, tropes, and 'readymades'.[12]

This arguably sits at odds with how the sentimental has for a long time been firmly aligned with a 'depth model of reality', whether with respect to its early alignments with the subject's innate, core virtue, or its entire opposite in a feigned, mannered gentility. To an extent, the postmodern announces the death of emotion altogether, owing to both the omnipresence of simulacra and a pervasive collapse of subjectivity. For Frederic Jameson, there is a profound 'waning of affect' in the present-tense images of postmodern culture, aligned with a fundamental undermining of humanist and metaphysical models of truth, progress, and history. Like postmodern images, emotions for Jameson are 'free-floating and impersonal and tend to be dominated by a peculiar kind of euphoria' (16). Such pronouncements are echoed in the title of Steven Shaviro's article, 'The Life, After Death, of Postmodern Emotions' (2004). Meanwhile, Jeffery Sconce identifies an entire genre of the 1990s, which he coins the 'Smart Film', that is distinguished by its contemporary nihilism and 'blankness' of style. Through a static deployment of mise en scène and longer shot lengths (that contrast with classical Hollywood editing), such films 'are highly stylized, their sense of authorial effacement and blank presentation achieved not through a feigned verité but through a series of stylistic choices mobilised to signify dispassion, disengagement and disinterest' (359).

Moral philosophers like Alasdair MacIntyre meanwhile echo the revisionist impulses of postmodernist theory by announcing the failure both of the Enlightenment individual and its nihilistic aftermath, in favour of a return to an Aristotelian understanding of morality founded in man's interaction with society. Identifying the same late-nineteenth-century moment of the Enlightenment's collapse in Nietzsche's attacks on a universalist morality, MacIntyre nevertheless attacks the latter's own emphasis on the individual as an *Übermensch*. While a faith in Enlightenment's universalism was bound, he argues, to fail, solutions resting on the political philosophy of Nietzsche to John Rawls fail owing to their reliance on 'emotivism', a philosophical movement that MacIntyre implicitly aligns with the modernist age and its rejection of nineteenth-century Victorian culture. Thus, he asks:

> What was it about the culture of the late nineteenth century which made it a burden to be escaped from? . . . But we ought to notice how dominant the theme of that rejection is in the lives and writings of the Woolfs, of Lytton Strachey, of Roger Fry. Keynes emphasised the rejection not only of the Benthamite version of utilitarianism and of Christianity, but of all claims on behalf of social action conceived as a worthwhile end. What was left? The answer is: a highly impoverished view of how 'good' may be used. (MacIntyre 2007: 16)

Without unpacking all of MacIntyre's arguments, which remain outside the scope of this chapter, I would emphasise that the period identified in the above largely coincides with the period of proto- or high-modernism discussed at length in the chapters above. Philosophically, it becomes aligned with a vitriolic, Nietzchean retreat from moral discourse altogether: by rejecting the baby of Enlightenment reason, it throws out the bathwater of the possibility of a social theory of the 'good'. Ironically, MacIntyre refers to this movement with the term 'emotivism', yet this is not intended as a repudiation of emotion per se but rather a critique of what he argues constitutes a downsizing of moral discourse to the mere 'feelings and attitudes' of writers who nevertheless purported to make philosophically objective claims.

The sentimental as such comes to represent an Enlightenment doctrine that is rejected in the twentieth century by a movement that paradoxically is not so much too rational as too subjectivist. If all prior models of the 'good' had to be rejected for their false claims to universal truth, MacIntyre argues that emotivism leaves us with little but our own untestable preferences and feelings. His solution nevertheless returns to Aristotelian notions of the 'moral' as grounded in shared standards of social life, or '*telos*', a criterion with which the sentimental has always itself been associated, despite its own reputation with vulgar subjective irrationalism.[13] It remains, however, continuously problematised by its conflation of the objective and subjective, the rational, and the irrational. This becomes most evident in Macintyre's critique of Hume's concept of 'sympathy' as a 'philosophical fiction' that cannot bridge these binaries. While Hume subjected 'rationality' to qualification and Kant discounted the 'passions', Macintyre argues that both major Enlightenment philosophers failed to found morality in rational discourse and precipitated emotivism. Thus:

> The project of providing a rational vindication of morality had decisively failed; and from henceforward the morality of our predecessor culture – and subsequently of our own – lacked any public, shared rationale or justification. In a world of secular rationality religion could no longer provide such a shared background and foundation for moral discourse and action; and the failure of philosophy to provide what religion could no longer furnish was an important cause of philosophy losing its central cultural role and becoming a marginal, narrowly academic subject. (50)

The above passage echoes claims made by such scholars as Peter Brooks that use a philosophical context to explain the advent of melodrama, an aesthetic that could be considered to make 'ethical forces' legible (Brooks 1976: 20) in the absence both of religion and, as MacIntyre claims, an adequate moral theory. Yet just as Hume and Kant both fail to fully account for morality, so the sentimental has always courted accusations of its attempting to provide evidence for an ungrounded and unfoundable 'sympathy', an issue that has always made the theorisation of the sentimental a difficult one, and arguably also prefigures the modern problematics of sentimental art.

For MacIntyre, then, emotivism has been both an inevitable and inadequate response to ethics writ large, and requires renewed efforts to found moral discourse as something more than the relativistic conflict of individual preferences. This, however, has not stopped many other contemporary philosophers from engaging in the codification, explanation, and recuperation of emotions. No longer the blind spot of rationalist enquiry, the question of emotion's interdependence with reason has now come centre stage, producing a wealth of work concerning the validity of emotional experience. Key to such interventions has been the critical debunking of emotion's subjectivist connotations.[14] Martha Nussbaum has analysed compassion, for instance, alongside a tradition of its detractors, who since Plato and the Stoics have assumed a fatal association between compassion and the particularism of individual preference. Arguing against the disinterested judgement of the influential Stoical approach, Nussbaum provides evidence of a strong counter-tradition (or 'pro-compassion'). Of particular interest to discussions of melodrama is Nussbaum's dismantling of what she terms the Stoic's 'egalitarian cosmopolitanism' (2003: 359). The family, for example, within this rubric, represents a unit that wrongfully courts a 'disproportionate measure of our concern and energy' (374) in its members, who attend to a particular sub-group of community at the expense of society's wider, cosmopolitan circle. Echoing communist ideology of course, it is compassion that is blamed here for prompting the subject to attend morally only to those perceptually close to him. When individuals outside of such close circles (whether family, national territory, imagined community) are out of sight, they are also out of mind, and receive undeserved neglect on the part of a subject overly focused on the nearest and dearest.

Of course, such has been a key rationale in relation to the promotion and distribution of films and other art projects that bring the experience of marginal or under-represented groups to the attention of film-goers deemed overly accustomed to sentimental Hollywood entertainment and its allegedly narrow repertoire of characters and heroes. Because the American family and its white, heterosexual patriarch suffers from over-representation, the broadening of the spectator's field of experience has rightfully constituted a core ethos of arts funding, the festival circuit, and quality film criticism for a long time. Such policy of course rests on the notion that a broad-minded subject must be persistently apprised of marginal figures and minority experiences in order to act morally in the interest of the wider social and global community. While compassion is certainly invoked in such a process, representation and the being made aware come first and foremost, or else compassion (as one, and perhaps not the most necessary, of various appropriate responses) will be immorally constricted to a limited set of objects.

Yet it is precisely the common assumptions often underpinning such thinking that Nussbaum has sought to problematise in her defence of compassion itself. Rather than attack such a policy in its own right, her pro-compassion position seeks to defend the emotions of compassion in all its evocations, irrespective of interest group. While sentimentality is often associated with compassion felt in relation to an over-represented figure of sympathy, Nussbaum is careful to point out that it can't be the emotions of compassion itself that are to blame here, but rather the nexus of values and politics that bring about such interactions, due to either the Hollywood movie factory or the spectator who wants a cheap cry for its own sake. In itself, however, compassion is defended as having an intimate connection to a 'core theory' of value. Thus:

The standard occasions for compassion, throughout the literary and philosophical tradition – and presumably in the popular thought on which the tradition draws – involve losses of truly basic goods, such as life, loved ones, freedom, nourishment, mobility, bodily integrity, citizenship, shelter. Compassion seems to be, as standardly experienced, a reasonably reliable guide to the presence of real value. (Nussbaum 2003: 374)

In itself, therefore, and as Hume wrote long ago, moral sentiment is a rather dependable human activity that, if at times problematic, is too important to be dispensed with on the grounds of its closeness to sentimental abuse. Compassion and its regular evocations ground the subject as a properly social being that, only through such pedagogically inflected experience, can become a truly moral agent. Evaluation and discrimination are necessary checks to unencumbered compassion, but they do not necessarily for Nussbaum undermine the emotions associated with the compassionate process itself. Indeed, such rational checks on compassion are ultimately also reliant on compassionate impulses focused elsewhere, as part of an overall economy of 'real value'. She thus asserts a vital link between 'compassion' and such 'agency', because it is 'only when we see to what extent need for external goods is involved in the development of agency itself that we have the deepest possible basis for respecting and promoting human freedom' (385)

The dangers of sentimental abuse are not ignored, however, wherein the enjoyment of neediness or victimhood for its own sake through cheap signification is acknowledged as an ancient objection on the grounds of unwarranted or self-indulgent compassion. In response to such objections, Nussbaum is once again careful to qualify their traditional implications in relation to condemning compassion tout court. This she does first through the denial that compassion's cognitive component need necessarily be the desire to maintain misfortune and disaster as a means of ensuring a perpetual flow of pitiable objects. As proof, she allows compassion a cognitive component that understands 'need' and 'victimhood' to be normal phenomena of everyday life while at the same time able to allot value to their elimination or reduction. Once more asserted as the 'reliable guide to the presence of real value', compassion is here given the benefit of the doubt through Nussbaum's assertions concerning the mutual interdependence of emotional and systemic thought. She argues that 'compassion needs to be combined with an adequate theory of the basic human goods: but there is no reason to assume that it must have a bad such theory' (376). Put simply, compassion in Nussbaum's reasoning need not undermine or impair the subject's ability to discriminate between the various claims to 'need' that he encounters, but instead constitutes the core motivation to such acts of discrimination. Compassion requires us to 'get it right' (387), in order to avoid a regressive sentimentality (among other unfavourable consequences such as anger and violence, see below), but there is nothing according to Nussbaum in its own mode of action that should prevent this from happening. Informed by an 'adequate theory of the basic human goods', sentiment can and must operate despite the possibility of various manifestations of sentimental distortion, either as textual or subjective phenomena.

It is here that we discern most clearly a set of shared concerns between moral philosophy and postmodern visual culture, for here is expressed the possibility that real and imagined experiences of pathos can coexist with the subject's ethical discriminations. If postmodern culture immerses the spectator in an array of images and texts that have apparently lost their relation to the 'referent', we may follow Nussbaum's theory by saying that this need not necessarily imply that 'dampened affect' operates independently of compassion. Being hyper-aware of the array suggests not that compassion itself is eliminated as a cinematic affect but rather that the postmodern spectator has merely become *more* discerning and discriminating as to how 'need' should be recognised and verifiable. Images of 'need' and pathos do not become irrevocably lost or meaningless in this array, which sometimes seems to be suggested by such terms as 'blank style' or 'dampened affect'. It would be truer to suggest that our compassion and sentiment represent important components in generating an overall 'theory of basic human goods', parts of a cognitive system that can process kitsch or the gratuitous without needing to dispense with compassion wholesale.

However, and as discussed before turning to the philosophers discussed presently, compassion and empathy continue to carry connotations that are not so easily defended when read against issues debated in the context of the 'New Humanities'. In a post-Freudian, post-Marxist intellectual landscape, compassion remains the property of the 'subject', a concept that invokes a philosophical humanism that has been forcefully challenged by Michel Foucault and the 'deterritorialising' theories of Gilles Deleuze and Felix Guattari. Owing to various institutional and discursive differences (as implicitly questioned by MacIntyre above), such theoretical work is rarely considered directly alongside academic moral philosophy. If this is still attributable to an ongoing demarcation between Continental and Anglo-American philosophy (related no doubt also to distinctions between the 'leftist' humanities and the more 'conservative' Empiricist or Analytical philosophy traditions), the last thirty years has seen qualified efforts to bridge this divide.[15] For despite methodological, and certainly

ideological, differences that make comparison a thorny affair, shared genealogies can be found between such theorists. For instance, Deleuze and
Guatarri's critiques of Oedipal identity in some ways rehearse the Stoical
condemnation of the family in favour of larger communal formations.
Frequent appropriation of philosophical 'immanence' by Deleuze and
Guatarri implicates such alternative spheres as being in a more perpetual
state of 'becoming', arguably radicalising the Stoics' sense of a tangible
communal formation. If the Stoics may have been happier to validate
society over family, a similar concept of disinterest and nullification of
subjective preference is nevertheless still implicit here, where compassion
continues to constitute an inadequately moralistic discourse.

For Deleuze and Guattari, codes of morality inherited from Christianity
and other institutional clusters are thus rejected in favour of a Nietzchean
anti-rationalism, wherein static codifications of the moral give way to the
perpetual flux of the ethical. Where morality is posed as an inherently
conservative set of regulatory impositions on the subject, the ethical comes
to signify a more abstracted and fluid set of interactions between bodies.[16]
Appropriating Bergsonian psychology, Deleuze and Guattari undermine
the integrity of the subject, positing subjective experience as a series of
neuronal firings between sensory and motor activity, inputs and outputs
with little scope for mediation. A philosophical anti-humanism displaces
any sense of common-sense individualised morality (with which compassion has so often been aligned) in favour of a 'deterritorialised' aesthetics.
Bergson's concept of 'affect', as distinct from the more humanist category
of emotion, is central here, for while 'emotion' is felt by a subject, 'affect'
suggests above all an irreducible interaction between what moves (exemplified for Deleuze in cinema) and the body that is moved by it. Taking the
psychoanalytic premise that locates desire or libido as abstracted drives,
Deleuze and Guattari reconfigure the Enlightenment subject as a 'desiring machine', a cluster of impressions and impulses that share vital attributes with cinema, which itself approximates the body as an analogous
'sensorium'. While image and body are still qualitatively different objects,
their modes of action both resemble each other and serve as channels for
an ongoing flow of impressions.

Nussbaum's formulation of compassion, then, sits in tension with
Deleuzian theory above all in terms of agency. Where Nussbaum depends
on a conception of the subject as active, self-determining, and compassionate, Deleuze and Guatarri follow the Nietzchean premise of dehu-
manising the body for more expressly radical purposes. Capitalism still
looms very large here as a commodifying logic that serves to concretise
and identify bodies in the name of material consumption, a process that

also includes such aspects as the continued demarcation between private and public or family and wider notions of community. Destabilisation of bodily integrity constitutes a vital counter-logic here, whereby the collapsing of constructed boundaries (in Foucaultian terms, of gender, criminality, sanity and so forth) can serve to reconfigure perceptual experience.[17] Where compassion between subjects still necessitates a boundary between subjective and objective, these anti-humanist formulations seem to call for a more radical collapse of such boundaries, reinforcing rather the role of a 'materialist' post-Freudian unconscious.

Paradoxically, it is precisely in the extent to which Deleuze and Guatarri engage with affect over emotion that leads a literary historian specialising in eighteenth-century sentimental 'languages', James Chandler, to claim Deleuze and Guattari as the true heirs of its critical project. The crux of the sentimental in such regards pertains not to moral discourse or discourses of compassion as such, but rather to the philosophical problems foregrounded by sentimentalism with regards to defining emotion and affect. Cinema, as for Deleuze, serves as an ideal paradigm of such indeterminacies, for as a sign of Chandler's 'vehicularity', it serves to materially embody emotion as motion. The cinematic close-up, or 'affection-image', for instance, becomes a metaphor for movement despite its dependence on stillness. Thus:

> The fact that the affection-image is associated with an absence of locomotion becomes less significant when we understand that the movements in each case are meta-movements to begin with. The resonance of this language with the discourse of the vehicle – the discourse from which A Sentimental Journey initially emerged as a form – seems to me too strong to ignore, especially in light of Deleuze's self-proclaimed, Bergson-derived materialist account of affectivity. (2013: 38)

Situating sentimental theory within a theoretical tradition of 'materialist affectivity' (22), Chandler claims Deleuze's discussion of the 'movement image' as a continuance of sentimentalism's preoccupation with moving and being moved, thematised notably for him by both 'moral sentiment' theory and Sterne's Sentimental Journey. The famous Maria of Moulines episode in Sterne's novel, for instance, invokes for Chandler the Deleuzian 'affection-image' in its thematisation of Yorick's response to the face of a distraught woman he meets and its foregrounding of a handkerchief that becomes a repository for their commingled tears, moments that Chandler aligns with the cinematic close-up and insert. What matters for this analysis revolves, as with Deleuze and Guatarri, less on the how it is that Sterne or the cinema belong to a sentimental or melodramatic tradition of pedagogy and communication and rather more on how the sentimental tableau problematises distinctions between the static and the moving, and how a language of emotion that begins with Shaftesbury and Sterne persists as a philosophical problem regarding the representation of 'matter and motion'.

Of equal importance to such debates are Stanley Cavell's writings on film and its negotiation of Enlightenment 'scepticism', wherein the demise of a shared rational or foundation for moral discourse (as with McIntire) is reflected in the modern subject's alienation from the world. Cinema serves in such respects as both a paradigm of our alienated isolation or 'screening' from the world, and one another, while serving as a potential catalyst to its overcoming. In *Pursuits of Happiness: The Hollywood Comedy of Remarriage*, Cavell insists that the 1930s 'Comedy of Remarriage' envisions the possibilities of connection between married people despite the ways that modern institutions like marriage and the cinema are predicated on the intransigencies of personal experience. What becomes of key importance to the relationships Cavell analyses in such films is not, to rehearse a shared rationale for union in the form of legal documents, social institutions or moral codes, but the phenomena of constant renegotiation and rearticulation of common perceptions and goals between fundamentally discrete subjects. Thus:

> Our genre emphasises the mystery of marriage by finding that neither law nor sexuality (nor, by implication, progeny) is sufficient to ensure true marriage and suggesting that what provides legitimacy is the mutual willingness for remarriage, for a sort of continuous reaffirmation, and one in which the couple's isolation from the rest of society is generally marked; they form as it were a world elsewhere. (Cavell 1981: 142)

Cinematic remarriage serves here for Cavell then as 'reaffirmation', a model that relies far less on static codes of morality or law and more on a continuous world-building between subjects. If, as Cavell and others argue, post-Enlightenment modernity is typified by a vital division between subject and world, Cavell positions (re)marriage and cinema as conditions of potential re-connection and alliance, allowing the subject access to a sentimentality that must persist beyond his or her own frames of reference. The cinema is posed as an essential model of 'remarriage', in other words, because it serves ambivalently as both screen and portal, a 'world elsewhere' that is nevertheless vital in its reflection of shared experience.

Camp, or 'Sympathy for a Kitsch Devil'

What is shared by theorists like Cavell, Deleuze, and other philosophical contributions to film theory is a recasting of film that I suggest is animated by compromises and correspondences with sentimentalism. They emphasise processes of 'becoming' and re-engagement over the more static legitimacies of rationalised discourse and institutionality, while acknowledging the inadequacies of ignoring a popular, sentimentalist cinema and its invocations of moral legibility. In reference to the principal protagonist of *Stella Dallas*, for instance, around which so much debate was fuelled in 1980s feminist film theory, Cavell is concerned with the possibilities attached to the subject's transcendence and self-knowledge as opposed to the spectator's mere apprehension of Stella's suffering and its political determinants. The 'melodrama of the unknown woman', as he writes of such a film, must be structured around topoi analogous with the Deleuzian 'unbearable', both of which are bound up with the subject's acceptance of non-being and the negotiation of one's isolation from humanity. However, rather than pose such a condition as grounds for the exercise of an austere critical detachment and a rationalised ethics, aesthetic experiences of this kind are framed rather as modes of potential freedom and openness to the world. Once again, the emphasis here is less on the risks of emotional over-identification with Stella (and a possible 'submission-response'), or of an intellectualising political Stoicism, and more with the epistemological condition of unknown-ness that the film invokes in its articulation of loss, possibility, and self-knowledge.

The philosophical return represented by such thinkers, and the 'affective-turn' more broadly understood, signals thus an ongoing negotiation between the necessary acknowledgement of epistemological doubt and the cinema's speculative dimensions as an embodied medium. In this, we are on the terrain of a more ambiguous and reflexive sentimentalism animated at its core by the problematic relation of subject and object. Cinema's movements become analogues of emotion itself, feeling *for* the spectator and thus undermining the extent to which the latter constitutes a subject at all. Just as with the conditions that produce Jameson's 'waning of affect' and its seemingly antithetical 'euphoria', the emotions of postmodernism become indissociable from the material conditions of image production: desubjectivised, free-floating, and unmoored from the referent. That which is moved and that which moves become equivalents, neither privileged ontologically over the other, with such 'depth' rubrics as sympathy, compassion, or morality becoming necessarily evacuated of specific content or value as such. Related to the disinterest or 'nihilism' often raised in relation to the postmodern spectator, such affect undermines any sense of authenticity to emotions, allowing only for a subjective experience that is necessarily 'promiscuous' (or heterogeneous) in taste, desire, and politics.

This pluralistic affectivity and its 'euphoria' share elements indeed with 'camp' and its dismantling of standards of originality and artistic innovation. A certain 'classical' mode of address is challenged in particular by the camp attitude for its own policing of 'excess', whether of the sentimental, the effeminate, the violent, the amateurish, the cheaply made, or the plain 'bad'. The camp spectator is characterised as such in terms of a 'particular reading protocol' (Sconce 1995: 372), where a healthy postmodern distrust of classical pathos is paramount, seeing all appeals to 'conventional' emotions as precisely that – appeals, and, moreover, ones that the spectator always sees coming. The laying of inverted commas over any such appeal and the 'dampened affect' (Sconce 2002: 359) that results, characterises a spectator who has seen it all before and cannot be impressed upon in the same way that more classical audiences may have been. Only through parody (or what Jameson calls 'blank parody' (1991: 17)) can the postmodern spectator be reminded of that appeal, albeit one that is now distorted and unmistakably self-reflexive and knowing.

Camp thus rejects the 'organic unity' (Buckland 2006: 31) of the well-made Hollywood film in favour of excess and irony, substituting its harmony of form and content for a more hysterical and pluralistic affective experience. Of course, if one were to offer an example of the aforementioned aesthetic against which camp rails, one may be tempted to suggest *Schindler's List* or any one of Spielberg's 'serious' films. It has the technical virtuosity, sophisticated mode of address, and emotional seriousness that exemplifies the common-sense 'quality' against which so many other films are deemed inferior. The latter are consumed with glee, however, by a camp sensibility that relishes such stylistic shortcomings and reclaims them as 'paracinema' (372), and it is with a punkish sneer at the mainstream canon that such films are applauded as unintentional masterpieces. Although *Schindler's List* is discussed above precisely in terms of its sentimentalism, and was both recognised and repudiated by various critics as such, such an attribute cannot possibly qualify it here for recuperation as camp. Displaying mainstream Hollywood's high production values, its emotional appeals are considered *calculatedly* excessive rather than accidentally or ironically so. While postmodern in terms of its intertextuality and self-conscious referentiality, the film necessarily contrasts in tone with the 'Smart' cinema (Sconce 2002) of such film-makers as Tarantino or Solondz discussed below. While the latter stand as paradigms of an ironic and über-stylised approach to the melodramatic mode, Spielberg remains committed in such films as *Schindler's List* to more traditional invocations of pathos, meaning, and 'sincerity' (Collins 1993: 257).

It is often therefore with an ambiguous disdain for mainstream sincerity that camp differentiates itself, favouring the unintended, unconscious, or ironic attributes of paracinema over the deliberate, didactic, and sometimes manipulative features of sentimentalism. In sympathy with the feminine and 'queer' identities historically repressed by an ideologically patriarchal, heteronormative system of aesthetic value, camp aligns with an ironic championing of unjustly derided discursive forms and speaking positions. As Steven Shaviro notes of camp, its

> affectations and exaggerations . . . ridiculed the straight world's values and norms. But at the same time, they also secretly allowed gay men to affirm those values, an affirmation that was otherwise forbidden to them. The camp value of bad performance lies in the way that it both expresses forbidden desires and simultaneously protectively disavows those very desires through parody and excess. In this way, camp is deeply ambivalent: it has both a subversive, desiring edge and a conservative, conformist edge. (Shaviro 2004: 131)

Camp's recuperation of the 'bad performance' rests here then on a promiscuity of subject position, a desire to inhabit and perform conservative codes while insured and protected by the irony and artifices of their staging. Such play has in turn itself gone mainstream, an attitude that Barbara Klinger refers to as 'mass camp' (1994: 132) owing to its pervasiveness in contemporary culture, wherein postmodern images and performances are casually tried on for size and just as quickly cast off. Surface, image, and subjective fluidity are clearly foregrounded here, at the expense of more traditional reading protocols that emphasise more long-term ethical investments or political allegiances.[18]

If the camp sensibility recuperates 'trash' for its ephemeral pleasures, it is still, however, a certain category of 'melodrama' that wins out here over sentimentalism as such. Camp functions in postmodern culture as a hermeneutic attuned to excessive signifiers of desire, denial, and hysterical repetition that an abstract high culture has failed ultimately to register. In a curious turnaround of what one may be tempted to call camp's inverted snobbery, the sentimental remains conservative in its wrong-headed aspiration to 'high moral tones'. Where camp revels in the provisional realities of a disposable image culture, sentimentalism is still often deemed to strain for feeling and deeper, more static, truths and certainties. If camp valorises John Wayne, the Queen Mother, the films of John Waters and Todd Haynes, daytime soap operas, and a whole host of rediscovered paracinematic classics, it is because their 'schlock' is either unintentionally gratuitous or intentionally, ironically parodic.[19] Yet camp, even 'mass camp', is rather less concerned with melodrama that remains within a sentimental category of taste, the latter delivering pathos without the apparent irony and parodic intent that so defines a 'trash' aesthetic of its own. Chaplin's patheticism and Spielberg's redemptive models do not connote camp as the above examples have, for they still embody a classicism that is neither archly 'smart' nor casually 'incompetent'. Indeed, humanistic sentimentalism is more often associated with full intentionality, and indeed seriousness, the chief grounds upon which charges of emotional manipulation are levied. Amidst the increasingly complex image economies within which sentimental tropes circulate, as outlined above, it is still in terms of the sentimental's connotations of earnest or didactic pedagogy, in accordance with its genealogical roots, that its own effects continue to court dismissal.

So the sentimental seems not to have lost all conceptual significance within a culture of emotion characterised for Jameson, quoting Lyotard, as the fleeting 'intensities' (Jameson 1991: 16) of an image culture perpetually in flux. One can indeed say with some certainty that the sentimental clearly has survived conceptually for a very long time and most likely will continue to do so, albeit in forms guided by a contemporary postmodern sensibility. The aesthetic 'bracketing' of emotions need not in such a context imply a loss of potency but a rather more complex interaction between subject, technology, and memory. In such respects, Steven Shaviro's deployment of 'sentimentalism', in his article on 'postmodern emotions', rests on a 'terminal irony' that foregrounds and celebrates the failure of sentimentalism's more humanistic epistemologies. Because our emotional lives have changed from the enthralled immersion of cinema to Warhol's distracted spectatorship of a television that's always switched on, postmodern emotions allow for a wider spectrum of aesthetic experience, signified by image cultures that perpetually feed on 'feeling'.

With disaffected irony now thus the virtual precondition of a postmodern sensibility, the sentimental project of guaranteeing moral civility through art's transmission of particular moral values remains a largely bankrupt idea. Getting 'beyond the bounds of irony' (as called for, for instance, by an online 'Patheticism Manifesto'[20]) requires a sympathy that must still not be equated with a conservative moralism, necessitating a shift towards the abstract, for which Shaviro is quite right to invoke Kant. From tears as tangible evidence of moral character to tears as a momentary bodily reaction cued by a particular constellation of stimuli, the latter is nevertheless accorded importance as the 'affect' generated by aesthetic experience. If it is not subversive, affect can no longer be dismissed as apolitical either. Neither progressive nor regressive, the political promiscuousness of sentiment becomes its most promising attribute, as experienced by a subject unmoored from both rigid ideology, and, if the most radical postmodern voices are to be believed, from herself. If irony and media-literacy deflate the newness of experience and any notion of a naïvely moral spectator, po-mo sentimentality must necessarily be considered within a more expansive rubric than that defined within reductive moral parameters.

In what follows in the two final chapters below are analyses that therefore work within the spirit of a 'radical pluralism' (Martin-Jones 2016: 10) that for scholars working within the 'film-philosophy' field serves as the most promising direction for film's negotiation of analytic and continental approaches. Both chapters seek to account for cinema's continued negotiation of sentimentalism in its post-classical phase, both in terms of the modern art film's negotiation of the melodramatic imaginary (Chapter 6) and the embrace of the more 'ridiculous' or deterritorialised affects of Tarantino's cinema (Chapter 5). In such a vein, and being mindful of the expansive field of affect within which film sentimentalism is negotiated, a distinctly post-classical set of films from the last twenty years can be identified that reflect the indeterminacies of its legacy. The chapters can be delineated by gender, wherein Chapter 5's focus on the classical masculinity of the war/combat film is counterposed by Chapter 6's appropriation of the 'maternal melodrama'. What is demonstrated overall, however, are post-classical forms of genre hybridity and reflexivity that nuance these gendered distinctions. Camp, in particular, plays a key role in each of the films discussed below, operating less in terms of a specifically queer aesthetics and rather more in terms of a populist postmodernism of parody and pastiche.

Notes

1. Oscar Wilde is famously said to have remarked, 'One would need a heart of stone to read of the death of Little Nell without laughing.'
2. Echoed in Althusser's theory of 'interpellation', that in turn draws on the concept of misrecognition in Lacan's mirror stage theory. See Louis Althusser, 'Ideology and Ideological State Apparatuses', Ben Brewster (trans.), in *Lenin and Philosophy & Other Essays*, New York: Monthly Review Press, pp. 127–86.
3. The homogenous character of mass identity under Fordist standardisation is problematised by theories of postmodernist culture, where difference is fuelled by capitalism's ability to cater to diverse, niche markets, suggesting ostensible heterogeneities of (consumer) identity. See 'Interview with Stuart

Hall', in *Jameson on Jameson*, edited by Fredric Jameson and Ian Buchanan, Durham, NC: Duke University Press, 2007, pp. 113–34.

4. Buck-Morss poses Benjamin's essay as a response to the 'anaesthetising' effects of commodity culture on an industrialised society that threatens the modern subject with the bodily dangers of the factory, war, and their attendant technologies. See Susan Buck-Morss, 'Aesthetics and Anaesthetics: Walter Benjamin's Artwork Essay Reconsidered', *New Formations* 20 (1993), pp. 123–43.

5. Miriam Hansen discusses the 'therapeutic' function allocated to the mouse by Benjamin in relation to the subject's encounter with 'military and industrial technology'. She notes, in particular, Benjamin's caution and fear about the Disney character's Utopianism, and his ambivalence as to whether the character represents a 'therapeutic discharge or prelude to a pogrom'. See Miriam Hansen, 'Of Mice and Ducks: Benjamin and Adorno on Disney', *South Atlantic Quarterly* 92 (January 1993), pp. 27–61.

6. Adorno has been critiqued often enough for his negativistic indictment of mass culture, yet his theory has undergone significant re-readings that question what seems an initial dismissal of any kind of alternative artistic practice. See Miriam Hansen, Introduction to Adorno, 'Transparencies on Film', *New German Critique* 24/25, Special Double Issue on New German Cinema (autumn 1981–winter 1982), pp. 186–98.

7. See Jean-François Lyotard, *The Postmodern Condition: A Report on Knowledge*, Geoffrey Bennington and Brian Massumi (trans), Manchester: Manchester University Press, 1984.

8. See Jean Baudrillard, *Simulacra and Simulations*, Sheila Faria Glaser (trans.), Ann Arbor: University of Michigan Press, 1994.

9. For instance, Foucault dismisses a Hegelian 'transcendental subject' in favour of attending to the 'various enunciative modalities' that 'manifest his dispersion'. Methodologically, therefore, an 'archeology of knowledge' is foregrounded over and above a more teleological 'history of ideas'. (See *Archeology of Knowledge*, London: Routledge, 2002, pp. 55–61).

10. Jacques Derrida's term for the post-structuralist emphasis on textuality and the infinite permutations of identity inherent to a world structured by language. See 'Différance', in *Margins of Philosophy*, Alan Bass (trans.), Chicago: University of Chicago Press, 1982, pp. 1–28.

11. As discussed by Martin Jay in *Marxism and Totality: The Adventures of a Concept from Lukács to Habermas*, Berkeley and Los Angeles: University of California Press, 1986, p. 54.

12. Although Duchamp's 'readymade' of course epitomises the self-critical collapsing of high and low art as a chief aspect of modernism itself, such a figure has proven particularly resilient in postmodern discourse in terms of the already-existent status of tropes in contemporary media culture.

13. Conceptualisation of a communitarian ethics that opposes the individualism of John Rawls' *A Theory of Justice*, is central also to the thought of such

philosophers as Charles Taylor. See Charles Taylor, *Sources of the Self: The Making of the Modern Identity*, Cambridge, MA: Harvard University Press, 1992.

14. For an overview of contemporary philosophical approaches to emotion, see Robert C. Solomon (ed.), *Thinking About Feeling,: Contemporary Philosophers on Emotions*, 1st edn, United States: Oxford University Press, 2004.

15. A preponderance of journals and conferences have thus emerged, seeking to instigate dialogue between these two traditional camps. Within Film Studies in particular, significant inroads have been made into analytic philosophy (see Richard Allen and Murray Smith, eds, *Film Theory and Philosophy*, USA: Oxford University Press, 1997) and cognitive philosophy and psychology (see Bordwell and Carroll's *Post-Theory*, cited above), the discipline having been traditionally associated most firmly with continental theory and cultural studies models.

16. For Deleuze and Guattari's appropriation of 'Immanence', see Gilles Deleuze and Félix Guattari, *What is Philosophy?*, Graham Burchell III (trans.), New York: Columbia University Press, 1996. For good overviews of Deleuzian concepts see Patricia Pisters (ed.), *Micropolitics of Media Culture: Reading the Rhizomes of Deleuze and Guattari*, Amsterdam: Amsterdam University Press, 2002.

17. A key figure of such bodily fragmentation is termed the 'Body without Organs', which is related to the 'desiring machine', both concepts discussed in particular in Gilles Deleuze and Félix Guattari, *Anti-Oedipus: Capitalism and Schizophrenia*, Robert Hurley, Mark Seem and Helen Lane (trans.), New York: Penguin Classics, 2009 and *A Thousand Plateaus: Capitalism and Schizophrenia*, Brian Massumi (trans.), New York: Continuum International Publishing Group, 2004.

18. The 'pathetic' has been appropriated in some sectors as a new aesthetic unto itself, one that revels in the camp appropriation of sentimental kitsch, for which even an online manifesto of 'patheticism' exists. Patheticism is defined here 'as a desire to move beyond the bounds of irony via an unapologetic occupancy of a position which is from the outset acknowledged to be untenable in any heroic sense yet very human'. While at the same time asserting that 'pathetic art hates the ethical and the moralistic' such a manifesto approaches kitsch through the lens of 'camp' humanism or in its own terms – a 'sympathy for a kitsch devil'. As with the Surrealists and their lost objects, it is in the pure triteness of the pathetic that a camp sensibility finds aesthetic value, connoting freedom in the collapsing of aesthetic criteria invoked by such acts of contemplation in relation to kitsch. See http://www.kurtbrereton.com/pathman.html, accessed 3 July 2010.

19. See Richad Dyer's brief list of camp icons in 'It's Being So Camp as Keeps Us Going', in Fabio Cleto (ed.), *Camp: Queer Aesthetics and the Performing Subject*, Ann Arbor: University of Michigan Press, 1999, pp. 110–16.

20. See note 18.

CHAPTER 5

The Sentiments of War in Spielberg and Tarantino

This chapter seeks to examine the contours of the new sentimental-ism outlined above by focusing on the rise of camp as an increasingly popular 'reading protocol' of Hollywood's post-classical period. Aligned with the era's hybridisation of genre, style, and attitude, camp very much characterises the mood of much 'postmodern' Hollywood cinema in its persistent acts of self-reference and media re-appropriation, while fore-grounding 'disinterest' as its vital affective corollary. The discussion below focuses specifically on two treatments of combat during the Second World War: Steven Spielberg's *Saving Private Ryan* (1998) (hereafter *SPR*) and Quentin Tarantino's *Inglourious Basterds* (2009) (hereafter *IB*), and demonstrates how they can be profitably differentiated in terms of their recourse to sentimentality and camp. The purpose of such comparisons is not to evaluate the artistic merit or quality of these films, but rather to analyse and interrogate these films' distinct appeals to emotion and moral virtue as contemporary American depictions of wartime sacrifice and trauma. It seeks not, in other words, to favour one film over the other, but rather to consider what is gained or lost by contemporary rhetorical variations in the 'war/combat film' (Langford 2005: 107), particularly in its post-classical phase. I argue in particular that a more traditionally sen-timental film like *SPR*, through its reverential honouring of fallen Allied soldiers, serves to clarify the moral legitimacy of warfare in a way that still challenges the moral indeterminacies and aporia of *IB*'s more post-modern, camper, approach. The essay speculates thus on the feasibility of *IB*'s approach as any kind of affective alternative to *SPR*, while ultimately asserting the importance of understanding both films as postmodern, or post-classical, films.

A crucial emphasis relates here to the temporal dimensions of senti-ment, specifically cinema's nostalgic but no less complex invocation of mythic pasts, or golden ages. Christine Gledhill has argued, for instance, that Hollywood melodrama follows a dual logic, showing what 'is' alongside what 'should have been', often doing so through affirmations of a 'golden past' (1987: 21). In many ways exemplified by the depiction of the Second World War's 'Greatest Generation' in numerous war films, this particularly Hollywoodian form of rhetoric has also been discussed by Jim Collins with reference to certain 'New Sincerity' films of the 1990s. Films displaying 'New Sincerity' are, for Collins, 'hyperconscious' of the postmodern 'array' of images circulating in contemporary image culture, and respond through a nostalgic reassertion of lost 'authenticity' (257), revealing fantasy spaces that are anterior to the world's and cinema's own commodification of images. Thus:

> Rather than trying to master the array through ironic manipulation, these films attempt to reject it altogether, purposely evading the media-saturated terrain of the present in pursuit of an almost forgotten authenticity, attainable only through a sincerity that avoids any sort of irony or eclecticism. (Collins 1993: 257)

In films such as Phil Alden Robinson's *Field of Dreams* (1989), Kevin Costner's *Dances with Wolves* (1990), and Steven Spielberg's *Hook* (1991), the recovery of a 'never-never land of pure wish fulfilment' (257) symbolically redresses for Collins the problems of the present through the longed-for return to an imaginary and impossible past. Needs for self-actualisation, often on the part of male characters who have lost a sense of direction in middle age, impose themselves on the re-writing of past 'folk culture' (260), as represented by the idealisation of Native Americans, early baseball players, or childhood itself. Through the 'fetishising of "belief" rather than irony as the only way to resolve conflict' (259) such texts posit 'escape' and 'fantasy' as alternative responses to 'ironic mastery' of the postmodern array, both on the part of characters or spectators.

Collins thus notes a distinction between modes of address where eclecticism predominates (his examples include Robert Zemeckis' *Back to the Future Part III* (1990), Ridley Scott's *Thelma & Louise* (1991), and *Blade Runner* (1982)) and those alongside which paradigms of a forgotten, abandoned virtue are foregrounded. While the former mode emphasises play and 'eclectic irony' (257), the latter re-constructs a sense of authenticity and virtue that is felt to be lost to modernity, and on certain levels resists modernity's epistemic complexities. While the first class of films not only revise genres but fuse genres, the latter class approach genre itself as an opportunity for nostalgic re-integration with timeless iconographies and authentic forms of being that transcend the postmodern array.

The limitations of 'sincerity' films often emerge therefore as failures to reflect the complex discursive terrain of postmodern media, appealing more to the heart, or the gut, than to the head. Critics such as Jeffrey Sconce and Steven Shaviro, for instance, who foreground irony and pastiche in the previous chapter as key attributes of a postmodern or 'smart' (Sconce 2002: 349) cinema, both express caution with regards to the security or reassurances of genre, and underline the tendency of postmodern films to bracket the emotions invoked by nostalgia, sentiment, or 'sincerity'. Shaviro, in particular, as discussed in the last chapter, recovers 'sentimentalism' as a kind of modern, sensual eclecticism, aligned in turn with the 'Kantian disinterest' (2004: 137) of camp as a key feature of modern gay identity. Differentiated conceptually from the austere emotions of political-modernism, camp becomes salient above all here in terms of the double-edged humour of the 'bad performance' (131), with its deliberate foregrounding of affectation and artifice. Rejecting the classically heteronormative values of continuity, action, and sincerity, the camp performance (as exemplified perhaps by Christoph Waltz's performance in *IG*) foregrounds theatricality and reflexivity. At the same time, it foregrounds a nostalgia for the problematic certainties of patriarchal hegemony, often invoked by an affected or hyperbolic reproduction of generic signs. The ongoing adoption of camp by mainstream culture, or 'mass camp' (Klinger 1994: 132), speaks by extension to a pervasive postmodernism of affect in Western culture more generally, a *de rigeur* irony aligned in many ways with the intellectual 'distance' critiqued by cognitivist theorists. It at once allows for the 'resistant' or 'oppositional' readings so celebrated by cultural theory in relation to dominant representations of gender, race, or sexuality, while foregrounding equally the profound ambivalences of contemporary spectatorship in its remove from a traditional ethics, a structure of feeling aligned in turn with the 'waning of affect' (1991: 11, 16) described by Frederic Jameson in late capitalist culture.[1]

The questions addressed above relate therefore to how emotions can be invoked by postmodern cinema without the méconnaisances of a recovered authenticity that is always–already problematic in historical terms. To use Peter Wollen's terms, the sentiment-as-sincerity model seems most applicable to Hollywood films that veer towards the 'closure' of a monologic mode of address in its recovery of authentic pasts, while Shaviro's 'sentimentalism' seems more applicable to films that foreground a more radical eclecticism of address and invoke the 'aperture' (Wollen 1986: 125) of more polysemic forms. In order to test these positions, I situate the two films under analysis as useful examples of the contrasting sentimentalisms outlined above by Collins and Shaviro, while maintaining the importance of the postmodern 'array' to both films' depiction of war and combat. The initial discussion of *SPR* establishes the films' foregrounding of a 'Greatest Generation' discourse, and goes on to examine the debates engendered by critics who have found the film's invocation of humanist redemption and sentiment problematic. I then turn to *IB* as a war film that in many ways responds to Spielberg's historical film projects with a far more strident dismissal of sincerity, at the same time as it attempts (like Tarantino's more recent film *Django Unchained* (2012)) to move away from his usually non-historical material. The discussion focuses also, however, on how *IB* becomes itself constrained by the melodramatic stakes of war and its victims, and thus itself struggles to cohere as any kind of ethical alternative to Spielberg,

Saving Private Ryan and 'Sincerity'

As a film-maker who operates firmly within Hollywood's melodramatic 'mode' (Williams 1998: 42), Steven Spielberg ensures that spectator engagement with characters is as important as 'action' and special effects. *Saving Private Ryan* arguably exemplifies Spielberg's mastery of showing how grand events, specifically the Normandy landings, impact on individuals, through his focus on a small band of soldiers who are re-deployed from the grand offensive to rescue the eponymous private whose brothers have all been killed in action. In such respects, the film conveys the experience of war on individuals within largely respectful, reverential parameters. This is demonstrated in almost the first shot of the film as the elder Ryan walks in front of his family towards the present-day Normandy cemetery that houses the graves of his fallen comrades. The disapproving look that Ryan's son receives from his wife, as he raises a camera to take a photo of his solemn father walking towards the cemetery, seems to epitomise Spielberg's overall vision as one that mandates (as Collins argues in relation to the 'fantasy technophobia' (1993: 262) of New Sincerity) an authentic, unmediated expression of reverence for the fallen that dispenses with technologies that may detach us, and characters, from such experiences.

Ironic therefore that Spielberg is nevertheless widely accused precisely of such mediations in those of his films concerned with recounting real historical events and traumas, such as *SPR*, where male heroism and comradely honour are foregrounded.[2] Bill Nichols comments, for instance, that Spielberg's historical films of the 1990s have 'replaced ethics with spectacle and history with fantasy', (11) targeting *SPR*'s stereotypical supporting characters, the idealisation of 'white male heroes of gentle character', and a Manichean divide between good (Allied) and bad (Nazi) characters. A good example of these tendencies is the sequence where General Marshall signs off on the rescue mission to save Ryan, delivering a morally stirring speech that draws on the authority of Lincoln. In medium close-up, and accompanied by the swelling strings of John Williams' score, Marshall reads (and then recites from memory) a letter written by Lincoln to an American woman, conferring honour on five sons she lost in the Civil War. A moral rationale is provided here for Ryan's rescue as the redressing of a historical wrong, a means by which national guilt can be assuaged by a virtuous act in analogous situations.

However, such scenes as this are also often deemed problematic in terms of their ideological legitimation of patrician figures, the honour code, and American militarism. Nichols argues with palpable irony, for instance:

> Great wars serve great principles. Individual soldiers, though, don't trust the noble rhetoric of their leaders. Still they know real values when they see them. They willingly sacrifice for others. They give their lives to a greater cause. And those who survive combat, slavery or the Holocaust dare not forget the price others paid so that they might live. Pvt. Ryan, for example, in the bookend scenes of flashback plaintively asks his wife, 'Am I a good man?' There is nothing like war to produce a sense of honourable conduct and noble purpose in citizens, if they survive. (Nichols 2000: 11)

Nichols' comments exemplify here how Spielberg's melodramatic treatment of history is met with cynicism in some critical quarters. The moral angst of the elder Ryan honouring his fallen comrades in Normandy at the film's end is problematically couched within a sentimental scheme of reverential distance from the trauma and moral idealisation of the bourgeois family. The chief flaw of the film for such critics is the alleged grafting of redemptive meaning on to war, despite the opening scene's graphic depiction of battle and death. Through classical melodrama's emphasis on character development and the recognition of virtue, the film identifies war as an opportunity for individual development and moral lessons, effacing for certain critics the rhetoric of nihilistic meaninglessness that conventionally characterised the 'anti-war film'. For Krin Gabbard therefore:

> Spielberg departs from the more recent paradigm of war films in the 1970s and 1980s by suggesting, sentimentally and without irony, that war is about building character and not about brutality and stupidity. Most disturbingly, he joins those who have promoted conservative retrenchment through nostalgia for the war years. (Gabbard 2002: 132)

Such criticisms as Gabbard's are particularly mindful then of the more explicitly anti-war films of 1970s and 1980s auteur cinema (Robert Altman's *M*A*S*H** (1974), Francis Ford Coppola's *Apocalypse Now* (1979), Oliver Stone's *Born on the Fourth of July* (1989), Stanley Kubrick's

Full Metal Jacket (1987), and possibly Michael Cimino's *The Deer Hunter* (1978)). *SPR* is widely deemed by such criticisms to approach the Second World War (and the more abstract category of American warfare) without the necessary irony, ambiguity, or nihilism of such predecessors, often read moreover as a particularly untimely mythical legitimation of the American military in the light of its continued deployments in Bosnia and the Middle East during the 1990s).

A problem arrives, therefore, when defenders of *SPR* and other Spielberg films detect ambiguity and aporia in the same scenes that other critics find to be smugly simplistic and/or triumphalist. For Lester Friedman, *Private Ryan* problematises the brutality of war and its sacrifices precisely owing to what he considers its negotiation with the disillusioned, post-Vietnam perspective that informed war films of the New Hollywood, finding in it a jaded cynicism worthy of such auteurs as Kubrick, Scorsese, or Coppola. Friedman responds to criticisms like those by Nichols and Gabbard above by aligning such critique with an inadequate 'retreat into abstract logic' (241) that fails to acknowledge the consequences of war on individuals and the particular historical context (and justification) for the Allied invasion of Nazi-occupied Europe. Such defences of *SPR* are echoed by Nigel Morris, who argues:

> as the film aspires to canonical status within its genre, it dialogises movie warfare to challenge assumptions. Gung-ho masculinity of John Wayne movies, 'anti-bourgeois and anti-authoritarian dropout values' of the Vietnam generation and 'patriotism, nationalism and militarism' of the 1980s all constitute the discursive formation mediating warfare, and veterans' experiences in the 1990s. (Morris 2007: 296)

In order to visualise the human costs of war, the film is argued here then to invoke a variety of discursive positions that (rightfully) fail to cohere with one another in either formal or ethical terms; the combat genre's battle sequences contend with 'anti-war' scenes of protest and potential 'fragging', which are in turn offset by more sentimental sequences of noble rhetoric and reverence. Such hybridity of address is argued to intensify, rather than undermine, the film's overall pedagogy, where the spectator understands the mechanics of sacrifice and honour even if the characters therein fail to. If *SPR*'s postmodernism, in the opinions of more sceptical critics, merely in Morris' terms, 'inoculates itself against criticism' (288), he and other critics defend the film as a melodrama that seems now closer to the kinds of jaded sentimentalism outlined by Shaviro above.

However, do such arguments adequately address the criticisms outlined above from such critics as Nichols, Gabbard, and others? Is it necessary, for instance, that such defences ignore, or minimise, the extent to which *SPR* adheres to a 'Greatest Generation' discourse, despite nods to the Vietnam sub-genre's anti-authoritarianism? Following the character development of Private Reiben (Edward Burns) is instructive here, as a character who speaks in the early portions of the film for the more dissident members of the platoon and most overtly questions the choices of Captain Miller, to the point of his eventually inciting a near mutiny of all platoon members. For, if an individualist, anti-authoritarian discourse seems most represented in such sequences (as well as in Reiben's near desertion of his platoon), it is also notably tempered and largely effaced, by Miller's words and actions in the remainder of the film. Miller's long speech about his life back home as a school teacher and husband (recalling the tone and rhetorical effect of General Marshall's speech and many of Lincoln's speeches in Spielberg's more recent *Lincoln*, 2012), neutralises the tension between Reiben and Sergeant Howarth in the above scene, such that the latter lowers his gun on a would-be deserter and Reiben chooses to not abandon the group. Moreover, Spielberg is quite emphatic in choosing Reiben as the one other character alongside Ryan who hears Miller's dying words in the final battle sequence, and markedly shows him weeping more bitterly upon Miller's death than Ryan himself does, mourning Miller as the all-too-recently acquired father-figure he'd probably needed all along.

Such an analysis allows us to argue then that a model of sentimental instruction remains very much a dominant discourse in *SPR*, deployed in such sequences as a less than ambiguous riposte to 'drop-out' values rendered dishonourable, or, at best, a fallacy of the young. It is, moreover, difficult to ignore the extent to which *SPR*'s ideology has become something of a template in terms of its revival of the war/combat genre in mainstream cinema and television of the last fifteen years. In the wake of *SPR* came a slew of productions (many if not all Spielberg-produced) that rehearse its blend of graphic violence and educational patriotism (Clint Eastwood's *Flags of Our Fathers* (2006) and *Letters from Iwo Jima* (2006)) and successful TV series and mini-series (*Band of Brothers* (2001) and *The Pacific* (2010)). In all such examples, violence is represented as a necessary evil for the triumph of democracy over tyranny. The soldiers of *SPR* and these other texts serve in such respects as paradigms of a socially and ethnically diverse (albeit problematically male) nation that finds common cause at times of war.

The platoon also undeniably represents the kind of 'folk' morality that Collins writes of as key to 'New Sincerity' films. Negotiating directly with the fragmented subjectivities of a 1990s amnesiac media culture, Spielberg and the revived war film teach America a set of (forgotten?) cultural values, deploying a didacticism that asks the spectator to see beyond the postmodern present of MTV and cable TV (but not HBO), and appreciate the ethical substance of nation and its institutions. In Thomas Elsaesser's terms, Spielberg can 'redeem the past, [and] rescue the real' (31) by revealing those signs of humanity and benevolence that persist in nation, family, and the individual, in order that the 'real' of history need not lead us to the most pessimistic, individualist, and godless of outlooks. The 'Greatest Generation' of *SPR* is communicated in such respects as a synecdoche of America, where differences of class, ethnicity, and lapses of good manners and honour are ultimately trivialised, and ideologically neutralised, under the larger sign of a historically validated paradigm of moral good.

Pulp War Fiction

True to 'New Sincerity', therefore, Spielberg's approach to wartime history acknowledges the postmodern array of subject positions in order to all the more 'redeem' us from its discursive indeterminacies, enabling the subject to take a well-reasoned stand and believe in something as it once was, and perhaps ought to be again. *SPR* seems also thus to fall short of the new 'sentimentalism' advocated by Steven Shaviro, invoking a selective nostalgia and monumentalisation of American military heroism that contrasts with a more robust, and critical, form of 'disinterest'. Because it asks Ryan, Reiben, and implicitly us, to 'earn' the 'this' of our contemporary democracy, the film more than implicitly inhibits our disinterest in the world/society in which we live, demanding rather that we have 'values', that we take a side, and that there is essentially nothing inherently wrong in those values being American values. *SPR* thus revises the 'war/combat' genre only to return it to an earlier 'classical' phase of development, where history can yet again yield a lesson even in its most ostensibly 'FUBAR' (*SPR*'s abbreviation for 'fucked up beyond all recognition') of arenas.

Inglourious Basterds by contrast is distinguished by its almost complete inability to stand on ceremony and honour those fallen, and uses war rather as the backdrop for a sublime historical revisionism. I use the term 'sublime' here advisedly, but I would suggest that such a term has pertinence, not least with regards to the imaginative liberties that Tarantino's film takes with what for Hollywood now constitutes well-trodden historical material. Spielberg's realist exposition of war and its now familiar foregrounding of Western humanitarian values is substituted by something both more personal, owing to its direct emphasis on a persecuted, angry Jewry, and more disinterested in its delirious fabrication of events and rewriting of war and Holocaust history. If *SPR*'s 'Greatest Generation'

appeals to the worthy pedagogy of the museum exhibit or the bowed reverence before the war memorial, *IB* seems informed above all by a cinephilia
that reclaims the war on its own self-referential terms, where cinema in
many ways (and certainly in the last sequence of the film, analysed below)
has the last word.

Yet at the same time as *IB* demonstrates Tarantino's usual appropriations of Blaxploitation and Western genres and Hong Kong cinema, his
choice of historical subject matter represents a rather unprecedented shift
towards the kind of discursive territory charted by Spielberg himself. As
such, a question arises as to the kinds of 'sincerity' that *IB* itself introduces
into Tarantino's work, considering in particular the film's explicit foregrounding of the Holocaust and thematisation of Jewish victimhood. Such
comparisons with Spielberg's work leads, I suggest, to unclear demarca-
tions between the two directors' treatments of history, despite Tarantino's
more strident historical revisionism and stylisation. I suggest in fact that
the film, in its foregrounding of Holocaust victims (and black slaves, as in
Tarantino's *Django Unchained*), resists, or certainly problematises, invocations of 'disinterested' affect in a way that runs against the grain of
Tarantino-esque affectivity. While the gangsters of Tarantino's *Reservoir
Dogs* (1992) and *Pulp Fiction* (1994), or the former assassin-turned-mum
of the *Kill Bill* films (2003, 2004) court our attention as entirely fiction-
alised, comic-book heroes or villains, Tarantino's latest film brings the
spectator to something of a dilemma, bringing his usually 'disinterested'
and/or 'smart' style to material that conventionally demands an ethical,
moral, or political response in its foregrounding of racial persecution and
historical trauma. In such respects, Tarantino's war film is necessarily, and
almost uncannily, structured in uncharacteristically melodramatic terms,
and continuously risks yielding to the weight of the historical phenomena
it represents. Put differently, while Tarantino's usual style often collapses
distinctions between heroic and villainous characters in favour of their
mythical-poetic, cinephiliac functions, *IB* is almost inevitably and necessarily lent (or even burdened by?) the sobriety of the 'Holocaust movie'
and the now problematic cultural values attached to it within contemporary Western culture.

IB is, thus, I suggest, structurally melodramatic while remaining
stylistically unsentimental in comparison to *SPR*, a claim that can be
demonstrated without falling back on unclear distinctions between the
two terms. With regards to the sentimental as a purely stylistic consideration, *IB* remains very much a film of disinterest. The film is perhaps at
its most self-reflexive at its climax, when cinema itself (and cinephilia)
serve as the chief catalysts for victimhood and vengeance. Like the climax

of Sam Peckinpah's *The Wild Bunch* (1969), *IB*'s final sequence depicts an inferno of guns and explosions as the Nazi high-command (Hitler, Goering, Goebbels, Himmler, and so on) are massacred in a Parisian cinema by various 'Basterds' (an American-Jewish guerrilla platoon) and the cinema's Jewish proprietor, Shoshanna (Mélanie Laurent), whose family have been murdered by the SS. The raw material of cinema itself, a pile of nitrate film, is ignited behind the screen of a locked cinema auditorium full of Nazis watching Goebbels' latest propaganda 'masterpiece', the latter a most unimaginative film showing a German sniper monotonously picking off Allied troops from a vantage point. IB's conceit revolves here then around a punishment of the Nazis that serves as much to redress their unimaginative cinematic tastes (crimes against cinema) as for their historical crimes. As Goebbels' tampered film cuts to Shoshanna's face in extreme close-up, she states to the Nazi audience her true Jewish identity and their imminent fate, whereupon the film stock located behind the screen ignites and two uncaptured 'Basterds' begin machine-gunning the already fleeing Nazis, while Shoshanna laughs maniacally on-screen. Cinema emerges as the key to *IB*'s climax, facilitating an intervention that contrasts with both the historical reality of Jewish extermination and with Shoshanna's subsequent murder in the film (shot by her Nazi admirer, would-be suitor, and star of Goebbels' film, Private Zoller). Only through cinema's conflation of war, Holocaust, Western, and comic-book genres does Hitler get the death he 'deserves'. Rather than the dignified suicide of historical fact, Hitler's face is graphically pummelled by the pepper-spray of an American Jew's machine-gun, subjected thus to a particularly melodramatic delivery of vengeance.

Cinema is posed here, therefore, as the last bastion of imaginary justice in a world (and media culture) where virtue is inadequately put to a disadvantage by history, where trauma and tragedy can only be effectively re-engineered through the guerrilla tactics of Tarantino's postmodern approach to history. Focused both on Jewish-American soldiers on a 'guerrilla' mission in Normandy and a Holocaust survivor seeking revenge, *IB* speaks of the annihilation of 'home' and 'nation', and in Adorno-esque terms, of the evaporation of the humanitarian values that could truly redeem them. As with *Django Unchained*, history's villains are mercilessly punished for their crimes by Jews driven to inhuman lengths, who lack the grace and detachment of Spielberg's patrician leaders and unknown soldiers. Indeed, *IB* seems often to respond directly to Spielberg's beloved 'Greatest Generation' of multiple ethnicities and classes (the intellectual writer, Midwest schoolteacher, Brooklyn Jew, Southern evangelical) and its appeals to a universalist, humanitarian spirit of (American) justice.

IB's focus on wartime Jewry here substitutes ethnic for national identity, centralising revenge as the key engine for a usually more rationalised military violence. Unlike *SPR*'s platoon, the 'Basterds' replicate the inhuman ruthlessness of the 'Nazis', intent on immediate, bodily violence and torture without compassion, forgiveness, or rationalisation. While *SPR*'s writer-intellectual Private Upham judiciously reserves the only bullet he fires in the film for a German soldier who his platoon had humanely spared (who then voluntarily returns to the Wehrmacht and fatally shoots Captain Miller), the extreme violence of the 'Basterds' is directed at nothing more specific than any 'Nazi', irrespective of individuality or moral nuance. They are led, moreover, by a character who serves in no way to embody the ethically balanced liberalism of *SPR*'s Captain Miller. In the part-Apache Lieutenant Aldo Raine (Brad Pitt), who demands of each of them the delivery of 100 Nazi 'scalps', the 'Basterds' find common cause with a minority persecuted by 'America' itself, once more destabilising the national contours of the conflict. The detached dignity of the reluctant teacher-turned-soldier Miller is supplanted by the professional Raine's unhinged remove from reality, and, it also seems in the film, any higher authority. Like the invocations of contemporary Jewry by the 'Basterds', Raine is scarred by a historical trauma that cannot be redeemed, but can be addressed only in terms of a melodramatic excess of assaults to real Nazi bodies.

Filtered through the revenge fantasy of 1970s Blaxploitation and Spaghetti Western genres, the violence of the 'Basterds' is thus affective, exhibitionist, and, above all, camp, rather than instrumental or rational, signifying the fantasy of 'terror' and (im)personal revenge over the paralysis of victimhood and personal 'trauma'. Both in temporal and ethical terms, the 'Basterds' embody a pathology or 'schizophrenia' that mirrors today's mediatisation of war, where the spectacle (and reception) of 'terrorist' acts becomes as significant as their effective consequences 'on the ground'. With German officers punished within a self-conscious rubric of mass entertainment (Raine says to one of his German officer victims, 'Frankly, watchin' Donny beat Nazis to death, is the closest we ever get to goin' to the movies'), war is subjected here to a radical virtualisation that recalls the showbiz aesthetics of the WWE (World Wrestling Entertainment) or *American Idol*. Like these contemporary texts, the 'melodramatic mode' is applied in its fullest sense of making both good and evil aggressively performative, or as Ben Walters notes of the film's overall tone, 'fun' (par. 9). While defences of *SPR* outlined above, such as by Lester Friedman, emphasise its refusal to fall back on abstraction in favour of showing war's effects on individuals, *IB* skews such logic, such as in the character of Colonel Landa (Christoph Waltz), whose enjoyment as an SS interrogator approaches the comically ironic. While Goeth, the camp commandante of *Schindler's List*, commits murder in a state of confused, pathological obedience, Colonel Landa plays games with his victims, relishing his performances of 'Nazi' evil with playful nods to the audience. Described by J. Hoberman, for instance, as the film's 'master of revels', Landa's characterisation evades any kind of naturalism in favour of the 'knowing' typology of the Basterds themselves, sharing their love of teasing those in his power and withholding any sense of ethical rationale for violence.

Dispensing thus with Spielberg's universe of honourable men in history, Tarantino animates the symbolic and mythical potentials of war, such that any sentimental appeal to character virtue becomes redundant. Rather than tastefully redeem humanity through the exceptionality of Schindler, for instance, *IB* demands playfulness in its postmodern bracketing of the Nazis as the ultimate villains of history. While *SPR*'s dying Captain Miller delivers 'character-building' speeches to his now hushed platoon-members, *IB* has Lieutenant Raine carve a swastika into Landa's forehead, making history speak of itself rather than be redeemed by paradigms of virtuous humanity. With the mythical anarchy of the Spaghetti Western and Blaxploitation etched similarly on to the Second World War, both history and the body must serve in *IB* as manipulable materials, yielding to instruments of violent inscription (Raine's hunting knife and cinematic stylisation) that deny them the integrity of historical truth. When Landa is mutilated in this way (because he nearly gets away with his crimes as a Nazi Jew-hunter through a savvy deal with the Allied HQ), the film asserts the importance of inscription and marking, of manipulation over any faith that history can yield its own moral lessons if only we look hard enough, and filter out its complexities.

The 'New Sincerity' of *SPR*'s honourable camaraderie is thus ostensibly collapsed by *IB*'s insistence on disinterest, a 'sentimentalism' that goes beyond notions of sacrifice and 'good men', towards a more radical sublimation of destructive energies and ethnically partisan scores to settle. As if responding to the demolished death camps shown in Claude Lanzmann's *Shoah* (1985), covered up by the Nazis and thus all the more reliant existentially on the testimony of traumatised survivors and other witnesses, *IB*'s utopia is one where history yields not the conventional signs of humanist consolation for slaughter, but generates its own hyper-destructive logic within the present tense of the 'FUBAR' moment. Responding more overtly to contemporary society's affective remove from war and our current paralysis at its ongoing mediatisation, *IB* adheres more closely to Shaviro's revised 'sentimentalism' in its embrace of the 'futile', 'wasteful' pleasures of a post-ironic cinema. As with the generic hybridisation referred to by Collins, *IB*'s mode of address favours the media 'array' over any fidelity to history, invoking a world gone mad with spectacle and violence, one that cannot support the sincerity of a 'Greatest Generation' discourse, and its sturdy moralisms.

And yet, while Tarantino's film avoids the sincerity of a Spielbergian redemption of the real, the extent to which *IB* functions as any kind of ethical alternative to Spielberg remains highly debatable. While *SPR* speaks for the 'unknown soldier' within a conventional rubric of reverence and sacrifice, *IB*'s attempt at fusing the 'epic war movie' with a comic-book aesthetics remains problematic precisely owing to its engagement with the politics of history and trauma, and the seriousness of tone and taste encoded by such endeavours. The film remains tied to a traditional sentimental scheme, at least to the extent that its characters belong to such over-determined categories of historical good and evil as the Jews and the Nazis, and thus it in many ways cannot fully embody the kinds of disinterest we have come to expect from Tarantino in such films as *Kill Bill* or *Death Proof* (2007), where the comic-book aesthetic usually reigns supreme. Because it seeks to dismantle received images of a persecuted Holocaust Jewry, the film makes a political statement that runs against the amoral grain of Tarantino's own corpus, its characters inevitably standing in for historical victims who still carry the weight of trauma and loss. Negotiating a racial politics in this way, we can say that the film takes on a moral position in many ways despite itself, a sincerity not of style to be sure, but a sincerity nonetheless, that speaks to its inevitable, and unflappable, engagement with really existing ethnic groups and identities.

The above analysis demonstrates, therefore, the extent to which the moral and political stakes of war and genocide continue to cause critical problems for post-classical film-makers like Spielberg and Tarantino alike, albeit owing to the different emotional appeals of their corpora. The structures of feeling invoked by these films speak to very different, and in many ways, opposing approaches with regards to the place of the sentimental in Hollywood film and its mediatisation of war and trauma. *SPR*'s sentimentalism remains problematic precisely in terms of the objectivising rubrics within which the war has been contextualised in earlier forms, where a 'finest hour' rubric persists through the film's reverence of wartime sacrifice and national honour. *IB*, by contrast, represents the war and the Holocaust alongside a more promiscuous, destructive self-referentiality, attempting in many ways to dispense with sentimental sincerity entirely, while retaining and intensifying Hollywood's basic melodramatic scheme. In *IB*, cinema achieves what is beyond the subject and history, foisting disorder and chaos, but also joy, on some of the most unchangeable (and generic) images in cinematic history, not least of which include the persecuted Jewess and the figure of Hitler himself.

At the same time, and unlike Tarantino's earlier films, the weight of the Holocaust and the Second World War impose themselves on *IB* in a way that allows melodrama to complicate this film-maker's usual frame of reference, and thus itself somewhat problematises his usual abnegation of sentiment. In its more radical re-envisioning of a conventionalised history, where Hitler is brutally killed by American Jews, and the Nazi top-brass perish in an inferno triggered by a European Jewess, *IB* embraces our immersion in the postmodern 'array' but ultimately finds that it cannot be as 'dysfunctional' or 'futile' as it wants, grounded as it is in the more 'serious' terrain of war, its victims, and the politics of their descendants. In its reversion to the macho principles of the war/combat genre, *IB* in many ways indicates the limits to which the camp ironies and affectations of gay culture are assimilable to the melodramatic structures of Hollywood cinema. For if *IB* in many ways represents the 'mass camp' of a now mainstream postmodernism of affect, it reveals, too, the constraints that persist in Hollywood with regards to the representation of war, honour, and the suffering of real historical groups.

The complex historical 'real' looms, in other words, above both films discussed here and, in many ways, resists the abstractions and/or simplifications of either rhetorical manoeuvre. This 'real' can be conceived first in terms of the raw actuality of the war itself, against which neither film can ultimately compare, notwithstanding *SPR*'s commitment to recreating events surrounding the Normandy landings. The films also flounder against the 'real' of contemporary opinion, whether in terms of the continued consensus of approval with regard to the Allied campaign as a war worth fighting or in terms of the particularism of Jewish victimhood that fuels the moral rationale for revenge in *IB*. The real, in short, sits uneasily both with the idealistic rhetoric of a Greatest Generation discourse and with the postmodern revenge fantasy of Tarantino's approach, a tendency that remains problematic despite recent reimaginings of the melodramatic mode and its sentimentalisms.

Notes

1. Richard Dyer (2003), for instance, notes the parodic excesses of camp as a key feature of both underground gay and lesbian cinema, while remaining a key

attribute to other underground films that aren't specifically gay in content, such as the films of John Waters.

2. Other films in such regards would include *Amistad* (1997), *Schindler's List* (1993), and *War Horse* (2011).

CHAPTER 6

Sentiment and the 'Smart' Melodrama

Notwithstanding the significant tonal differences between the films examined in the previous chapter, both serve as examples of a post-classical Hollywood cinema that displays a 'knowingness' with regards to the genres and typologies it draws on. Their status as fundamentally post-classical films is predicated indeed on their tendency, like that of many contemporary Hollywood films, to negotiate the 'array' of perspectives and subject positions that characterise a postmodern culture of hybridity and eclecticism. The 'New Sincerity' of *Private Ryan* represents not simply a reversion to classical film-making, but rather a specific reaction and negotiation of the eclectic tastes and literacies of modern cinema-going audiences. Refracted through Tarantino's style, the post-classical war/combat genre takes on elements of a 'mass camp', signalling an aesthetics of disinterest and irony that is far from confined to the gay subcultures from which it may have emerged. What is indicated above all by such tendencies, whether of new sincerity, camp, or interactions between the two, is the extent to which postmodern processes of recycling and hybridity have become entirely familiar to us as modern spectators.

Sentimentality, as discussed above, becomes a significant term within this discussion precisely at the point therefore at which the 'Law of the Heart' and its emphasis on 'fellow-feeling' is challenged as any kind of aesthetic dominant within US cinema and its broader media culture. Examining the eclecticism of both *Saving Private Ryan* and *Inglorious Basterds*, it is shown that the 'submission-response' that characterises the sentimental, as cognitivists have identified as a response to melodramatic devices, is one that is challenged by film's very materiality as a medium of spectacle, and suffers indeed another 'decline'. As much as the widely melodramatic conventions of Hollywood film seek as always to overwhelm the spectator with 'awe-inspiration' or the quasi-religious triumph of unalloyed virtue, it now contends with various affects of disinterest and post-classical sophistication. This 'waning of affect' as Frederic Jameson refers to it, takes camp and disinterest as a defining condition of late-capitalist consciousness, and true to its theoretical forebears in poststructuralist notions of difference and discontinuity, finds solace in the idea of a logos (or for our purposes, an ethics) that is productively undermined.

However, as discussed in Chapter 4, it is precisely this problem of deferred meaning or legibility in critical debates that has prompted a wide-ranging critique of the austerities of political-modernism and its methods, and its apparent politics of 'unpleasure'. If post-structuralist paradigms of aporia and polysemy have become predominant as critical paradigms, scholarly attention has also shifted to alternative, less politicised frames of reference for the study of film culture. In a 'Post-Theory' Film Studies, for instance, analysis of ideology and hegemony in films gives way to expressing more easily hypothesised questions about narrative, style, characterisation, and spectator biology. Alongside this more 'piecemeal' approach to film spectatorship, comes a scepticism with regards to the utility of 'Grand Theory' as a way of delineating film as an object worthy of study. Chief among its objections is the 'cinema as illusion' model and the implied modes of alternative desire that its theorists wished to mobilise through a modernist aesthetics. Sentimentality all too often indeed becomes correlative to this dismissed model in its connotations of 'submission' or manipulation, and in its invocations of an ideological criticism that ignores the spectator as an active maker of meaning.

However, what has come to be understood as the 'affective turn' of the last twenty years means little if not the renewed effort on the part of 'orthodox' film theory (and the wider humanities) to nuance the 'apparatus' paradigm, too, albeit without the wholesale dismissal of the speculative methodology and tradition that it continues to draw upon. Nuancing notions of our imprisonment to difference and postmodern recycling, 'affect theory' at its core rejects, in crude terms, the reduction of 'affect' to 'emotion'. As Steven Shaviro, following Brian Massumi, argues:

> Affect is primary, non-conscious, asubjective, unqualified, and intensive; while emotion is derivative, conscious, qualified, and meaningful, a 'content' that can be attributed to an already-constituted subject. (Shaviro 2010: 3)

Drawing on Deleuze's theories of immanence and asubjectivity, Shaviro and Massumi centralise 'affect', or the 'affective', as a mode of productive ambivalence and creation that resists the 'already-constituted' paradigms of cognitive analysis. For Shaviro, such a mode becomes integral to a media-culture that continues to resist a neoliberal logic of individuation and rationalised consumption (or 'subsumption'), as manifest for him particularly in cinema's shifts to a post-cinematic, transnational, and transmedial phase of development.

The 'affective' turn, as argued in above chapters, thus potentially returns to sentimentalism the broadness that its contemporary valences have occluded for some time. In its foregrounding of the subject's intrinsically unique encounter with the object as a creative process, affect is advanced (over emotion) as key to processes of differentiation and creation. Finding common ground with psychoanalysis in its bracketing of the 'conscious', affect theory lays the groundwork for a sentimentalism that is reducible neither to the spectator's cognitive experience nor to its alignments with a narrative genre or 'mode', even one as broad as Linda Williams' melodramatic mode. The *affective* represents, in other words, neither a return to what Claudia Breger refers to as the 'modernist and postmodernist foci on critique, distanciation, and difference' (66) nor a re-embrace of problematically universalist, or humanist, paradigms. It is marked instead, as Breger claims, by the 'challenge' of 'how to integrate the affirmative insistence on human commonality and connection with a continued critique of contemporary regimes of exclusion and inequality' (67). In the case of Breger's analysis, such a tension is illustrated by the 'complex world making' (87) of Fatah Akin's *Auf der anderen Seite* (English: The Edge of Heaven) (2007) in its treatment of Turkish-German immigration and labour, where the 'affective' is aligned with the film's refusal to privilege 'negativity and distance' (68) as a preferred reading protocol. In opposition to such paradigms, as manifest for Breger in a modernist-influenced dismissal of the film (and similar examples) as 'apolitical', Breger defends the 'good feelings' (68, 81) the film invokes through its narrative of victimhood, abandonment, and reconciliation.

The influence of Deleuze recurs here as an important consideration, borne out by Breger's emphasis of the 'affirmative inquiries' (66) that a 'transnational' cinema can enact from the standpoint of the 'New Humanities'. It is well known that Deleuze aligned his 'Time' and 'Affection' images quite directly to the European auteur cinema of such figures as Bergman, Antonioni, and Renais, all of whose ouevres are marked by the privileging of absence and asubjectivity over 'good feelings'. Such films, and the theory they engendered, nevertheless remain important considerations with regards to the vicissitudes of narrative, or to use Breger's terms, 'signification' (68), in twentieth-century film culture. To deploy Deleuze's own terms with regards to the 'Time-Image', characters of the art cinema are 'objectively emptied: they are suffering less from the absence of another than from their absence from themselves' (2005: 9). Breger's analysis, by contrast, foregrounds a film that is less easily assimilable to the 'anti-signification' (68) model, commending a narrative cinema that is predicated on 'a (performative) process of world-making' (69) in its attention to both a European politics of hatred and a Utopian universalism. At the same time, she retains in Deleuze and his various interlocutors the categories of 'emotion and experience' (69) as vital intermediaries between the critical and humanist registers of contemporary film. Put differently, the imaginative work of spectatorship is foregrounded as a mediating structure between 'signification' and 'anti-signification' cinematic traditions.

The rest of this chapter seeks in a similar vein to examine two US-produced art films that foregrounds an 'affective' cinema of melodramatic reflexivity, focusing in particular on their vexed responses to issues of sincerity and sentiment in US culture. The films discussed below specifically nuance the sentimentalism attached to women, children, and the domestic sphere. What they have in common are modes of affect that may best be described as 'post-ironic' in their assessment of the American pastoral. In contrast to the melodrama and anti-melodrama of the war films discussed in Chapter 5, these art films offer more nuanced assessments of the melodramatic legacy and its signature tropes of 'Virtue in Distress' and 'Virtue Triumphant'. These films remain highly politicised in their condemnation of suburban and pastoral American life, dramatising a melodrama that has always struggled to negotiate the problems of gender and childhood in American society, particularly in terms of the domestic or pastoral setting. These films do not so much therefore condemn small-town America as defamiliarise the coordinates within which the American pastoral is conventionally framed, shifting focus from issues of religion and politics to questions of genre, gender, and violence.

The Arthouse Musical: *Dancer in the Dark* (dir. Lars von Trier) (2000) (Denmark, Spain, Germany, Netherlands, Italy, USA, France, Sweden, Finland, Iceland and Norway)

The films examined below pay particular attention to the visualisation of women and children within small-town America, particularly those who are shown to come into such communities from various elsewheres. Driven by modes of address that foreground an emotionally 'blank style', as described by Jeffrey Sconce in relation to the American 'Smart Film' (2002: 359), *Dancer in the Dark* (2000), and *Palindromes* (2004) depict female characters who are at first welcomed but are eventually cast out by American provincial communities. Such despairing endings are particularly interesting in these films in their ultimate refusal to privilege one side of America over another, such that both the urban and the pastoral participate in their own, discrete systems of exclusion and prejudice. I suggest indeed that the nihilism of such endings speak revealingly to the current affective climate of America's vexed cultural politics, as well as to the problems of melodrama as a mode of moral legibility.

Lars von Trier's film, for instance, displays all the postmodern play with textual conventions and extra-textual contexts that characterises much of his film-making and marketing. At the same time, *Dancer* adheres to the melodramatic trope of female imperilled virtue. Its jarring shifts between musical and melodrama mark it out as a key work of 'camp', too, with von Trier's use of the Icelandic pop star Björk (as the film's heroine Selma) foregrounding intertextuality while still maintaining focus on the tragedy of the fictional character she portrays. Such stylistics earned the film much praise (and the Cannes film festival's Palme d'Or) yet there was also much criticism of its camp irony, such as in the following:

> For its sheer effrontery, for its browbeating melodrama and pseudo-tragedy, Lars von Trier's Dancer in the Dark has to be the most sensationally silly film of the year – as well as the most shallow and crudely manipulative. Everything about it is silly, from the faux naivety and implausibility of its plot to the secret little idiot savant smile on the face of its Victim Heroine played by Björk – a squeaking, chirruping diva turn sufficient to curdle every carton of milk within a 10-kilometre radius. (Bradshaw 2000: B12)

Rehearsed in the above of course are standard critical objections to melo-drama – the energy of such condemnation stemming from the sense to which von Trier deploys its clichéd tropes ironically, yet with still a certain degree of sincerity. The film-maker is here understood to be living up to his reputation of self-stylised prankster, as evidenced most notably by his playful publication in 1995 of the Dogme 95 manifesto along with fellow film-maker Thomas Vinterberg. The film's ability to 'curdle every carton of milk within a 10-kilometre radius' is deemed thus both a serious flaw and a mark of auteurist indulgence. Both 'silly' and 'manipulative', the film could be neither written off as a Hollywood genre piece nor did it conform to a more stable, if not by now conservative, standard of art cinema.

Dancer in the Dark was the third film in von Trier's 'Golden Heart' trilogy, which also included *The Idiots* (1998) and *Breaking the Waves* (1996). The films were inspired (von Trier claims) by a book he read as a child telling the sentimental tale of a girl who goes into the woods and gives away all her possessions to animals.[1] Each of the trilogy's films feature then a 'Victim Heroine' who sacrifices her own interests to save or help others, only to be severely punished by a society that fails to recognise such virtue. *Dancer*'s central character, Selma, an immigrant to the US from Czechoslovakia, works in a factory in the US state of Washington in order to save up money for an eye operation for her son, Gene, so that he will not go blind. Selma suffers from the same condition, and the film follows the deterioration of Selma's sight to blindness. Her initially friendly relationship with her landlord Bill meanwhile develops into an exploitative one, such that he steals her hard-earned savings in order to fund his wife's overspending. When Selma demands the stolen money back, he ashamedly exhorts Selma to kill him, and because she eventually does so under extreme duress, she is subsequently caught, put on trial, and finally executed for murder at the film's end. Although she commits murder, her act becomes one of both compassion (Bill begs her to do it) and justified retribution, with an aura of martyr established around her from the film's outset.

As with other von Trier films about rural to semi-urban life in America in particular, the narrative of *Dancer* begins with the possibility that members of a capitalist society can help and support one another, even where poverty seems entrenched (a similar premise of von Trier's subsequent film *Dogville* ((2003), for instance). When Selma is not able to buy a present for Gene's birthday, Bill and Linda buy him a bicycle, a gift that Selma warily accepts despite its ostensible foregrounding of her failings as a mother. Similar goodwill is apparent in her factory work, a place where Selma becomes increasingly unable to perform her duties owing to failing eyesight. While her supervisor Norman excuses mistakes that could possibly lead to a machine breakage, Selma's friend and colleague Kathy (Catherine Deneuve) turns up to help Selma perform her night shift without being paid. However, as the film progresses, such acts of benevolence prove either insufficient to preventing catastrophe (Selma still loses her job) or indeed prove more directly instrumental to her downfall. Despite the bicycle gift, we learn only two scenes later from Bill's conversation with Selma that it is precisely such expenditure on the part of Linda that has brought him (as breadwinner) to financial ruin. A society of goodwill functions fine in von Trier's films as long as conditions remain unrealistically stable, with poor individuals shown to benefit from the kindness of more wealthy neighbours and friends. Yet it is precisely owing to the untenability of such stability, where poverty comes to dominate without any welfare on the part of state or employers that crime and murder start to encroach on such pastoral idylls. Bill's theft of Selma's money and his death follow as direct consequences of such changes in circumstances. That Bill is too ashamed to admit to Linda that they're broke and that this financial situation has arisen from Bill's failure to curb her consumption serves to underline failings on the part of the married couple and its traditional propagation of imbalanced gender roles. The film shows that if such an anachronistic scheme of marriage is permitted to subsist, the wider society, represented by friends, neighbours, and colleagues, suffer equally if not more. While the status of American, landlord, paid employee, and husband affords Bill a certain respectability, it becomes nothing short of parasitical on those around him that fall short of such criteria. Such figures as the stranger, the immigrant, or the destitute (exemplified by Selma) become subjects at risk of abuse in such conditions. In the film's courtroom scene, for instance, where Selma is put on trial for Bill's murder, the prosecuting lawyer brands Selma a 'communist', invoking the knee-jerk, mindless accusation of mid-twentieth-century American society.

In such respects, as recognised of Douglas Sirk's films and other classic melodramas, the film serves as a critique of American society. It does so, moreover, while appropriating and arguably celebrating two of its principle genres: the melodrama and musical. As European art cinema, *Dancer* may be construed as another instance of anti-American rhetoric emanating from countries and film-makers who perceive themselves as more closely aligned with socially democratic principles. As winner of the Palme d'Or at the Cannes film festival, such a film inevitably becomes aligned with other recent winners that have mounted powerful ideological critiques of American capitalist society, such as Michael Moore's *Fahrenheit 9/11* (2004). However, it is precisely in *Dancer*'s evocation of Hollywood melodrama and the musical that situates its project as one more of negotiation with American movie culture and its sentimentalism. The musical in particular is subject to postmodern re-appropriation in *Dancer*, in which it maintains a shallowness of affect in its incomplete validation of the genre's ideology. Selma's rehearsals for an amateur production of *The Sound of Music* (1965) are shown, like the film's musical numbers, to break up the monotony of alienated, factory labour or, later on, the miseries of social isolation and rejection. While factory work imposes a crushing solitude on its workers, the rehearsal scenes show drama and music as episodes of social cohesion, support, and love. Moreover, it is the musical numbers themselves that provide marked ironic counterpoint, as often with the traditional musical, to the grim conditions that surround them. In musicals such as *West Side Story* (1961), *Oliver!* (1968), and *The Sound of Music* (1965), to name but a few, musical numbers provide relief from the tense events of their plots, invoking moral legibility and Utopian idealism despite the profusion of tragic events that take place around them. Moreover, the classic musical number often clearly serves a pedagogical purpose, bringing characters together romantically or socially despite their initial disagreements and conflicts. In *Dancer*, however, music serves to unite characters as a more direct counterpoint to how they interact in the film's non-musical segments. Characters in the latter sequences are either as indifferent to one another as atomised factory workers, or are more likely actively working against each other's interests, such as Linda in relation to Selma after Bill's death or the death-row officers that transport Selma to the execution room. During musical numbers, such differences become effaced in the spirit of larger ideals, where characters act with greater compassion and express sympathy with one another's motives – emotions that are later exposed as expressions of idealistic unreality in non-musical segments.

The moral legibility of the Hollywood musical thus becomes blurred, as musical escapism fails to bring people together in the non-musical episodes that follow. In the same scene in which Bill confesses his bankruptcy to Selma while she reveals her saving plans for Gene's operation, they discuss Hollywood musicals and their capacity to transport the spectator. A discourse is here foregrounded that poses music as a transcendent force over oppressive conditions (poverty for both Selma and Bill) so that they may survive psychologically. Yet when such escapism fails to prevent the theft, deceit, and murder between these characters, such a discourse is at least partially shown to fail. Likewise, despite the extent to which Selma and Katherine are shown to enjoy their amateur rehearsals of *The Sound of Music*, their rehearsal space becomes a place of distrust and danger later on in the film. Informed by the police of Selma's crime, Selma's director deceptively stalls her at rehearsal so that the police have time to arrive and arrest her, underlining the way that music can only be justified for its own sake rather than in more moral terms. Betrayal and deceit more often than not persist in non-musical segments of the film and we are thus confronted with the failure of moral legibility to translate beyond the formal confines of the musical number. Unlike *West Side Story*, for instance, where tragedy and music eventually precipitate recognitions of thwarted love and virtue between the two warring New York gangs, music remains interior, even delusional and psychotic in *Dancer*, ensuring nothing but its own abstracted logic.

Closer to *Dancer*, therefore, are the revisionist musicals of Dennis Potter's TV series for the BBC such as *Pennies from Heaven* (1978) (UK, aired on BBC television) and *The Singing Detective* (1986) (UK, aired on BBC television). These programs were notable for their intermingling of grim social realism and surreal musical numbers. In *Detective*, for instance, such numbers express the writer/detective Marlowe's delusional imaginings and can be contrasted with the more literal bursts into song by characters of the traditional musical. Performances by the doctors, nurses, and other patients surrounding Marlowe echo a similar kind of psychosis shown by Selma when she re-imagines the grim environments she inhabits as places for music, dance, and spectacle. Using standards from the 1930s, *Detective*'s excursions into song both allude to the long-established escapism of Hollywood and jazz while underlining the extent to which such songs (and the imaginer's psyche) signify an irrecoverable past and Utopian idyll. Like *Dancer*, therefore, such series revel in camp parody, suggesting that such musical forms can no longer be trusted as sites of genuine emotional reality. Interiorised as the imaginings of a sick man (immobilised in a hospital bed by severe psoriasis), the musical number here becomes a key symptom of a profound identity confusion and mental disorder. Such instabilities apply to *Dancer*, too, such as when Bill's corpse (his head having been graphically bludgeoned by Selma) comes back to life with the onset of the song 'Smith and Wesson' (Björk) in order to reassure Selma about the killing. The film immediately becomes saturated with colour compared to the washed-out resolution of the film's non-musical sequences and Selma's appearance becomes magically cleared of blemishes from her struggle with Bill. With the music still playing, Linda appears outside of the house and helps Selma escape from the police who she's just called in the film's non-musical narrative, now seemingly aware that Selma needs to get the money for a doctor for Gene's eye operation. With Gene himself then circling on his bicycle singing the refrain 'You Just Did What You Had to Do', the entire sequence here becomes dominated by the musical number's struggle to reconcile the otherwise restricted and antagonistic perceptions of characters, despite the impermanence of such a condition within the actual story.

In such respects, *Dancer* appropriates and defamiliarises the conventions of a sentimental Hollywood genre, calling attention to how the musical number in particular functions ideologically, and nuancing a simpler kind of melodramatic pathos. While Selma is certainly misunderstood and unjustly punished (as a 'Victim Heroine'), it is her unhinged remove from reality (her blindness serving as a good metaphor) that motivates the musical number's entertainment function and puts the spectator in a contradictory position emotionally. The film asserts that while the number may be diverting for Selma and entertaining for the spectator, there is a price to be paid for its artificial consolations, in the form of Selma's ultimate execution. Furthermore, rather than allowing for such punishment to be perceived as the sad conditions of a melodramatic universe of destiny, sacrifice, and martyrdom, *Dancer* implicates the spectator him- or herself as an integral element of that unjust economy. Unless our enjoyment of the musical number is one of camp detachment, it just may be possible that we ourselves are as much part of the problem as the state apparatus that ostensibly destroys Selma. By recognising the genre and being entertained, we are implicated in such a process at the same time as being permitted an ironic subject position. As with Sirkian melodrama, sentimental tragedy is counterposed with formal excesses in music and colour, yet the latter are now foregrounded as more overt symptoms of delusion and escapism than a subtle stylistic gloss on narrative. Embodying a rather grosser kind of postmodern parody, *Dancer* invokes sympathy for Selma while complicating the extent to which identification is truly possible. Is this Björk or a fictional character? To what extent are we supposed to sympathise with her off-kilter character? In such respects, *Dancer* certainly succeeded in distancing a fair number of critics and spectators, yet as the Cannes jury seemed to acknowledge, such a fostering of camp detachment seemed to be part of von Trier's game all along.

American Independent Cinema – *Palindromes*
(dir. Todd Solondz) (2004) (USA)

If von Trier's project suggests that such experimental approaches to narrative cinema require the seasoned familiarity with modernist technique that comes with a European background, America's own independent cinema has for some time also subjected the melodramatic tradition to a kind of 'Smart' irony. Todd Solondz's *Palindromes* addresses issues of underage sex between children and between children and adults. In its foregrounding of children as objects of the adult gaze, the film addresses America's unstable relationship with child sexuality, with a pastoral setting once again no longer excluded from the pervasive dysfunctions of American society. Invoking a mode of address with frequent recourse to the parodic and camp, *Palindromes* also epitomises the 'dampened affect' (Sconce 2002: 259) of the American 'smart' film, particularly in relation to its ambiguous framing of another 'Victim Heroine'. It tells the story of a thirteen-year old girl, Aviva, who runs away from her middle-class suburban home once she is forced by her parents to have an abortion. The character is played by seven different actors, varying in age, race, and even gender, who play Aviva through different stages of her picaresque journey. Such experimentalism in casting problematises the extent to which Aviva constitutes a subject. While at one level the spectrum of identification is widened, such casting also disrupts a more coherent framing of character in its failure to deliver visual continuity across narrative. The film thus undermines a more immersive model of spectatorship in favour of more episodic engagements and an intensified consciousness of film form.

As a middle-class teenage girl desperate for a baby from a young age, Aviva deliberately gets pregnant with the teenage son of family friends. Once Aviva very reluctantly goes through with an abortion, and is unknowingly given a hysterectomy due to medical complications, she runs away from home and hitchhikes to an undisclosed location in the American Midwest where she ends up at a rural foster home run by evangelical Christians. This extended middle section of the film, a camp and dark parody of 'bible-belt' values, serves less as validation of East Coast or notionally (sub)urban values, than as a more wide-ranging extension of the film's critique of American communal values *writ large*, where location and religious affiliation give way to a more general callousness towards child subjectivity as a key determinant of dysfunction. Both spaces, the suburban and the rural, are essentially debunked as places of ostensible security and nurture alongside such framings.

The Midwest section of the film sees Aviva initially happily accepted into a troupe of disabled orphans who have apparently found sanctuary from a cruel world, loved and cared for by their surrogate evangelical mother, Mama Sunshine. Happily going about household chores, children's games, and rehearsing performances of pop music numbers for the gospel circuit, the Sunshiners' home invokes so excessively saccharine a vision of Utopian innocence and moral values that an ironic perspective becomes inescapable. Typical of an evangelical Christian dance group, the Sunshiners appropriate the songs and performances of modern popstars and boybands like Madonna, NSYNC, and Britney Spears, and redirect them in relation to Jesus. Such re-appropriations retain, however, the traces of their earlier signification in terms of sexualised lyrics ('Nobody else could ever love me this way, Nobody, Jesus, but you') amidst emulation of such performers' sexualised dance movements. Jarring though it is when such numbers are performed by children, such performances are shown to be enjoyed in a particularly unironic way by their foster mother Mama Sunshine, a seemingly responsible, morally upstanding adult. Where the spectator is permitted a knowing irony in relation to the film's recourse to parody, it becomes apparent how their diegetic counterparts do not share this distance (aside from Aviva herself who is rather more mutedly enthused). A discomforting kitschy upbeatness and innocence remains in such a scene, challenging the 'smart' spectator to examine the extent to which her own sophisticated distaste may itself require qualification. If the kids are happy, the film slyly intimates, who are we to object to such an idyll with our own irony-inflected standards of taste? How is it also that spectators such as us are more sensitive to the jarring sexuality of such performances than their on-screen mother, the embodiment of Madonna-like (the biblical one) Christian virtue?

The film thus clearly provokes the spectator to take on subject-positions that it only ambiguously itself endorses, and invokes an above all postmodern loss of critical perspective. One of the world's most popular grand narratives, Christianity, is subjected to the simulacrum, its value system still expressed in terms of charity for the weak, poor, and vulnerable, but now made legible through a glitzy sensationalism as much as mere sentiment, via music video and modern celebrity culture. Such kitschy performances epitomise Frederic Jameson's 'blank parody' (Jameson 1991: 17), conflating the pop culture of MTV video with Christian rhetoric, and clashing a shallow culture of image, fame, and 'bling' with the depth model invoked by melodrama and its search for moral value through story and character. Yet while both modes are subject to critique emanating from different aesthetic agendas, their fusion in some way inoculates them from criticism altogether, one apparently redressing the excesses of the other. Camp allows us here to laugh at the tacky and the grossly clichéd, while it also has the double-edged attribute of taking pop culture at more than face value, that is, seriously.

Childhood virtue, therefore, also shares this double-valence in the film. While its sentimentalisation is suggestive of the potential for exploitation and mass-marketing, its imagery remains cloyingly sanitised of, although connotative of, what it effaces discursively. While Solondz's depiction of the suburban family and the devoutly Christian home are constituted by children and adults participating in a carnival of sentimentalisms and clichés, they are offset by the ubiquity of the extreme, the graphically explicit, and the criminal. As in David Lynch's films, Solondz has a fascination with detritus and trash as places of intensified social reality, including a scene where Aviva comes across a pile of aborted foetuses dumped en masse. In another sequence, Aviva finds a baby doll in a dumpster with its anal orifice violated by a beer bottle. In Lynch's *Blue Velvet* (1986), the idealised American suburban garden (complete with an absurdly artificial chirruping Robin) is similarly counterposed with the image of a human ear being broken down by hordes of insects just below the lawn's surface. With both film-makers then, an aesthetic is foregrounded wherein the lost commodities of Western mass culture are juxtaposed with aspects of the rotten and dead. This inevitably allows us to draw comparisons between the commodity form and the lost children of *Palindromes*. Despite the sunny charity of Mama Sunshine's home and its seeming epitomisation of a naïvely sentimental goodwill among its young residents, Aviva's stay is punctuated by reminders of imminent obsolescence and exchange value. The dumpsite for aborted foetuses serves as a portentous symbol of the disposal economy the Sunshiners are forced to negotiate, highlighting their performances as efforts to market themselves within an image-saturated culture of charity-as-consumption.

Foregrounding the instability and exchange value of children is compounded only further therefore by Aviva's discovery of plots to assassinate abortion doctors organised by Mama Sunshine's husband, Bo. With murder plotted downstairs alongside cruel proclamations of Aviva as a 'child-whore' and 'slut' in the basement of the house, the Sunshiners' homestead becomes a place of danger to be escaped. The first floor's self-consciously saccharine tableaux of childhood happiness serve as unconscious over-compensations for acts of murder and terror plotted one level below. Seen within such a scheme, the Sunshiners' performances merely efface the defilements and dogmas of a pastoral underground, even though such anti-abortion activities still proceed under the sign of childhood (Pro-Life) sanctity. What emerges overall then is a sense of instability in relation to any fixed meaning for childhood, indeterminacies that are mirrored by the extreme divergences in discourse that Aviva encounters within the different spaces of the pastoral setting.

Aviva's story calls less therefore for the recognition of an unalloyed childhood innocence and serves rather more as a pervasive questioning of how innocence (especially that of children) can be reliably represented at all. Child sexuality becomes the critical subject here, in relation to which Aviva's sexuality becomes paradigmatic. Subject to sentimentalisation as spectacle and repression as morally inappropriate, child sexuality is omnipresent but still problematic for American society. Aviva's overt sexuality makes her not the 'child-whore' of radical evangelical discourse but neither does it allow her to signify an ideal of rewarded virtue. Indeed, it is ultimately made clear that Aviva cannot herself remain a purely virtuous subject within the conditions of exchange and disposal through which her story proceeds. Surviving a variety of dangerous contexts, her life is one of chance and self-preservation, offering few opportunities for her own benevolence and altruism. In her insistences that the appointed hitman, Earl, goes through with the killing of the doctor who aborted her own foetus, Aviva's own moral compass is clearly here shown to have shifted from passive victim to retributive agent. Rather than forgive, Aviva here takes on the self-righteousness of Bo's evangelical libertarianism, resorting to murder for justice. The revenger's role may elsewhere serve to deliver moral legibility, yet here it is taken on by an underage victim of trauma who has been keeping bad company. Her actions are shown not to have the moral validity usually expected of the melodrama, whether justice is enacted or remains in the register of the 'if only'. We are left instead with a postmodern sense of existential uncertainty concerning a moral outcome, a state of mind symbolised indeed by the palindrome that cannot but end as it begins.

That the violent events of *Palindromes*' closing scenes turn out to constitute an unexpected tragedy (the accidental killing of the abortion doctor's daughter) serves only therefore to compound the film's evocations of chaos and chance at the expense of any sense of moral justice. With violence and moral retribution revealed as blunt, destructive instruments of justice, often instead leading to further tragedies, the film offers few indications as to where to gain a more morally legible viewpoint. The film's foregrounding of the abortion debate and its intractable moral complexities sets the tone for the entire film, wherein divisions in contemporary American society between liberal and libertarian, urban and pastoral, are underlined in terms of an ongoing reversion to aporia, inertia, and palindrome. Aviva, in such respects, serves as paradigm for the film's 'dampened affect', her fragmentation into several actors undermining any sense of a coherent subjectivity in formal terms, while the narrative's picaresque trajectory foregrounds a logic of chance at the expense of moral legibility.

Sentiment and Violence

The two films examined above demonstrate a postmodern framing of provincial America on the part of film-makers who foreground violence and the role of the media in relation to a mainstay of the American mythos: the small town or community. Deploying the conventions of melodrama in self-reflexive ways that foreground textuality and genre, *Dancer in the Dark* and *Palindromes* offer visions of a provincial America in crisis, leaving a sense of qualified and uncertain hope in those who both suffer and are tainted by its inequities. The films thus align alterity and American social exclusionism specifically with the American imaginary's unstable designation of virtue in relation to women and children.

This imaginary is of course well recognised beyond the territorial borders of America, and is attached to ideologies of freedom and individualist private enterprise. Hollywood's classic genre par excellence, the Western, demonstrated Hollywood's dream of rural America as fertile, unoccupied expanse, an uncharted wilderness that allowed man to forge his own destiny and establish private enterprise and home. The classics of the genre animated key tensions between civilisation and wilderness (the 'Garden/Desert' dichotomy), usually resolved amid elegiac nostalgia for the blank canvas of an unoccupied West and those that roam(ed) it.[2] At the crux of the genre was the ideal of the individual loner outlaw as paradigm of rural existence and subsistence. In *his* dismissals of social conformity and manners and adherence to a distinctly personal moral code, the outlaw stood outside the contradictions of a civilised, but tamed, America. Women and children in the Western remained, by contrast, problematically peripheral in the genre's narrative economy. Owing to their conventional exclusion from the phallic violence played out along the frontier, and aligned much more with the familial and domestic, they existed outside its narrative scope. The outlaw hero may either embrace or dismiss the domestic life she represents after the climactic accomplishment of his mission, but, in any case, the women are dismissed as autonomous economic or sexual agents.

The women (and children) discussed in the above films, however, are both violent and violated. Their violence lacks, however, the intentionality and instrumentalism of the classical, phallic male hero, induced rather by chance and misfortune than by a clear mandate of justice or revenge. In both films, violent acts on the part of women are still sanctioned in fact by the men in their lives, nuancing a simpler reversal of the usual terms regarding gendered passivity. The violence of the quite recent female action-hero tradition, exemplified by films like Tarantino's *Kill Bill* films, or Lara Croft, is nuanced here by the melodrama's traditional foregrounding of virtue and 'good feelings' in its main protagonists. 'Smart' melodrama of this kind foregrounds thus a key tension between a politics of hatred and a more affirmative universalism, where the domestic space of the mother and child is foregrounded as a case of 'virtue in distress' owing to the intransigent difficulties of being an economic agent in the contemporary US. This scenario of victimisation is one that is not easily resolved by the mere assumption of phallic authority.

The American pastoral in these films is acknowledged then as a context that has connoted ideals of comfort, virtue, and freedom in media culture, but that now must be combined and understood alongside signifiers of its more unconscious economies and desires. In the case of *Dancer*, such negotiations are staged at the level of genre revisionism, whereby a musical fails to live up to melodrama's redemptive coordinates. The melodramatic recognition of a woman's virtue remains confined to the diegetic parameters of the musical number and its fantasy spaces, while the grim oppression of the American pastoral in relation to the vulnerable and needy proceed unabated and in hysterical fashion. In *Palindromes*, the music video becomes equally implicated in the increasingly free-floating idealisms and iconographies that characterise contemporary media culture.

Children here function as fundamentally sentimentalised objects, as understood within the rubrics of Christian pop, abstinence, and organised charity, while their real counterparts are subjected to the realities of the repressed sexual economies they help to reproduce. Aviva comes thus to represent both victim and accomplice within the film's narrative logic, a figure the film is at pains to emphasise as being identity-less so as to emphasise her/his status as both child and sexual agent.

These films do more, therefore, than simplistically align American rural life with aspects of backwardness or the uncivilised, establishing rather how the problematics of provincial life both derive from, and can be deconstructed by, representational practices. They foreground problems of articulating the nature of justice and morality in contemporary American society, expressing above all a jaded kind of affect in relation to quasi-Christian signifiers of sacrifice and imperilled virtue. In contrast to melodrama's insistence on moral legibility via recognition/validation of the classical hero's virtuous actions and sensibility, such films frame female and childhood virtue within a darker, relativistic frame. They appropriate both the art cinema's tendencies towards experimentation in style and narrative and the American 'smart' film's recourse to parody and ironic intertextuality. The pastoral setting in both becomes thus unmoored from its more conventional semiotic function within America's well-rehearsed self-image and becomes subjected to the broader critiques of American capitalist society writ large. As Eisenstein recognised, 'Super Dynamic' and 'Small-Town' America are two sides of the same coin, a fact that these smart melodramas are at pains to underscore in relation to problems of gender and the recognition of virtue.

Notes

1. Von Trier comments on the DVD audio commentary of *Dancer* (New Line Platinum Series) that his father (a man he later found out not be his true father) would repudiate the sentimentality of the end of the children's book that inspired the trilogy, thus motivating von Trier to ask, 'Was it so stupid after all?' as a driving question of the 'Golden Heart' trilogy.
2. See, for instance, Matthew Bernstein, 'Stagecoach (1939)', in Jeffrey Geiger and R. L. Rutsky (eds), *Film Analysis: A Norton Reader*, New York: W. W. Norton & Company, 2005, pp. 318–38.

Conclusion

In a 2010 article for *The New York Times*, literary theorist Stanley Fish comments on recent manifestations of the 'crisis in the humanities' in the form of language department closures at US universities such as at the State University of New York at Albany. Defending a 'liberal arts' education amid the neoliberalist reality of higher-education funding and knowledge production, Fish is nevertheless highly critical of a fellow respondent's claims concerning the value of the humanities. This respondent asks in his letter, 'What happened to public investment in the humanities and the belief that the humanities enhanced our culture, our society, our humanity?' Fish advises caution concerning this line of defence, arguing:

> Well, it won't do to invoke the pieties informing [the above respondent's] question – the humanities enhance our culture; the humanities make our society better – because those pieties have a 19th century air about them and are not even believed in by some who rehearse them.
>
> (Fish 2010)

In the above, Fish foregrounds the problematics of a humanist defence of the arts and humanities, recognising issues in the respondent's statement that relate intimately to the problematics of sentimentalism in film theory and cultural criticism. This 'improving' discourse is one that is now almost indissociable from the exclusive focus on Western (male) individualist subjectivity and its sense of universalised progress and purpose in society. This is challenged by a more modern(ist) voice that has been long emergent since culture was conceived less in terms of moral improvement and more in terms of the autonomy that Adorno defended of the artwork in its evocation of self-reflexive knowledge production. It is this ambiguous discursive space that the chapters above have shown sentimentalism to occupy, as a concept invested in both the affective and ethical dimensions of cinema. Indeed, it has not been my intention here to mount a strident defence for the civilising, improving influences of the humanities, or indeed of film, in the face of Fish's comments, for as I hope to have shown in the above chapters, such 'sentiments' do indeed derive from the problematic hopes and aspirations of an era different to our own. The

Victorian era indeed was all too comfortable with rigid divisions in class and imperial colonial ambitions, where the study of the humanities (or rather classics, theology, and philosophy) was very much a privilege of an upper bourgeois class that could make pronouncements on the betterment of society as a function of their own tastes, values, and economic interests. Bolstered by an expanding bourgeois class, the humanities and such aesthetic doctrines as 'realism' and 'didacticism' developed alongside a sentimentalism of women, children, the family home, and one's home nation. Sentimentalism is often indeed aligned with a 'static' idealism or 'fantasy' (Mullan 1988: 118) that all too easily persists through the reproduction of the Victorian era's classic fetishes: hegemonic in its appeals to the universality and timelessness of innocence and virtue (as exemplified of course by Little Nell and her many imitations). As a 'Characteristic' that once defended the rights of the subject from the abuses of intellectual libertinism and feudalist privilege, it came to invoke as early as the mid-eighteenth century a rather more 'sickly' form of self-indulgent moralising, a taste category divorced crucially from post-Kantian notions of disinterest, impartiality, and aesthetic autonomy.

Sentimentalism has indeed been situated in the above as a theory and practice aligned closely with the problematics of ethical discourse and its narrativisation, something for which it has courted critical scorn and suspicion since its very earliest manifestations.

It persists as a category that continues to connote aspects of gentility and moral 'character', as inherited from 'Moral Sense' philosophy, the literary trope of 'Virtue in Distress' and the behavioural codes of the 'Cult of Sensibility'. The history of melodrama illustrates furthermore the resilience of this 'sentimental humanism' in American cinema and culture specifically, a mode of 'moral legibility' that demands the unambiguous articulation of justice, virtue, and community through the overt staging of their imperilment and rescue. Chaplin's films, for instance, can be understood as 'social comedies' (Musser 1988: 62) precisely owing to their bittersweet outlook for the social outsider who stands by his individualism of spirit. Invoking the melancholic hopes of the humanist individual, the tramp embodies a complex Utopian persistence of the body that stands in opposition to industrial modernity and its mechanisation of time and space. Charges of Chaplin's retrograde sentimentalism emerge indeed precisely as a function of this iconicity, whereby the tramp's embodiment of melodramatic virtue can be simplistically assumed to undermine, or even occlude, any further data the films offer by way of critique or 'excess'.

If Peter Brooks' formulations still hold then, there remains a sense to which the 'melodramatic imagination' (as exemplified by Chaplin's films) continues to stand in for and provide succour for the loss of belief and value that characterises a 'post-sacred era'. From the quasi-highbrow discourses of cultural humanism above to the everyday displays of pathos, popular psychology, and self-help that characterise daytime television, the Utopian inflection of sentimental discourse is omnipresent in audiovisual culture. This discourse of the 'heart' is frequently met, however, by a pervasive disenchantment that resonates with a variety of post- (feminist, Marxist, Freudian) positions in film and cultural theory. The discussion above connects the 'charge' of sentimentalism in such respects with strands of political modernist thought that repudiate the 'humanist' subject, both in favour of a more naturalistic aesthetics or a more formalist anti-representationalism. While I do not fully agree with a framing of film theory as a tradition mired in 'ideological Stoicism' (Plantinga 1997), nor adhere to cognitivist tendencies against continental philosophy, arguments running through this account have foregrounded persistent tensions between intellectual and embodied approaches to theorising film, and the resultant neglect of aesthetics in critical discourse. This tension is discussed by Rosalind Galt, for instance, in her account of the dismissal of the 'pretty' as a valid category in Western culture. Describing the 'iconophobia at the heart of postclassical film theory', Galt argues that within 'this influential theoretical field, an image that is ugly, sparse, or imperfect performs a formal critique of ideology that is in many ways precluded or actively undermined by spectacle, beauty, or visual pleasure' (178). In her invocation of 'beauty' and 'visual pleasure' as counter-logics to ideological critique, Galt's work shares this book's focus on the 'aesthetic' (or in her terms, the 'decorative image') as a still problematic category for contemporary criticism. Both the 'sentimental' and the 'pretty' are deemed to insist on 'surface' over substance, escapist fantasy over grim reality, and female subjectivity over a more robust male disinterest. Furthermore, just as Galt aligns this 'anti-aesthetic' sensibility with a rhetorical 'negation of studio perfection, stultifying formalism, or bourgeois aesthetic pleasures' (177), so the discussion above has situated the sentimental as a mode of feeling that is similarly dismissed in terms of kitsch, the generic, or the over-produced. Whether in terms of a 'humanist' framing of Chaplin, the 'Greatest Generation' of the Hollywood's war/combat genre or the virtuous heroines of Richardson's novels, the sentimental has long been bound up with an iconographic idealism that supposedly 'strains' for sincerity and feeling at the expense of socio-political accuracy or a deconstructive attitude.

Nevertheless, with the aid of theorists whose modernism may never have been so inimical to the sentimental as may be assumed, the discussion has also examined how film allows us to 'think both with and through our bodies' (Williams 1998: 47). It demonstrates how some of even the most formalist positions of classical film theory could accommodate certain forms of sentimentality, whether manifest in Eisenstein's ambivalent examinations of Dickens, Bazin's ontological realism, or Balázs' insistence on a diegetic hero for what he considered film's best deployment, the narrative film. While not wishing to discount or invalidate such positions as Brecht's or Adorno's in relation to the emotional conditions of Hollywood entertainment and the necessity for critical detachment, I have nevertheless striven to underscore positions that were themselves less rigidly stoical than is often assumed. Adorno would realise, for instance, despite his cultural elitism, that 'autonomous' art and the 'cultural industry' were 'torn halves of an integral freedom, to which however they do not add up' (2001: 130). In this is surely an acknowledgement that sentimentalism, for all its fallacies and contrivances, could not merely be dismissed, and indeed contained what Richard Dyer has discussed in relation to the 'Utopian' elements of entertainment (1985). More recently, the 'affective turn' in film theory, shifting attention away from the eye and cognition to the sensory, embodied experience of cinema, has further raised the stakes of discounting emotion and 'affect' by emphasising the importance of film's non-cognitive dimensions and the materialist ethics that lie at its core. While sentimentalism comes under renewed scrutiny here as a mode compromised precisely by its signature clichés of style, it nevertheless persists as a legitimate challenge to approaches that neglect the body and emotion.

If all this brings us to a moment of great ambivalence concerning the sentimentalist dimensions of cinema, I would suggest alongside other scholars of melodrama that such a situation is of course preferable to the great dismissals of kitsch that characterised an earlier era's more rigid divisions between high and low culture. Assumed alignments of the sentimental with the feminine, the genteel, or middle-class respectability, have been fundamentally nuanced by an established revisionism concerning the cultural politics of feeling. The final chapters of this book demonstrate how the 'heart' continues to present conceptual difficulties for postmodern critical approaches while nevertheless providing a vital category of interest to contemporary film and cultural theory. While the 'heart' invokes the cognitivised gut reactions of the humanist spectator, the 'body' constitutes its vital corrective as a mere boundary, surface, or screen, a site of disinterested 'affect' and becoming. This reconfigured sentimentalism foregrounds rubrics of pluralism and deferred meaning over more static frameworks of human connection and compassion, accommodating both a modernist attention to innovation and originality, and a postmodern appropriation and combination of genres, media, and affects. Films of 'mass camp', such as *Inglorious Basterds, Dancer in the Dark*, and *Palindromes* are addressed in the above, for instance, as examples of a 'smart cinema' (Sconce 2002: 352) that fuse genres and allow for an expanded, 'camp' sentimentalism of artifice and excessive emotion. A straightforward 'allegiance' towards morally conventional heroes and heroines is nuanced in favour of more ambiguous 'alignments' (Smith 1995: 187) with character trajectories and perspectives – a particularly postmodern approach to story, character, and style characterised by the signature quotation marks of 'blank parody'. A related aesthetic of the 'ugly' or 'imperfect', as discussed by Galt above, persists alongside such treatments in its negations of Utopian beauty and plenitude, from the visually explicit scalpings of *Inglourious Basterds* to the hyperreal musical numbers of *Dancer in the Dark* that both reproduce and break the musical genre's conventions of continuity and escape. As discussed in both Chapters 5 and 6, such postmodern texts do not presume to generate an entirely new mode of spectatorship, but rely rather on a model of parody, quotation, and excess that negotiates or plays with received models of virtue, sacrifice, and honour in the cinematic canon. Such postmodern play yields a form of disinterest that is more, not less, embodied, owing to its visceral breaking down of taboos and cliché and its refusal to 'stand on ceremony'. This sentimentalism, if it can be called that, is truly a grand departure from the saccharine model of sincerity and pathos, its virtue derived from its irreverent honesty about our deepest fantasies and longings.

It is this deconstructive attitude then, aligned with 'camp' and other rubrics of 'cool' disinterest, that the above discussion has situated as a complex rejoinder (if not antidote) to the sentimentalism of more classical humanist forms. As noted of *Inglourious Basterds*, it is a form of disinterest that still relies on the melodramatic model of justice and virtue imperilled (murdered Jews, an evil Hitler) but pushes for a significantly different resolution to more classical or Spielbergian modes. While Spielberg's violence is (ostensibly) defensive and cut to the measure of an honourable cause, Tarantino's is performative, mediatized, and always exceeds its initial rationale. Its excess is analogous to the more radical philosophy of Slavoj Žižek and others examined above, in its refusal to venerate a liberal-humanist mode of 'respect' and emotional correctness, insisting rather on a spiteful uncovering of humanity's true face. In *Palindromes*, this spite is reproduced in Aviva's appropriation of white supremacist, anti-abortion ideology in her willingness to kill her abortion doctor, and it is once again a decision taken in opposition to the suburban, liberal values of her parents and the hokey homespun wisdom of the Midwestern pastoral home. In both films, America's unconscious and problematic negotiation of race and identity politics are foregrounded, wherein the tolerant liberalism of *Saving Private Ryan*'s Captain Miller and the saccharine multiculturalism of Mama Sunshine's home are foregrounded as fantasy spaces that inadequately contain the violence and resentments of the domestic setting.

If the more hysterical or dysfunctional violence of such films signal a worrying rejection of liberal tolerance and the classical humanist subject, the examination of sentimentalism above nevertheless provides a framework for contextualising this turn towards a more visceral, embodied, and irrational cinema (and even its corrolary in American politics). At its core is a rejection of the various instrumentalisms that have always concerned critics and theorists about sentimentalism and its excessive insistence on the 'heart'. The discussion shows in such respects how sentimentality is semantically attached to melodrama by virtue of its always implicit 'brutality' (Midgley 1979) – a mode of 'pathos' that is in many ways indissociable from the 'action' of Hollywood melodramatic film. Our resistance to sentimentalism and its 'submission response' is always nuanced by melodrama's robust rejection of status quo and victimhood, despite the ever-present danger of violence and hatred that it can, and does, yield. If the sentimental all too often insists on the adequacy of 'high moral tones', a stylised lip-service to ideals and values that cannot be actualised in the mise en scène, the 'action' of melodrama and its great persistence in cinema *re-visualises*. Despite the ever-present possibility of violence, cinema insists on a 'becoming' that nuances the more 'static' forms through which the liberal-humanist subject has come to understand itself.

The liberal-humanist sentiments critiqued by Fish in the comments above remain therefore very much in quarantine when it comes to postmodern cinematic representations of America's imaginary. Films by von Trier, Solondz, and Tarantino are aligned in their refusal to 'make society better' but they reproduce such anti-humanist perspectives through specific attacks on our sentimentalised objects and practices. Virtue triumphs in these films, or it may not (nothing new there). Such outcomes, however, emerge crucially through a rejection of grace and forbearance and an acknowledgment of the violent fantasies and hatreds that animate our raced, gendered, and sexualised bodies. A universalised model of genteel tolerance is forfeited in favour of more melodramatic enactments of fantasy and ethical promiscuity. Cultural studies has certainly concerned itself for some time with the intersections of melodrama, race, and nationality in contemporary media, but future work may seek in such respects to more specifically address the role of sentimentalism in the construction and reproduction of nationalistic or factional ideologies, particularly in terms of the sentimentalist 'fetish' (Ahmed 2004: 11) that so often gives rise to such loyalty and doctrinal obedience. A particular focus here would be how such binaries as self and other are staged in different media cultures, and the problematic role of media in constructing a multiculturalist community while inadequately addressing problems of identity and trauma.

Indeed, in awareness of the increased emphasis on globalisation in film and media studies, a key avenue for future research concerns the discourse surrounding neglected media cultures that conform to sentimental models. Whether in terms of a post-colonialist theory that continues to shed insights on the rhetorical status of global Others, in terms of 'Orientalism' (Said 1994 [1978]) or otherwise, or the related conceptualisations of Third World cinema as alternative public spheres, the sentimental constitutes a very significant model for comprehending the placement of virtue and good at the geopolitical level. Already manifest in projects on the melodrama of race in US culture (Williams 2002) and of post-9/11 national self-image (Anker 2014), the sentimental has remained of key interest to scholars working on the ethics of global warfare, race, and identity. Of particular interest, I suggest, are the ways that actants within these rhetorical fields invoke tropes of imperilled virtue to make sense of highly complex histories of conflict and tension, and the vexed means by which these (his) stories are reproduced.

I would also like to stress the importance of genre as a still significant framework through which to make sense of our contemporary media, despite this study's foregrounding of 'mode' as a term that points to broader genealogies and traditions. Future research may be fruitfully applied, for instance, to understanding the quarantine of sentimentality in genres like film noir and science-fiction, both of which can be situated alongside 'hard' rubrics of technological modernity, alienation, and dystopia. I see this study indeed as one that shares continuities with work already undertaken in science-fiction studies, for instance, that has sought in various ways to recuperate the 'body' and the 'social' in response to the genre's traditional tendencies towards technological determinism and scientific verisimilitude. At the same time, the contested place of film within the science-fiction canon speaks to ongoing debates concerning the traditionally 'intellectual' virtues of the genre, elements of which seem problematically curtailed by the casual appropriation of science-fiction narrative devices in many contemporary blockbuster franchises and the renewed role of spectacle and melodrama in these texts (see Bould 2014).

Lastly, however, and shifting back towards this study's methodology, I would like to stress the importance of further studies that continue to examine the intersections between film, theory, and culture from the standpoint of a radical pluralism of approaches to film and media studies. As the humanities face an uncertain fate alongside the rise of the neoliberal, corporatised model in university governance, it seems imperative to emphasise the value of this work without reverting to a defensive instrumentalism in the name of either liberal or neoliberal values. While the humanities are often enough conceived as the ineffectual 'Man of Feeling' in an otherwise uncaring, technocratic world order, it is imperative to foreground the importance of their speculative and imaginative functions in producing models of resistance and critique. I hope in such a vein to have shed some light on a term that has for some time wallowed in semantic and conceptual limbo and, by doing so, made a small contribution to our collective critical vocabulary. To coin the terms that Fish dismisses above, it may not make our 'society better', but it adds I hope to the conversation concerning the categories and concepts with which we continue to think about our moving-image cultures.

Bibliography

Abrams, M. H. *A Glossary of Literary Terms*. Edited by G. G. Harpham. Boston: Heinle and Heinle, 1999.

Adorno, Theodor W. *Prisms*. Cambridge, MA: The MIT Press, 1983.

Adorno, Theodor W. and Walter Benjamin. *The Complete Correspondence: 1928–1940*. Cambridge, MA: Harvard University Press, 2001.

Ahmed, Sara. *The Cultural Politics of Emotion*. Edinburgh: Edinburgh University Press, 2004.

Affron, Charles. *Cinema and Sentiment*. Chicago: University of Chicago Press, 1982.

Allen, Richard and Murray Smith, eds. *Film Theory and Philosophy*. New York: Oxford University Press, 1997.

Althusser, Louis. 'Ideology and Ideological State Apparatuses'. In *Lenin and Philosophy, and Other Essays*, translated by Ben Brewster, 127–86. New York: Monthly Review Press, 1972.

Althusser, Louis. *Lenin and Philosophy, and Other Essays*. Translated by B. Brewster. New York: Monthly Review Press, 1972. Altman, Rick. 'Dickens, Griffith, and Film Theory Today'. *South Atlantic Quarterly* 88 (1989): 321–59.

———. *Film/Genre*. London: British Film Institute, 1999.

Anderson, Carolyn and John Lupo. 'Hollywood Lives: The State of the Biopic at the Turn of the Century'. In *Genre and Contemporary Hollywood*, edited by S. Neale, 91–104. London: Routledge, 2000.

Andrew, Dudley. *The Major Film Theories*, Oxford: Oxford University Press, 1976.

Anker, Elizabeth. *Orgies of Feeling: Melodramatic Politics and the Pursuit of Freedom*. Durham, NC: Duke University Press, 2014.

Aristotle. *Poetics*. London: Nick Hern, 1999.

Arnheim, Rudolf. *Film as Art*. Berkeley and Los Angeles: University of California Press, 1957.

Arnheim, Rudolf, Walter Benjamin, and John Mackay, trans. 'Walter Benjamin and Rudolph Arnheim on Charlie Chaplin'. *The Yale Journal of Criticism* 9, no. 2 (fall 1996): 309–14.

Balázs, Béla and Edith Bone. *Theory of the Film*. London: Dennis Dobson, 1952.

Bartov, Omer. 'Spielberg's Oskar'. In *Spielberg's Holocaust: Critical Perspectives on Schindler's List*, edited by Yosefa Loshitzky, 41–60. Bloomington: Indiana University Press, 1997.

Baudrillard, Jean. *Simulacra and Simulation*. Translated by Sheila Faria Glaser. Ann Arbor: University of Michigan Press, 1994.
Baudry, Jean-Louis. 'Ideological Effects of the Basic Cinematographic Apparatus'. In *Film Theory and Criticism: Introductory Readings*, edited by L. Braudy, M. Cohen, and G. Mast, 355–65. 5th edn. Oxford: Oxford University Press, 1998.
Bazin Andre. *What is Cinema? Vol. 1.*, Translated by Hugh Gray. Berkeley: University of California Press, 2005a.
———. *What is Cinema? Vol. 2.*, Translated by Hugh Gray. Berkeley: University of California Press, 2005b.
Bell, Michael. *Sentimentalism, Ethics, and the Culture of Feeling*. Basingstoke: Palgrave Macmillan, 2000.
Benjamin, Walter. *Understanding Brecht*. Translated by Anna Bostock. London: New Left Books, 1973.
———. *Charles Baudelaire: A Lyric Poet in the Era of High Capitalism*. Translated by Harry Zohn. London: Verso, 1983.
———. 'A Discussion of Russian Filmic Art and Collectivist Art in General'. In *Weimar Republic Sourcebook*, edited by Martin Jay, Anton Kaes, and Edward Dimendberg, 626–7. Berkeley: University of California Press, 1995.
———. *Selected Writings: 1913–1926*. Edited by Marcus Bullock and Michael W Jennings. Vol. 1. Cambridge, MA: Harvard University Press, 1996.
———. 'One-Way Street'. In *Selected Writings: 1927–1934*, vol. 2, edited by Marcus Bullock and Michael. W. Jennings, 444–88. Cambridge, MA: Belknap Press, 1996.
———. *Illuminations*. Translated by Harry Zorn. London: Pimlico, 1999.
Berlant, Lauren. *The Female Complaint: The Unfinished Business of Sentimentality in American Culture*. New York: Duke University Press, 2008.
Bernstein, Matthew. 'Stagecoach (1939)'. In *Film Analysis: A Norton Reader*, edited by Jeffrey Geiger and R. L. Rutsky, 318–38. New York: W. W. Norton & Company, 2005.
Best, Stephen and Sharon Marcus. 'Surface Reading: An Introduction'. *Representations* 108 (2009): 1–21.
Biskind, Peter. *Easy Riders, Raging Bulls: How the Sex-Drugs-and-Rock 'n' Roll Generation Saved Hollywood*. 1st edn. New York: Simon & Schuster, 1999.
Bolter, Jay David and Richard Grusin. *Remediation: Understanding New Media*. Cambridge, MA: The MIT Press, 2000.
Bordwell, David. 'A Case for Cognitivism'. *Iris* 9 (spring 1989): 11–40.
Bordwell, David. *On the History of Film Style*. Cambridge, MA: Harvard University Press, 1997.
Bordwell, David and Noël Carroll. *Post-Theory: Reconstructing Film Studies*. Madison, WI: University of Wisconsin Press, 1996.
Bordwell, David, Janet Staiger and Kristin Thompson. *The Classical Hollywood Cinema: Film Style & Mode of Production to 1960*. New York: Columbia University Press, 1985.

Born, Daniel. *The Birth of Liberal Guilt in the English Novel: Charles Dickens to H.G. Wells*. Chapel Hill: University of North California Press, 1995.

Boswell, James. *The Life of Samuel Johnson*. Ware, Ware: Wordsworth Editions, 2008.

Bould, Mark. 'Film'. In *The Oxford Companion of Science Fiction*, edited by Rob Latham, 155–68. . New York: Oxford University Press, 2014.

Bourdieu, Pierre. *Distinction: A Social Critique of the Judgement of Taste*. Cambridge, MA: Harvard University Press, 1986.

Bradshaw, Peter. 'Review of Dancer in the Dark'. *The Guardian*. London, 15 September 2000.

Breger, Claudia. 'Configuring Affect: Complex World Making in Fatih Akin's 'Auf der anderen Seite (The Edge of Heaven)'. *Cinema Journal* 54, no. 1 (2014): 65–87.

Breton, André. *Nadja*. New York: Grove Press, 1960.

———. *Manifestoes of Surrealism*. New York: Grove Press, 1972.

Brewster, Ben and Lea Jacobs. *Theatre to Cinema: Stage Pictorialism and the Early Feature Film*. New York: Oxford University Press, 1998.

Brissenden, R. F. *Virtue in Distress: Studies in the Novel of Sentiment from Richardson to Sade*. London: Macmillan, 1974.

Britton, Andrew. 'Blissing Out: The Politics of Reaganite Entertainment'. In *Britton on Film: The Complete Film Criticism of Andrew Britton*, edited by Barry Keith Grant, 97–154. Detroit: Wayne State University Press, 2008.

Brooke, Henry. *The Fool of Quality*. New York: Garland, 1979 [1770].

Brooks, Peter. *The Melodramatic Imagination: Balzac, Henry James, Melodrama, and the Mode of Excess*. New Haven: Yale University Press, 1976 [1915].

Brooks, Van Wyck. *America's Coming-of-Age*. Garden City, NY: Doubleday, 1958.

Brown, Herbert Ross. *The Sentimental Novel in America, 1789–1860*. New York: Pageant Books, 1959 [c.1940].

Browne, Nick. *Refiguring American Film Genres: History and Theory*. Berkeley and Los Angeles: University of California Press, 1998.

Buckland, Warren. *Directed by Steven Spielberg: Poetics of the Contemporary Hollywood Blockbuster*. New York: Continuum International Publishing Group, 2006.

Buck-Morss, Susan, 'Aesthetics and Anaesthetics: Walter Benjamin's Artwork Essay Reconsidered', *New Formations* 20 (1993): 123–43.

Burch, Noël. 'Charles Baudelaire versus Doctor Frankenstein'. In *Life to Those Shadows*, edited by Ben Brewster, 6–42. London: British Film Institute, 1990.

Calvert, Ben, Neil Casey, Bernadette Casey, Liam French, and Justin Lewis. *Television Studies: The Key Concepts*. New edition. New York: Routledge, 2001.

Carroll, Noël. 'The Specificity Thesis'. In *Film Theory and Criticism: Introductory Readings*, edited by L. Braudy, M. Cohen, and G. Mast, 322–8. 5th edn. New York: Oxford University Press, 1998.

Cavell, Stanley. *Contesting Tears*, Chicago: University of Chicago Press, 1996.

————. *Pursuits of Happiness: The Hollywood Comedy of Remarriage*. Cambridge, MA: Harvard University Press, 1981.

Chandler, James. 'The Historical Novel Goes to Hollywood: Scott, Griffith, and Film Epic Today'. In *The Birth of a Nation: D.W. Griffith, Director*, edited by Robert Lang, 225–49. New Brunswick, NJ: Rutgers University Press, 1994.

————. 'The Languages of Sentimen'. *Textual Practice* 22, no. 1 (2008): 21–39.

————. *An Archeology of Sympathy: The Sentimental Mode in Literature and Cinema*. Chicago: University of Chicago Press, 2013.

Choi, Jinhee and Mattias Frey. *Cine-Ethics: Ethical Dimensions of Film Theory, Practice and Spectatorship*. London: Routledge, 2013.

Cleto, Fabio. *Camp: Queer Aesthetics and the Performing Subject – A Reader*. Edinburgh: Edinburgh University Press, 1999.

Collins, Jim. 'Genericity in the Nineties: Eclectic Irony and the New Sincerity'. In *Film Theory Goes to the Movies*, edited by Hilary Radner and Ava Collins, 242–63. London: Routledge, 1993.

Cowley, Malcolm. *After the Genteel Tradition: American Writers, 1910–1930*. Carbondale: Southern Illinois University Press, 1964 [1937].

Crane, R. S. 'Suggestions toward a Genealogy of the "Man of Feeling"'. *ELH* 1, no. 3 (1 December 1934): 205–30.

Currie, Gregory. *Image and Mind: Film, Philosophy and Cognitive Science*. New York: Cambridge University Press, 1995.

Deleuze, Gilles. *Cinema 2: The Time-Image*. Translated by Hugh Tomlinson and Robert Galeta. London: Continuum International Publishing Group, 2005.

Deleuze, Gilles and Félix Guattari. *What Is Philosophy?* Translated by Graham Burchell III. New York: Columbia University Press, 1996.

————. *A Thousand Plateaus: Capitalism and Schizophrenia*. Translated by Brian Massumi. New York: Continuum International Publishing Group, 2004.

————. *Anti-Oedipus: Capitalism and Schizophrenia*. Translated by Robert Hurley, Mark Seem, and Helen Lane. New York: Penguin Classics, 2009.

Denby, David. 'FACE; OFF; Steven Spielberg meets Stanley Kubrick'. *The New Yorker*, 2 July 2001.Derrida, Jacques. 'Différance'. In *Margins of Philosophy*, translated by Alan Bass, 1–28. Chicago: University of Chicago Press, 1982.

Dickens, Charles. *Hard Times*. New York: Routledge, 1987.

————. *Great Expectations*. London: Wordsworth Classics, 1992.

————. *The Old Curiosity Shop*. London: Wordsworth Classics, 2001.

Diderot, Denis. *Essai sur le mérite et la vertu*. Paris: Desrey & Deterville, 1798. https://books.google.ca/books?id=kug9AAAAcAAJ&dq=Diderot%27s+Essai+sur+le+merite+et+la+vertu&source=gbs_navlinks_s, last accessed 4 October 2012.

————. *Diderot's Writings on the Theatre*. Edited by F. C. Green. Cambridge: Cambridge University Press, 1936.

————. *Selected Writings on Art and Literature*. Translated by G. Bremner. London: Penguin, 1994.

Doane, Mary Ann. *The Desire to Desire: The Woman's Film of the 1940s.* Bloomington: Indiana University Press, 1987.

Dodd, Charles. *The Curse of Sentiment.* Gale Eighteenth Century Collections Online Print Ediiton, 2012 [1787].

Donald, James, Anne Friedberg, and Laura Marcus, eds. *Close Up, 1927–1933: Cinema and Modernism.* Princeton: Princeton University Press, 1998.

Douglas, Ann. *The Feminization of American Culture.* New York: Knopf, 1978.

Dumas, Alexandre. *The Corsican Brothers: A Play in Three Acts.* Translated by Frank Morlock. Rockville, MD: Wildside Press, 2013 [1844].

Dyer, Richard. 'It's Being So Camp as Keeps Us Going'. In *Camp: Queer Aesthetics and the Performing Subject*, edited by Fabio Cleto, 110–16. Ann Arbor: University of Michigan Press, 1999.

———. 'Entertainment and Utopia'. In *Movies and Methods: An Anthology*, edited by Bill Nichols, 220–32. Vol. 2. Berkeley and Los Angeles: University of California Press, 1985.

———. *Now You See It.* 2nd edn. London: Routledge, 2003.

Eagleton, Terry. *The Ideology of the Aesthetic.* London: Blackwell, 1990.

Eig, Jonathan. 'A Beautiful Mind (Fuck): Hollywood Structures of Identity'. *Jump Cut* 46, no. 7 (2003). http://www.ejumpcut.org/archive/jc46.2003/eig.mindfilms, last accessed 20 March 2010.

Eisenstein, Sergei. *Film Form.* Translated by J. Leyda. New York: Harcourt Brace, 1977 [1949].

———. *Immoral Memories.* Translated by H. Marshall. Vol. 5. Boston: Houghton Mifflin, 1983.

———. *Nonindifferent Nature.* Translated by H. Marshall. Cambridge: Cambridge University Press, 1988.

———. *The Eisenstein Reader.* Edited by Richard Taylor. London: British Film Institute, 1998.

———. *Problems of Film Direction.* Honolulu: University Press of the Pacific Place of Publication, 2004.

Ellis John. *Visible Fictions.* London: Routledge,1992

Elsaesser, Thomas. 'Tales of Sound and Fury'. In *Movies and Methods. Vol. 2*, edited by Bill Nichols, 166–89. Berkeley and Los Angeles: University of California Press, 1985.

———. 'Film History as Social History: The Dieterle/Warner Brothers Bio-Pic'. *Wide Angle* 8, no. 2 (1986): 15–31.

———. 'Studying TV Audiences Today: Voodoo, Shamans and Prospectors?'. In *History of Moving Images*, edited by Kathrine Skretting and Jostein Gripsrud, 171–9. Oslo: Levende Bilder, 1994.

———. 'Subject Positions, Speaking Positions: From Holocaust, Our Hitler and Heimat, to Shoah and *Schindler's List*'. In *The Persistence of History: Cinema, Television and the Modern Event*, edited by Vivian Sobchack, 145–86, London: Routledge, 1996.

Erämetsä, Erik. *A Study of the Word 'Sentimental' and of Other Linguistic*

Characteristics of 18th Century Sentimentalism in England. Helsinki: Helsingin Liikekirjapaino, 1951.

Fish, Stanley. 'The Crisis in the Humanities Officially Arrives'. *The New York Times*, 11 October 2010.

Foucault, Michel. *Archaeology of Knowledge*. Translated by Alan Sheridan. London: Routledge, 2002.

Frazer, Michael. *The Enlightenment of Sympathy: Justice and the Moral Sentiments in the Eighteenth Century and Today*. New York: Oxford University Press, 2010.

Freud, Sigmund. *Civilization and Its Discontents*. The Standard Edition. New York: W. W. Norton & Company, 1989.

Friedman, Lester D. *Citizen Spielberg*. Champaign, IL: University of Illinois Press, 2006.

Gabbard, Krin. 'Saving Private Ryan Too Late'. In *The End Of Cinema As We Know It: American Film in the Nineties*, edited by Jon Lewis, 131–8. New York: New York University Press, 2002.

Galt, Rosalind. *Pretty: Film and the Decorative Image*. New York: Columbia University Press, 2011.

Garncarz, Joseph. '"Films That are Applauded All Over the World: Questioning Chaplin's Popularity in Weimar Germany'. *Early Popular Visual Culture* 8, no. 3 (2010): 285–96.

Gledhill, Christine. 'The Melodramatic Field: An Investigation"'. In *Home is Where the Heart is: Studies in Melodrama and the Woman's Film*, edited by Christine Gledhill, 1–39. London: British Film Institute, 1987.

———. 'Between Melodrama and Realism: Anthony Asquith's Underground and King Vidor's The Crowd.' In *Classical Hollywood Narrative: The Paradigm Wars*, edited by Jane Gaines, 129–67. Durham, NC: Duke University Press, 1992.

Goethe, Johann Wolfgang von. *The Sorrows of Young Werther*. London: Penguin Classics, 1989 [1774].

Grieveson, Lee. *Policing Cinema: Movies and Censorship in Early-Twentieth Century America*. Berkeley: University of California Press, 2004.

Griffin, Elizabeth. *The Delicate Distress*. Lexington, KY: University of Kentucky Press, 1997 [1757].

Grimsted, David. *Melodrama Unveiled: American Theater and Culture, 1800–1850*. Chicago: University of Chicago Press, 1968.

Grodal, Torben. *Moving Pictures: A New Theory of Film Genres, Feelings, and Cognition*. Oxford: Clarendon Press, 1999.

Gunning, Tom. 'An Aesthetic of Astonishment: Early Film and the (In)Credulous Spectator'. In *Viewing Positions: Ways of Seeing Film*, edited by L. Williams, 114–33. New Brunswick, NJ: Rutgers University Press, 1995a.

———. 'Buster Keaton, or The Work of Comedy in the Age of Mechanical Reproduction'. *Cineaste* 21 (1995b): 14–16.

———. 'From the Opium Den to the Theater of Morality: Moral Discourse and the Film in Early American Cinema'. In *The Silent Cinema Reader*, edited by Lee Grieveson and Peter Krämer, 145–54. New York: Routledge, 2004.

———. 'Chaplin and the Body of Modernity'. *Early Popular Visual Culture* 8, no. 3 (2010): 237–45.

Hammond, Michael. 'Saving Private Ryan's "Special Affect"'. In *The Action and Adventure Cinema*, edited by Yvonne Tasker, 153–66. 1st edn. New York: Routledge, 2004.

Hansen, Miriam. Introduction to Adorno, 'Transparencies on Film'. *New German Critique* 24/25, Special Double Issue on New German Cinema (autumn 1981–winter 1982): 186–98.

———. 'Of Mice and Ducks: Benjamin and Adorno on Disney'. *South Atlantic Quarterly* 92 (January 1993): 437–69.

———. '"With Skin and Hair": Kracauer's Theory of Film'. *Critical Inquiry* 19, no. 3 (1993): 437–8.

———. '"Schindler's List" Is Not "Shoah"': The Second Commandment, Popular Modernism, and Public Memory'. *Critical Inquiry* 22, no. 2 (1996): 292–312.

———. 'The Mass Production of the Senses: Classical Cinema as Vernacular Modernism'. *Modernism/Modernity* 6, no. 2 (1999): 59–77.

Hart-Davis, Rupert, ed., 'Sentimentality is merely the bank holiday of cynicism'. In *Selected Letters*, 501. Oxford: Oxford University Press, 1979.

Hawkins, Joan. *Cutting Edge: Art-Horror and the Horrific Avant-garde*. 1st edn. Minneapolis: University of Minnesota Press, 2000.

Heilman, Robert Bechtold. *Tragedy and Melodrama: Versions of Experience*. Seattle: University of Washington Press, 1968.

Heininger, M. L. S. 'Children, Childhood, and Change in America, 1820–1920'. In *A Century of Childhood, 1820–1920*, edited by Mary Lynn Stevens Heininger et al., 1–32. Rochester, NY: Margaret Woodbury Strong Museum, 1984.

Hillier, Jim. *Cahiers Du Cinema: The 1950's Neo-Realism, Hollywood, New Wave*. Cambridge, MA: Harvard University Press, 1985.

Hobbes, Thomas and Richard Tuck. *Leviathan*. Cambridge: Cambridge University Press, 1996.

Horkheimer, Max and Theodor W. Adorno. *Dialectic of Enlightenment: Philosophical Fragments*. Edited by Gunzelin Schmid Noerr. Stanford: Stanford University Press, 2002.

Howard, Dick. *The Primacy of the Political: A History of Political Thought from the Greeks to the French and American Revolutions*, New York: Columbia University Press, 2010.

Hume, David. *A Treatise of Human Nature*, reprinted from the Original Edition in three volumes and edited, with an analytical index, by L. A. Selby-Bigge, M.A. Oxford: Clarendon Press, 1896. http://oll.libertyfund.org/titles/hume-a-treatise-of-human-nature#Hume, last accessed 12 June 2011.

———. *Essays: Moral, Political and Literary*, edited and with a Foreword, Notes, and Glossary by Eugene F. Miller, with an appendix of variant readings from the 1889 edition by T. H. Green and T. H. Grose, revised edition. Indianapolis: Liberty Fund, 1987. http://oll.libertyfund.org/titles/hume-essays-moral-political-literary-lf-ed#Hume, last accessed 16 September 2016.

Hutcheon, Linda. *A Theory of Parody: The Teachings of Twentieth-Century Art Forms*. Champaign: University of Illinois Press, 2000.

Huxley, Aldous. *Vulgarity in Literature: Digressions from a Theme*. 1st edn. London: Chatto and Windus, 1930.

Huyssen, Andreas. *After the Great Divide: Modernism, Mass Culture, Postmodernism*. Bloomington: Indiana University Press, 1987.

Jacobs, Lea. *Decline of Sentiment: American Film in the 1920s*. Berkeley: University of California Press, 2008.

Jameson, Fredric. 'Reification and Utopia in Mass Culture'. *Social Text* 1 (1979): 130–48.

———. *Postmodernism, or, The Cultural Logic of Late Capitalism*. Durham, NC: Duke University Press, 1991.

Jameson, Fredric. 'Interview with Stuart Hall'. In *Jameson on Jameson*, edited by Fredric Jameson and Ian Buchanan, 113–34. Durham, NC: Duke University Press, 2007.

Jameson, Fredric and Ian Buchanan. *Jameson on Jameson: Conversations on Cultural Marxism*. Durham, NC: Duke University Press, 2007.

Jay, Martin. *Marxism and Totality: The Adventures of a Concept from Lukács to Habermas*. Berkeley and Los Angeles: University of California Press, 1986.

Jefferson, Mark. 'What is Wrong with Sentimentality?' *Mind* XCII (368) (1983): 519–29.

Jeffords, Susan. *Hard Bodies: Hollywood Masculinity in the Reagan Era*. New Brunswick, NJ: Rutgers University Press, 1994.

Jenkins, Henry. *What Made Pistachio Nuts? Early Sound Comedy and the Vaudeville Aesthetic*. New York: Columbia University Press, 1992.

———. 'This Fellow Keaton Seems to be the Whole Show: Buster Keaton, Interrupted Performance and the Vaudeville Aesthetic'. In *Buster Keaton's Sherlock Jr.*, edited by Andrew Horton, 29–66. Cambridge: Cambridge University Press, 1997.

———. 'Introduction: Childhood Innocence and Other Modern Myths'. In *The Children's Culture Reader*, edited by Henry Jenkins, 1–37. New York: New York University Press, 1998.

Kaes, Anton, Martin Jay and Ed Dimendberg, eds. *The Weimar Republic Sourcebook*. Berkeley: University of California Press, 1994.

Kaplan, E. Ann. *Women and Film: Both Sides of the Camera*, New York: Methuen, 1983.

Kendrick, James. 'Marxist Overtones in Three Films by James Cameron'. *Journal of Popular Film and Television* 27, no. 3 (1999): 36–44.

Kenner, Hugh. *The Pound Era*. Bloomington: University of California Press, 1973.

Kleinhans, Chuck. 'Notes on Melodrama and the Family under Capitalism', *Film Reader*, 3 (1978): 40–7.

Klinger, Barbara. *Melodrama and Meaning: History, Culture, and the Films of Douglas Sirk*. Bloomington: Indiana University Press, 1994.

Knight, Deborah. 'Why We Enjoy Condemning Sentimentality: A Meta-Aesthetic Perspective'. *The Journal of Aesthetics and Art Criticism* 57, no. 4 (autumn 1999): 411–20.

Knott, Sarah, *Sensibility and the American Revolution*. Chapel Hill: Omohundro Institute, University of North Carolina Press, 2009.

Kolker, Robert. *A Cinema of Loneliness: Penn, Stone, Kubrick, Scorsese, Spielberg, Altman*. 3rd edn. New York: Oxford University Press, 2000.

Koresky, Michael. 'Twilight of the Idyll'. *Senses of Cinema*, Special Issue: The Question Spielberg (2003).

Kracauer, Siegfried. *The Mass Ornament: Weimar Essays*. Translated by Thomas Y. Levin. Cambridge, MA: Harvard University Press, 1995.

———. 'Two Chaplin Sketches'. Translated by J. J. K. MacKay. *The Yale Journal of Criticism* 10, no. 1 (1997): 115–20.

Landy, Marcia. *Imitations of Life: A Reader of Film and Television Melodrama*. Detroit: Wayne State University Press, 1991.

Langford, Barry. *Film Genre: Hollywood and Beyond*. Edinburgh: Edinburgh University Press, 2005.

Lanzmann, Claude. 'Why Spielberg has Distorted the Truth'. *Manchester Guardian Weekly*, Le Monde. 3 April1994.

Leavis, F. R. *The Great Tradition*. London: Penguin. (Original work published 1948), 1993.

Locke, John. *An Essay Concerning Human Understanding*. London: Tegg, 1836.

Lutz, Tom. *Crying: The Natural and Cultural History of Tears*. New York: W. W. Norton & Company, 1999.

Lyotard, Jean-François. *The Postmodern Condition: A Report on Knowledge*. Translated by Brian Massumi and Geoff Bennington. Manchester: Manchester University Press, 1984.

MacCabe, Colin. 'Realism and the Cinema: Notes on Some Brechtian Theses'. *Screen* 15, no. 2 (1974): 7–27.

MacIntyre, Alasdair. *After Virtue: A Study in Moral Theory.*, 3rd edn. Notre Dame, IN: University of Notre Dame Press, 2007.

———. *The Man of Feeling*. Oxford: Oxford World's Classics, 1987.

McRobbie, Angela. *Postmodernism and Popular Culture*. 1st edn. London: Routledge, 1994.

Maland, Charles J. *Chaplin and American Culture: The Evolution of a Star Image*. Princeton: Princeton University Press, 1989.

Malcolm, Derek. 'Empire of the eternal kid/Profile of Steven Spielberg'. *The Guardian*. London, 17 June 1989.

Mannoni, Octave. 'Je sais bien, mais quand même'. In *Clefs pour l'imaginaire ou l'autre scène*, 9–33. Paris: Éditions du Seuil, 1969.

Marcus, Laura. *The Tenth Muse: Writing about Cinema in the Modernist Period.* New York: Oxford University Press, 2007.

Markley, Robert. 'Sentimentality as Performance: Shaftesbury, Sterne, and the Theatrics of Virtue'. In *The New Eighteenth Century: Theory, Politics, English Literature*, edited by Laura Brown and Felicity Nussbaum, 210–30. New York: Methuen, 1987.

Marks, Laura U. *The Skin of the Film: Intercultural Cinema, Embodiment, and the Senses.* Durham, NC: Duke University Press Books, 1999.

Martin-Jones, David. 'Introduction: Film-Philosophy and a World of Cinemas'. *Film-Philosophy* 20 (2016): 6–23.

May, Henry Farnham. *The End of American Innocence: A Study of the First Years of Our Own Time, 1912–1917.* Oxford: Oxford University Press, 1959.

Mencken, H. L. *Prejudices: A Selection.* Baltimore: Johns Hopkins University Press, 2006 [1920].

Mercer, John and Martin Shingler. *Melodrama: Genre, Style and Sensibility.* Annotated edition. New York: Wallflower Press, 2004.

Merck, Mandy, ed. *After Diana, Irreverent Elegies.* London: Verso, 1998.

Merritt, Russell. 'Nickelodeon Theaters, 1905–1914: Building an Audience for the Movies'. In *The American Film Industry*, edited by Tino Balio, 83–102. Madison: University of Wisconsin Press, 1976.

———. 'Melodrama: Postmortem for a Phantom Genre'. *Wide Angle* 5, no. 3 (1983): 24–31. Reprinted in *Home is Where the Heart Is: Studies in Melodrama and the Woman's Film*, edited by Christine Gledhill, 354. London: British Film Institute, 1987,.

Metz, Christian. *The Imaginary Signifier: Psychoanalysis and Cinema.* Translated by Ben Brewster. Bloomington: Indiana University Press, 1982.

Michelson, Annette. 'Introduction'. In Dziga Vertov, *Kino-Eye: The Writings of Dziga Vertov*, translated by Annette Michelson, xlvi–l. Berkeley: University of California Press, 1984.

Midgley, Mary. 'Brutality and Sentimentality'. *Philosophy* 54, no. 209 (July 1979): 385–9.

Moore, C. A. 'Shaftesbury and the Ethical Poets in England, 1700–1760'. *PMLA* 31, no. 2 (1 January 1916): 264–325.

Moretti, Franco. *Signs Taken for Wonders.* London: Verso, 1983.

Morris, Nigel. *The Cinema of Steven Spielberg: Empire of Light.* London: Wallflower Press, 2007.

Mrs Thomson. *Excessive Sensibility; or, the History of Lady St. Laurence. A Novel.* Gale Eighteenth Century Collections Online Print Editon, 2010 [1787].

Mullan, John. *Sentiment and Sociability: The Language of Feeling in the Eighteenth Century.* Oxford: Clarendon Press, 1988.

Mulvey, Laura. 'Visual Pleasure and Narrative Cinema'. *Screen* 16, no. 3 (1975): 57–68.

———. 'Notes on Sirk and Melodrama'. *Movie* 25 (winter 1977/8): 53–6. Reprinted in *Home is Where the Heart Is: Studies in Melodrama and the Woman's*

Film, edited by Christine Gledhill, 75–9. London: British Film Institute, 1987.

Musser, Charles. 'Work, Ideology and Chaplin's Tramp'. *Radical History Review* 1988, no. 41 (1988): 36–66.

Naremore, James. 'Love and Death in A.I. Artificial Intelligence'. *Michigan Quarterly Review* 44, no. 2 (2005): 256–84.

Neale, Steve. 'Melodrama and Tears'. *Screen* 27, no. 6 (1986): 6–22.

———. 'Melo Talk: On the Meaning and Use of the Term "Melodrama" in the American Trade Press'. *Velvet Light Trap* 32 (1993): 66–89.

Neale, Steve and Frank Krutnik. *Popular Film and Television Comedy*. London: Routledge, 1990.

Nichols, Bill. 'The 10 Stations of Spielberg's Passion: "Saving Private Ryan." "Amistad." "Schindler's List."'. *Jump Cut* 43 (July 2000): 9–11.

Nietzsche, Friedrich Wilhelm. *Ecce Homo*. Translated by Anthony M. Ludovici. New York: Courier Dover Publications, 2004.

———. *Thus Spoke Zarathustra*. London: Continuum International Publishing Group, 2005.

———. *On the Genealogy of Morality*. Edited by Keith Ansell-Pearson. Translated by Carol Diethe. Cambridge: Cambridge University Press, 2007.

Nowell-Smith, Geoffrey. 'Minnelli and Melodrama'. *Screen* 18, no. 2 (1977): 113–18.

Nussbaum, Martha C. *Upheavals of Thought: The Intelligence of Emotions*. Cambridge: Cambridge University Press, 2003.

Orwell, George. *Down and Out in Paris and London*. London: Penguin, 1999.

Oxford English Dictionary (*OED*). Online edition, 2017.

Pattee, Fred Lewis. *The Feminine Fifties*. New York: D. Appleton-Century Company, 1940.

Perkins, David. *A History of Modern Poetry, Volume II: Modernism and After*. Cambridge, MA: Belknap Press of Harvard University Press, 1976.

Perkins, V.F. *Film as Film: Understanding and Judging Movies*, New York: Da Capo Press, 1993.

Pisters, Patricia, ed. *Micropolitics of Media Culture: Reading the Rhizomes of Deleuze and Guattari*. Amsterdam: Amsterdam University Press, 2002.

Plantinga, Carl R. 'Notes on Spectator Emotion and Ideological Film Criticism'. In *Film Theory and Philosophy*, edited by Richard Allen and Murray Smith, 327–93. New York: Oxford University Press, 1997.

———. *Moving Viewers: American Film and the Spectator's Experience*. Los Angeles and Berkeley: University of California Press, 2009.

Plantinga, Carl R. and Greg M. Smith, eds. *Passionate Views: Film, Cognition, and Emotion*. Baltimore: Johns Hopkins University Press, 1999.

Rahill, Frank. *The World of Melodrama*. University Park, PA: Pennsylvania State University Press, 1967.

Rawls, John. *A Theory of Justice*. Cambridge, MA: Harvard University Press, 2009.

Rhu, Laurence F. 'The Cavellian Turn'. In *The Oxford Handbook of Transcendentalism*, edited by Joel Myerson, Sandra Harbert Petrulionis and Laura Dassow Walls, 549–58. New York: Oxford University Press, 2010.

Richardson, Samuel. *Pamela, or Virtue Rewarded*. Vol. 2. London: J. M. Dent, 1955.

———. *The Correspondence of Samuel Richardson*. Edited by Mrs Barbauld (Anna Letitia). New York: Abrahams Magazine Service Press, 1966.

———. *Pamela, or Virtue Rewarded*. Vol. 1. Boston: Houghton Mifflin, 1971 [1740].

———. *Clarissa, or the History of a Young Lady*. London: Penguin, 1985 [1748].

———. *The History of Sir Chares Grandison, Charleston, South Carolina in a Series of Letters*. Charleston, SC: Bibliobazaar, 2009.

Rodowick, D. N. 'Madness, Authority and Ideology: The Domestic Melodrama of the 1950s'. *Velvet Light Trap* 19 (1982): 40–5. Reprinted in *Home is Where the Heart Is: Studies in Melodrama and the Woman's Film*, edited by Christine Gledhill. London: British Film Institute, 1987..

———. 'Madness, Authority and Ideology: The Domestic Melodrama of the 1950s'. In *Imitations of Life: A Reader on Film and Television Melodrama*, edited by Marcia Landy, 237–47. Detroit: Wayne State University Press, 1991.

Rousseau, Jean-Jacques. *Julie, Or the New Heloise: Letters of Two Lovers Who Live in a Smll Town at the Foot of the Alps*. Edited by Philip Stewart and Jean Vache. Lebanon, NH: University Press of New England, 2010.

Rushton, Richard. *The Reality of Film: Theories of Filmic Reality*. New York: Manchester University Press, 2010.

Said, Edward Wadie. *Orientalism*. Toronto: Random House, 1994 [1978].

Santayana, George. 'The Genteel Tradition in American Philosophy'. In *The Genteel Tradition: Nine Essays*, edited by D. L. Wilson, 37–64. Lincoln, NE: University of Nebraska Press, 1967 [1911].

Sconce, Jeffrey. '"Trashing" the Academy: Taste, Excess, and an Emerging Politics of Cinematic Style'. *Screen* 36, no. 4 (1995): 371–93.

———. 'Irony, Nihilism and the New American "Smart" Film'. *Screen* 43, no. 4 (2002): 349–69.

Seldes, Gilbert. *The 7 Lively Arts: The Classic Appraisal of the Popular Arts*. Toronto: General Publishing Company, 1952.

Shaftesbury, Anthony Ashley Cooper, 3rd Earl of. *An Inquiry Concerning Virtue, or Merit*. Edited by David Walford. Manchester: Manchester University Press, 1977.

———. *Characteristics of Men, Manners, Opinions, Times*. Edited by Lawrence Klein. Cambridge: Cambridge University Press, 2000 [1711].

Sharma, Shailja. 'Citizens of the Empire: Revisionist History and the Social Imaginary in Gandhi'. *Velvet Light Trap* 35 (1995): 61–8.

Shaviro, Steven. 'The Life, after Death, of Postmodern Emotions.'. *Criticism* 46, no. 1 (2004): 125–42.

———. 'The 'Wrenching Duality' of Aesthetics: Kant, Deleuze and the "Theory

of the Sensible"'. 2007. (available as PDF at www.shaviro.com/Othertexts/
SPEP.pdf, last accessed 15 February 2014)

———. 'The Cinematic Body Redux'. 2008. (available as PDF at www.shaviro.
com/Othertexts/Cinematic.pdf, last accessed 22 June 2014)

———. 'Research Statement'. 2009. www.shaviro.com/Blog/?p=777, last
accessed 13 September 2014.

———. Post-Cinematic Affect. Washington, DC: Zero Books, 2010.

Shaw, George Bernard. 'The Cinema as a Moral Leveller: George Bernard Shaw
on the Role of the Cinema'. New Statesman. London, 27 June 1914.

———. 'Hard Times'. In Hard Times, edited by Fred Kaplan, 383. New York:
W. W. Norton & Company, 2001.

Simons, Jan. Playing the Waves: Lars von Trier's Game Cinema. Amsterdam:
Amsterdam University Press, 2007.

Singer, Ben. Melodrama and Modernity: Early Sensational Cinema and its Contexts.
New York: Columbia University Press, 2001.

Sinnerbrink, Robert. New Philosophies of Film: Thinking Images. London:
Continuum International Publishing Group, 2011.

———. Cinematic Ethics: Exploring Ethical Experience through Film. London:
Routledge, 2015.

Small, Ian, ed. Epistola, In Carcere Et Vinculis. Oxford: Clarendon Press, 2000.

Smith, Adam. The Theory of Moral Sentiments. Minneapolis: Filiquarian
Publishing, LLC, 2007 [1759].

Smith, Greg M. Film Structure and the Emotion System. New York: Cambridge
University Press, 2003.

Smith, Murray. Engaging Characters: Fiction, Emotion and the Cinema. Oxford:
Clarendon Press, 1995.

———. 'Film and Philosophy'. In SAGE Handbook of Film Studies, edited by
James Donald and Michael Renov, 147–63. London: SAGE, 2008.

Sobchack, Vivian. The Address of the Eye. Princeton: Princeton University Press,
1992.

Solomon, Robert C., ed., In Defense of Sentimentality. United States: Oxford
University Press, 2004.

———. Thinking about Feeling: Contemporary Philosophers on Emotions. 1st edn.
United States: Oxford University Press, 2004.

Sontag, Susan. Against Interpretation and Other Essays. New York: Picador, 2001.

Stam, Robert. Film Theory: An Introduction. Oxford: Wiley-Blackwell, 2000.

Steele, Richard. 'Preface to the Conscious Lovers' (1722). In The Plays of Richard
Steele, edited by Shirley Kenny, 299–301. Oxford: Oxford University Press,
1971.

Sterne, Laurence. The Life and Opinions of Tristram Shandy, Gentleman. London:
Penguin, 2003 [1767].

———. A Sentimental Journey. London: Penguin, 2001 [1768].

Stowe, Harriet Beecher. Uncle Tom's Cabin. London: CRW Publishing, 2004
[1852].

Strachey, Lytton. *Eminent Victorians*. New York: Penguin Classics, 1990.

Studlar, Gaylyn. *In the Realm of Pleasure: Von Sternberg, Dietrich and the Masochistic Aesthetic*. New York: Columbia University Press, 1988.

Tan, Ed S. *Emotion and the Structure of Narrative Film: Film as an Emotion Machine*. New York: Routledge, 1996.

Tan, Ed S. and Nico Frijda. 'Sentiment in Film Viewing'. In *Passionate Views: Film, Cognition, and Emotion*, edited by Carl Plantinga and Greg M. Smith, 48–64. Baltimore: Johns Hopkins University Press, 1999.

Tanner, Michael. 'Sentimentality'. *Proceedings of the Aristotelian Society* 77 (1976– – 7): 127–47.

Taylor, Charles. *Sources of the Self: The Making of the Modern Identity*. Cambridge, MA: Harvard University Press, 1992.

Thomson, David. 'Presenting Enamelware'. *Film Comment* 30, no. 2 (1994): 44–6.

Todd, Janet. *Sensibility: An Introduction*. London and New York: Methuen, 1986.

Tomasulo, Frank P. 'Empire of the Gun: Steven Spielberg's Saving Private Ryan and American Chauvinism'. In *The End Of Cinema As We Know It: American Film in the Nineties*, edited by Jon Lewis, 115–30. New York: New York University Press, 2002.

Tompkins, Jane. *Sensational Designs: The Cultural Work of American Fiction, 1790–1860*. New York: Oxford University Press, 1985.

Turvey, Malcolm.'Balázs: Realist or Modernist'. *October* 115 (winter 2006): 77–87.

Uricchio, William, and Roberta E. Pearson. *Reframing Culture: The Case of the Vitagraph Quality Films*. Princeton: Princeton University Press, 1993.

Vertov, Dziga. *Kino-Eye: The Writings of Dziga Vertov*. Translated by Annette Michelson. Berkeley: University of California Press, 1984.

Vincent-Buffault, Anne. *A History of Tears: Sensibility and Sentimentality in France*. New York: St Martin's Press, 1991.

Ward, Janet. *Weimar Surfaces: Urban Visual Culture in 1920s Germany*. Los Angeles and Berkeley: University of California Press, 2001.

Welter, B. 'The Cult of True Womanhood, 1820–1860'. *American Quarterly* 18, no. 2 (summer 1966): 151–74.

Wieseltier, Leon. 'Close Encounters of the Nazi Kind'. *The New Republic* 210, no. 4 (1994): 42.

Williams, Linda. 'Something Else Besides a Mother: "Stella Dallas" and the Maternal Melodrama'. *Cinema Journal* 24, no. 1 (autumn 1984): 2–27.

———. 'Film Bodies: Gender, Genre, and Excess'. *Film Quarterly* 44, no. 4 (1991): 2–13.

———. 'Melodrama Revised'. In *Refiguring American Film Genres: History and Theory*, edited by Nick Browne, 42 –88. Berkeley: University of California Press, 1998.

———. *Playing the Race Card: Melodramas of Black and White from Uncle Tom to OJ Simpson*. Princeton: Princeton University Press, 2002.

Wilde, Oscar. *The Picture of Dorian Gray and Other Writings*. New York: Simon & Schuster, 2005.

———. *Selected Letters*. Edited by Rupert Hart-Davis. Oxford: Oxford University Press, 1979.

Williams, Raymond. *Culture and Society 1780–1950*. Harmondsworth: Penguin, 1961.

———. *Modern Tragedy*. Stanford: Stanford University Press, 1966.

———. *Drama from Ibsen to Brecht*. New York: Oxford University Press, 1969.

Williamson, Jennifer A., Jennifer Larson and Ashley Reed, eds. *The Sentimental Mode: Essays in Literature, Film and Television*. Jefferson, NC: McFarland & Company, Inc., 2014.

Winston-Dixon, Wheeler. "Twenty-Five Reasons Why It's All Over'. In *The End Of Cinema As We Know It: American Film in the Nineties*, edited by Jon Lewis, 356–66. New York: New York University Press, 2002.

Woal, Michael and Linda Kowall Woal. 'Chaplin and the Comedy of Melodrama'. *Journal of Film and Video* 46, no. 3 (1994): 3–15.

Wollen Peter, 'Perhaps …,' *October* 88 (spring 1999): 43–50.

Wollen, Peter. 'Godard and Counter-Cinema: *Vent d'Est*'. In *Narrative, Apparatus, Ideology: A Film Theory Reader*, edited by Philip Rosen, 120–9. New York: Columbia University Press, 1986.

Wood, Robin. *Hollywood from Vietnam to Reagan*. New York: Columbia University Press, 2003.

Zavattini, Cesare. 'Some Ideas on the Cinema'. *Sight and Sound* 23, no. 2 (1953): 50–61.

Zelizer, Viviana. A. *Pricing the Priceless Child: The Changing Social Value of Children*. New York: Basic Books, 1985.

Žižek, Slavoj. *The Ticklish Subject: The Absent Centre of Political Ontology*. New York: Verso, 2000.

Index

EU Authorised Representative:

Easy Access System Europe Mustamäe tee 50, 10621 Tallinn, Estonia

gpsr.requests@easproject.com

Printed and bound by CPI Group (UK) Ltd, Croydon, CR0 4YY

26/05/2025

01882787-0001